THE GOSPEL OF THE GNOSTICS

Edited and almost wholly Newly Translated from the Coptic, Greek and Syriac of original and summarised Gnostic texts, in some cases for the first time into English; With a brief Introduction, explanatory Commentary on each Section, and very full Footnotes explaining all difficulties in doctrine and language, and four illuminating Appendices

---

BY

DUNCAN GREENLEES, M. A. (OXON.)

THE BOOK TREE
San Diego, California

Originally published
1958
by The Theosophical Publishing House
Adyar, Madras, India

New material, revisions and cover
© 2006
The Book Tree
All rights reserved

ISBN 978-1-58509-007-5

Cover layout and design
by Ben Riggs

Published by
The Book Tree
P.O. Box 16476
San Diego, CA 92176
www.thebooktree.com

We provide fascinating and educational products to help awaken the public to new ideas and information that would not be available otherwise.
Call 1 (800) 700-8733 for our *FREE BOOK TREE CATALOG*.

FOREWORD

Recommended by top scholars in the field of Gnostic studies for many years. This book is considered one of the best on the subject, essential for any serious researcher. Takes the reader through every facet of the Gnostic experience including sections on The Soul is Sent Forth, Glory of the Indwelling Light, The Way to the Higher Mysteries, The Final Secret of the Self, and The Soul Travels Home. Based on the rare, surviving works of ancient Gnostic teachers like *Pistis Sophia* and the two *Books of Ieou*. Sources include the Agnew Codex, Bruce Codex, Akhmim Codex, Jung Codex, Cairo Codex, the Gnostic Acts (of Peter, Andrew, John, Thomas and Philip), the *Chaldean Oracles*, and various Gnostic hymns, prayers, Gospels and papyri. A virtual gold mine of Gnostic material, some translated and presented here for the first time.

At the time this book was written some, but not all, of the Nag Hammadi texts had been made available. Those that were available are found within this collection, so that all known and accessible gospels of the Gnostics were collected together and either presented or paraphrased in this work.

What may at first seem to be a new text is the inclusion of "The Two Books of Ieou" (sometimes spelled Ieu), also known as the "Gnoses of the Invisible God", which is one of the two main texts found in the Bruce Codex. Also included are a few works that I have not personally seen elsewhere, but the vast amount of Gnostic material that has been released since this book's first publication precludes me from stating that it can be found here exclusively. It is best left up to the reader to make that determination.

What can be attested to with complete conviction is the quality of Greenlees' writing. I have never read more poetic yet sensible words regarding the Gnostics and their works. This book is a joy to read because of its clarity. He shows how and why church-sponsored writings, which were biased against Gnostic ideas, missed the entire point and Greenlees, who is trying to be completely unbiased and give credit where credit is due, is able to place these ideas in their proper spiritual and religious context. Reading this book is truly an eye-opening and mind-opening experience.

In scholarly texts similar to this the footnotes included are dry and factual, pointing to sources used and references cited. The notes included here, however, add a wealth of fascinating information beyond the text and serve to explain things more deeply. Instead of citing a reference, it often brings you into another level of learning. No matter how much one has read on the subject, they are still sure to come away more enriched by this work.

A good index can be found at the end, but to avoid confusion it must be noted that what seems like page numbers are, in fact, referring to numbered sections of the text itself, which is otherwise only explained in a small note at the very end of the Index.

As part of the book's Introduction there is an extensive overview of all the sources used, which provides a good foundation for the reader. It is useful information to go along with the actual text. The author also recommends two other books he wrote in this series in order for the reader to gain a complete understanding of the birth and infancy of Christianity. *The Gospel of Hermes* is also published by The Book Tree and *The Gospel of Mani*, which we hope to make available.

This book alone still goes far beyond others on the subject. One example of this follows as a last point is to be made. It points out in more than one place that the Gnostics (or at least the more popular Valentinian Gnostics) recognized three types of souls, and therefore three types of people. All three have fallen into Ignorance and the world of matter, the only difference is in the level of awareness they have. The spiritual soul recognizes the predicament and is aware of one's own soul and inner light. They have achieved a level of Gnosis, or awakening, but none have entered into it completely. We all reside in Ignorance due to the physical world and can never fully escape it while here. The psychic soul is willing to be prepared for the Gnosis-it knows it's there and is interested in progressing toward that aim. The fleshy soul has no appreciation of the Gnosis and anything one might do to arouse an interest in such a person fails.

When both ancient and modern critics of the Gnostics dismissed their ideas, they accused the Gnostics of claiming to be "better" than everyone else. The aim of the Gnostics, however, has never been to be part of an exclusive "club" meant to set themselves apart and be "better" in any way, but to help us all realize a higher level of consciousness or awareness involving who we really are, how we got here, and where we are going. The only people who truly bought the idea that the Gnostics were trying to be better than others were those who were fleshy--with no appreciation at all for higher spiritual work. It was a great way for such people to attack them, and remains to this very day.

Paul Tice

THE WORLD GOSPEL SERIES

Gather us in, Thou Love that fillest all;
Gather our rival faiths within Thy fold;
Rend each man's temple-veil and bid it fall
That we may know that Thou hast been of old.
Gather us in; we worship only Thee:
In varied names we stretch a common hand;
In diverse forms a common Soul we see,
In many Ships we seek one Spirit-Land.
Each sees one colour of Thy rainbow light;
Each looks upon one tint and calls it heaven;
Thou art the Fullness of our partial sight—
We are not perfect till we find the seven.
G. MATHESON

Apart from a few scholars and devotees, the modern public are unwilling to spend time on reading through the whole of the lengthy Scriptures of the world. This little Series is planned to offer them in a cheap, handy and attractive form the essence of all the world's great Scriptures, translated and edited by one who has a deep and living sympathy for each of them.

It is based on the inevitable conclusion of any fair student that all the great Religions and their Scriptures come from one Divine Source, in varying degrees of purity of transmission, and according to the needs and capacities of those to whom they came—the authentic Word of God to man.

The Publishers hope to issue two volumes yearly, each of about 400 pages, with short notes or running commentary, and a brief introduction to point out the significance of each Faith in the history of world thought. This is Volume Thirteen.

When the Series is completed, it will form a useful little reference library of the world's religious literature, which has done so much to mould the thought and culture of today, even though few individuals in each of the communities have perhaps been able to reach the ideal laid down in them.[1]

DUNCAN GREENLEES

---

[1] *Yet, as this is an objective study, aiming at a fair presentation of the Gnostic point of view, it is obvious that the writer does not thereby pronounce his own personal convictions or religious faith.*

THE GOSPEL OF THE GNOSTICS

GNOSTICISM is a system of direct experiential knowledge of God and the nature of the Soul and the universe; therefore it has no fixed dogmas or creed but naturally expresses itself in terms familiar to its environment. In the early centuries of this era, amid a growing Christianity, it took on the form of the Christian faith, while rejecting most of its special beliefs. Its wording is therefore largely Christian, while its spirit is rather that of the latest paganism of the West—pantheistic, esoteric, relying on a Divine Saviour to rescue the Soul from Matter.

Out of the Eternal formless and infinite One arose before all time, either by an exercise of will (Love desiring an object to be loved) or by a natural process of emanation (creativity inevitably creating out of itself) the Seed of this Universe, which has ever since been unfolding newer and finer forms to manifest the Divine. This Divine Element shone forth in an infinity of ' Light-Sparks ', the individual Souls, and these, in order to gain through experience of the darkness of Matter a direct knowledge and appreciation of the Light of Spirit, plunged into the prison of the body. Charmed by the manifold delights of outer form, the Soul forgot its spiritual aim and came to identify itself with that external body; hence it subjected itself to all the passions and to every kind of misery.

Being all Love, the Eternal Father of All cannot leave His Sons unaided in the wretchedness wherein they are now involved. So He sends, or Himself comes forth as, a manifestation of the Truth in human form; and so through the 'Gospel' or the 'Call' of a Divine Messenger He arouses the sleeping Soul to awareness of his plight and to the real purpose of immersion in the ocean of Matter. The Soul is filled with powers of Grace enough to overcome the inertia his Ignorance has laid upon him, and, having been born many times in ignorance, comes to be born with the passionate desire for Gnosis and for God. Thus he is able to recognise and receive God's Message, which is the Light of Gnosis that destroys the besetting darkness of his Ignorance; equipped with all the necessary virtues, he is initiated in the Mysteries and led step by step up the Ladder that leads to full realisation of the Cosmic Life, which is absolute unity with all that is. Having been thus at-oned with all life, he becomes himself the Cross that unites the Above and the Below, the Right and Left, spreading through the whole universe as infinite blessing to all beings; shining beyond our highest dreams of perfection, he becomes a part of the Infinite Light which is God Himself, nay, he becomes that Light.

Such is the Path the Gnosis has declared to all who care to hear, even though by its very nature it cannot be trod by all. It is only those who have realised the worthlessness of material aims and finally renounced the dominating lure of the flesh to devote themselves wholly to the Spirit, who can actually tread this Path to its end. Their reward is to be misunderstood and unvalued by the world, but they enter in and share the infinite perfection of Divinity, which they know for themselves and can enjoy in every moment of their unending lives. It is to invite all who can enter on this Path that the Divine Saviour comes down from God into our world of flesh; it is for those who would enjoy eternal bliss to learn what the Gnosis really is, and so to become themselves in time true Gnostics, whose very presence uplifts their fellows in the world.

PREFACE

IT was in 1919, when the old Christian orthodoxies seemed to have failed a world agonized by our first Great War's shattering blows, that Theosophy came to me, with its revealing of long-forgotten truths. And the form in which it first came to me was that of Gnosticism. So deep, so sweet, was its ancient hold upon my mind that I at once plunged into Mead's great book, so full of sympathy and vision, so wise in its view of the 'Faith Forgotten' which had so long had such a raw deal from the bigots and fanatics of its successors; and there I found unending delight. Those long-buried memories swiftly began to awake, taking shape in such poetic essays as 'The Spirit of Flame', printed in this volume.

Who, then, were these Gnostics? Like the Manicheans, they were long falsely styled Christian heretics, who fancifully added to and corrupted the divine revelations of the Apostolic Faith. So long as we knew nothing of them beyond what the not-over-clever refutators of the age of controversy (late 2nd to 5th centuries A.D.) chose to transmit, badly garbled, there was some excuse for this misunderstanding. It was the study of the 'Pistis Sophia', the strange Coptic codex so long treasured in the British Museum, which began to clear the way to the truth. Then came more and more discoveries in Egypt—the Bruce, Akhmim, Jung and Cairo Codices—together with a scholarly and sympathetic research in the apocryphal Acts, which unveiled the Gnostic origin of several; and this opened our eyes fully to the rich treasures stored away in these superficially unattractive cupboards.

Amélineau, Schmidt, Reitzenstein, Mead perhaps share the glory for unveiling the splendours of this 'Forgotten Faith'; and they have their successors in the many scholars of our own day. It is now clear that the Gnosis began long before Jesus walked in Galilee; its roots run back into the past of Iran, Egypt, Syria, Mesopotamia, and perhaps the Phrygian culture of which so little has yet been found. In the 'Gnosis' that we know, the Christian elements are mostly overwriting or editing of earlier 'pagan' forms which had lost their appeal in the 'sceptical' age of the decline of myth. It is time now that, as Volume Thirteen of this Series, we try to place the Gospel of the Gnostics alongside its fellows as a real Faith, built on ancient traditions and modes of thought, and on personal experience of the mystical life, and not as a congéries of fantastic mental speculations.

Who, then, were the Gnostics? The name (Gk. *gnōstikos*) is cognate with the Skt. *jñāni*, an adjective from the noun *Gnōsis*, by which was implied a direct experiential knowledge of God, the Soul, and their true relationship in the Universe. The Gnostic was not one who adhered to a set formula of faith, who accepted dogmas emanating from a certain school, by repeating which he could even without moral or mental capacity win to Heaven; he was one who after long preparation and training had fitted himself to be initiated into the direct knowledge of these things for himself. And the foundation for that training was the highest ethical standard, the renunciation of worldly aims, and the spiritualising of his whole life. Hence we find no one set of dogmas which may be styled as 'Gnosticism'—as in the case of Catholic Christianity—but rather a typical mode of thought, a flash of intuitional vision into the realities, an independence of verbal expression by means of traditional terms of what has been thus 'seen' and 'known'.

The reader of this book must not, therefore, be confused by the variety of approaches, by the difference in its cosmologies and soteriologies. The Gnostic was free to express such ineffables as he could, in any way which might seem suitable to him at the time. It was perfectly likely that the same Valentinus who could write the 'Gospel of Truth' at one time would later edit a primitive version of the 'Pistis Sophia', or draft the 'Gnosis of the Light', without the slightest feeling of incongruity or doctrinal instability. So our texts cannot be judged by the standards of literary criticism commonly applied by Western critics.

In this 'Gospel' we have a selected bouquet, as it were, culled from various Gnostic gardens. We see the majestic, almost Upanishadic, style of the Bruce Codex

'Apocalypse' alongside the puerility of magical invocations in the wrongly so-called 'Books of Ieou'; the Johannine simplicity and beauty, with infinite depths of thought, of the Gnostic Acts come alongside the almost childish rendering of the Soul's great epic from the 'Pistis Sophia'; the involved evolution of the Aeons in later (?) Valentinianism rubs shoulders with the profound advaitic truth of Monoimus's letter; and in the first Appendix we see how the Gnostics worked on earlier scriptures to prove the antiquity of the particular truths which they proclaimed.

Though illness somewhat helped to delay this volume, it has not lessened the joy its writing has brought myself. I have newly translated almost every word of the texts from the Coptic, Greek, Syriac or Latin of the versions spared to us by the ravages of time and vandalist opponents. And in this work I find my College studies of the Coptic language—mainly in the Sahidic dialect wherein most of the Gnostic texts have been preserved —justified and fulfilled. To my old teacher, Prof. F. Ll. Griffith, I would like to add a word of thanks and homage; he has long preceded me into that world where perhaps he has met with those who loved, who wrote, these scriptures; I too in my turn will presently join their company. My love for their work may prove to be a happy introduction to their surviving personalities when we meet—in a world of cultured leisure, free from the international hatreds and injustices, and the madness of atomic radiation, which have made a very hell of this lovely world of ours.

XV

The path the Gnostics blazed in their day is still wide open in our own. In a world of confusion, still those who draw aside into the calmness of contemplation can enter the gates of Initiation, pass through all the subtle planes of the Mysteries, and become citizens of the City Above, the glorious Kingdom of the Light. Let us be glad as we enjoy the gift they have left for us, as we share the inspiration of their vision, as we try to understand the subtleties of their thought; and then we too shall join them in the blinding glories of the 'Robe of Light', which every restored Soul wears in the dawn as it enters on the threshold of the Bridal Chamber of the King, its eternal Spouse.[1]

---

[1] As usual, in this volume words in brackets have been speculatively restored by me from indications of parallel texts or by the requirements of English idiom; words substituted for the sake of grammatical sequence or greater clarity for those in the text have been printed in a heavy type.

The Index deals with only a few representative topics and relates solely to the text of the 'Gospel' itself; no attempt has been made in this Series to index the commentaries, footnotes, introduction, appendices, etc.

I wish here to express my thanks to the authorities of the British Museum for allowing me to handle and copy the original MS. of "Pistis Sophia", of St. Mary's College, Kurseong, Bengal, for the free use of Migne's vast thesaurus of the 'Fathers', and of Adyar Library in 1943 for letting me copy certain other Gnostic texts not in my own possession.—D.G.

THE PATH OF FIRE

Before these worlds of matter first took shape,
The Heaven-Father of eternal Calm
Enshadowed Nūt, the holy Queen of Love,
With veiled power; so sprang forth to birth,
Amid the groanings of the depths of Space,
The dawning glory of a new-formed life.

His Thought enshrined in Form, all planes of life
Now swift surpassing, Earth appeared in fire;
And on its shore to find the Mystic Pearl
And to attain the Robe of spotless Light,
Through many sorrows striving yet to learn—
A host of Monads from the Silence flashed,
And downward sped through all the whirling Spheres.

One Spark of scintillating beauty watch
Descending to the realm of Nature's night;
From plane to plane, through darkness bred of sin,
It tries to enter on the carnal life—
Until at last it sinks to sleep, and flows
In all the heavings of the voiceless Deep;
It slumbers in the mighty rocks and stones,
Then stirs to gentle whispering in the trees
And softly murmurs in the rustling ferns.

Till one great Day the scene of life is changed,
Swift-rising through the grades of bird and beast
Until the dawning consciousness of Man
At last appears. Yet long in Matter chained,
The yearning Monad scarce can loose its bonds
And often sinks again to slumber deep
While ages pass—the tale of Earth unfolds.

At last the Hour of Fate; this wandering Soul
Perceives its true vocation, seeks the Light
And enters on the ancient Path to God.
Few struggles more; the agelong fight is won,
And rapid strides secure the shining Pearl,
While Angels gladly aid its hastening steps.
In giving all, it finds the Key of Heaven
And swiftly passes homeward on its way.

What shouts of joyful welcome cheer its path,
While all the Victors of the glorious Fight
Stand round with anthems. Now the King of All
Comes forth with such a smile of love, and bears
A shining Raiment glorious as the Sun,
And clothes it therewith, hails it as a Prince
At last returned from long-drawn travels far;
While every side resounds the shout of joy
That bursts from every hardened Warrior there;
They press around to greet the Victor-Soul;
They join its jubilation in the King—
The Father-Mother Lord of endless worlds,
Who through the perils of this chain of life

xix

Has guided and protected till the end
The Spirit leaning on His loving Breast
And drawn it into Union sublime.

Eternal Wisdom, Source of Love and Light!
The Heavens first arose at Thy dread will,
And with the glory of that deathless Might
They roll in splendour through the paths of Space;
While Thine own Sons are searching for Thee still
In every age, through every creed and race;
Against the many wiles of flesh they fight
And nobly strive to find the Soul of Right.
To Thee we bring our joyous meed of praise,
To Thee our King of Peace through boundless
    days!

16-8-1919

INTRODUCTION

GNOSTICISM belongs to one of the definite Religious Families, such as the Semitic Group, the Indian Group, the Ethical Group and the Autochthonous Group, with which we are not now immediately concerned. The Gnostic Group of Religions arose in the lands east of the Mediterranean, was non-evangelistic and intended mainly for individuals personally qualified for initiation into its Mysteries. We have already in this Series studied two Religions of this Group: Hermeticism (GH) and Manicheism (GPM), derived respectively from Egypt and from various elements in the popular religions of the Iranian Empire of the 3rd century A.D.; we now turn to Gnosticism itself, a definite attempt to blend the dawning philosophies of the age, the longing for a personal Saviour, and the immense prestige of ancient Scriptures, with direct experience of the Reality. We shall find in the course of our study how almost every sentence may be paralleled with one from the Gospels of Hermes and the Prophet Mani, and later with the subsequent Gospel of the Mandeans; the relationship between members of this Group is so intimate it is sometimes impossible to say from which a given sentence may have come. These three volumes, at least, should therefore be read together, if the student would have a true picture of the religious atmosphere surrounding the birth and infancy of Christianity.

In this volume, I have preferred to concentrate largely on a detailed exposition of the text, leaving only a short introduction. To do justice to the history of Gnosticism, one must plunge into thousands of pages of books, most of them not available to me here; and one must spend at least three years on the task, which would not repay the effort for one engaged in a Series of this magnitude, a religionist rather than a mere specialist in Gnosticism.

1. Background of the Gnosis

The old State cults had lost the faith of educated people; a welter of new religions were pouring into the vacuum left behind; the masses, and many of the philosophical, had begun to turn to the hope of a new life offered by the Soteric cults which had grown from the ancient Mysteries; the time was ripe for new revelations of the One Truth. The trend of the age is well shown by the fourth chapter in Gilbert Murray's ' Five Stages of Greek Religion '.

In his splendid ' Fragments of a Faith Forgotten ', G.R.S. Mead gives a most vivid account of Alexandria in the great days of the Gnostic schools; and here we see one of the main focal points of Gnosticism. Alexandria was mainly a Greek city but planted firmly on Egyptian soil, and though many of its people were Jews, the bulk must always have been Egyptian; the form of the Gnosis which chiefly flourished there must have looked back to ancient Egypt for its foundations. In two volumes of this Series, the 'Gospel of the Pyramids' and the 'Gospel of Hermes', we have already seen something of that Egyptian background. It was solidly laid in Egypt's ancient Mysteries—in the Solar Faith, realising the oneness of the Initiate with the Divinity of Light; and in the Osirian Faith, raising the spiritually dead through the Life of Incarnate Deity into spiritual and eternal Life. Until the ignorant arrogance of the Victorian age, no one doubted the reality of those Egyptian Mysteries, or the vast wisdom which ensouled them; even proud little Greece, intoxicated with Alexander's victory over a world, eagerly paid homage to the almost infinite antiquity of those Mysteries and their influence on religious thought in all the lands. They admitted themselves to be but children before the priests of Egypt who had been initiated therein. So the Gnosis found in Egypt a fruitful soil, and there it could perhaps longer than elsewhere survive the insensate bigotry of the new-growing Faith of the West.

But, as our first Appendix will tell us, the Mysteries of Phrygia—that is, of Asia Minor, parent of the prehistoric Cretan cult of Rhea, Mother-Goddess, and Zeus her Son—though perhaps influenced by Egyptian refugees from the founders of the Dynasties about 3400 B.C., claimed even greater antiquity for themselves. Because we have no written texts from Phrygia to compare with the marvellous scriptures in the Pyramids, we cannot now check upon this claim; it would be foolish on that account to deny it. Behind the old Greek culture and its myths, revealed in part in Homer's later epics and excavations in the Mycenean sites on the mainland, lay this vast tradition, stretching back beyond the limits of recorded time. In the Greek myths and legends of later date, we catch glimpses of the faith and rites of those old people; we find evidence of an appalling volume of human sacrifice, even as among the Aztecs of medieval Mexico; we trace orgiastic rites which recall tales of the decline of Atlantean religion; we discover a gradual development of kingship out of unions between gods and nymphs. Coming nearer to our own days, we meet the Mysteries of Eleusis, of which the same Appendix speaks, Mysteries of Orpheus wherein the candidate was made infinitely pure and immortal and so at-oned with his God, Mysteries ineffable wherein the initiates trod the ancient Inner Path to the Supreme.

Turning eastwards, we come to the focal centre of Ephesus, where the timeless worship of the Divine Mother of the Aegeans later had its home; here St Paul preached, and here St John settled down; and here arose one of the greatest churches of Christianity. Here too, it is clear that many Gnostic 'sects' arose, even in the days of the Evangelist himself (cf. 2 Jn); early legends associate his name with the mysterious Cerinthus or Merinthus—who bears a pre-Hellenic name suggesting Cretan origin—as one of the very first of the Christian Gnostics and 'heretics'.

Further east still, we come to Antioch and Edessa, long among the pillar-churches, where the old religions of Syria and the 'Chaldees' (cf. App. IV) flowered afresh in Hermetic and Gnostic forms; here lived Bardaisan, the poet of the Gnostics, and near by, in Harran, there were Hermetists till about the tenth century of our era.

Yet eastwards travel, and we come to that old old land of Babylonia, one of mankind's cradle-homes, perhaps the birthplace of magic, astrology and syllabic writing. Way back before the dawn of history they told there of how Tammuz descended to the lower world to slay Tiamat, the great Dragon of Chaos, and the Soul's betrothal to the King of Gods and Men—as Widengren has shown us in his fascinating books. Here in the 3rd century Mani found the Gnosis vividly alive; from it he drew much that inspired his own great Message to mankind from the King of Light. The vitality of the old Chaldean faith, taking ever fresh forms as among the Hebrews was a constant inspiration to those who sought to penetrate the mere husk of outer words to the living kernel within. How then could the Hebrews, whose faith grew and blossomed during the long exile on Babylon's hideous sands, fail to develop their own form of the Gnosis? Forbidden by the orthodox to ask about the origin or final end of things, yet the Jewish philosophers, like their brethren elsewhere, pierced the dusty words of the Mosaic Law to find the living waters of spiritual truth. Philo and his Contemplatives, the Essenes and Therapeuts of Egypt and the Jordan desert, did much to enlighten mankind, without breaking adrift from the anchorage of the divinely guided past.

And so we journey further eastward still, into the now almost treeless Iranian plateau, where, as we know now, so much of the Gnosis had its real source in the popular faith—divorced as it always was from the royal cult of Zarathushtra, even while using his holy name to gain additional authority for its teachings.

At last we come to India, the immemorial land of Yoga and the Jñānis, where spiritual realisation of the one Reality has always been upheld as the supreme aim of life, the one thing worthy of our utmost effort to attain. We have not yet worked out the actual influence of India upon the Western Jñānis, or as we call them Gnostics; yet it is clear to the sympathetic, and therefore to the honest, student it must have been very great. At times we can almost recognise a direct quotation from some Indian scripture; vaguer echoes meet us on every page. In speaking of how the Gnosis dawns upon the mind, Valentinus might have been a follower of Śaṅkara; in his defining of the path to self-realisation, Monoimus seems to echo Sri Ramaṇa Maharṣi; the unknown writer of the lovely 'Gnosis of the Light' seems to carry in mind the Vedas and

Upanishads. Even the more peculiarly Christian Gnosis of Leucius Charinus, of the Ephesian (?) school, would have found little alien in the main trends of Sanskrit philosophy.

Yet this is not to suggest any direct contact, any actual imitation. The Gnostics were not men who made up synthetic religions out of tatters from the old discredited past. Like their brothers taught of Hermes, God of wisdom, they were Seers in their own right, Rshis who described what they knew for themselves, out of their own direct experience; but like every human being they had to put that experience into human words which had been used before by others, with their own connotations. So it is that they drew upon the ancient myths and legends, the old religious concepts of the lands where they lived and worked and taught, much as did the writers of the Purāṇas. It is thus that they seem to group into 'sects' with various modes of expression of the same one truth; and it is thus that the ignorant, who were concerned not with understanding but with denial, refutation, ridiculing, imagined a welter of conflicting doctrines, where there was a total unity—only expressed in various ways for the understanding of Greeks, Egyptians, Syrians, and the rest. There were no Gnostic 'sects'; there was only Gnosticism.

And so it is that we find in our first Appendix the Jewish Gnostic commenting on, explaining, the barbarous myths of Greece, Phrygia and Egypt, and the

Mycenean poetry of Homer—to be himself later commented and explained by a Christian Gnostic, eager to show how Jesus had been truly foreshadowed by the pagans even as by the Jews, his own people.

This is the Gnosis—the realisation of truth for oneself, truth about God and the Soul, and how these react upon each other in the Universe; how the Soul fell into this unseemly slavery to Matter, and how it can at last, at the awakening Call and Teaching of the manifested Divine-Light, return to its heavenly Home Above where all is Light supreme. This has to be put in words; and the choice of words depended on the individual background of the Seer-teacher and his pupils. The language used was almost always the Greek of the day, for that was the language of cultured men everywhere; it is an accident that most of our sources are now Coptic translations from the lost original Greek, which fell victim to the senseless vandalism of orthodox inquisitors in the 4th and later centuries. Happy are we that the people of Egypt in those days gave so natural and hearty a welcome to this philosophy; thus it is that in the various crude and unphilosophical dialects of their language so much of this precious literature has survived to our day. It is now at last that men are again coming on the earth to read it with a modicum of understanding and appreciation, despite the mental degradation which uniform and utilitarian education threatens to bring upon mankind.

2. Sources of the Gnostic Gospel

1. The Coptic Codices:
First in importance for our Sources of Gnosticism, as it was to those who loved and studied it, are the five Codices which time has spared to us in the sands of Egypt. We shall glance at these in turn:

a. **The Agnew Codex,** preserved in the British Museum, London, which the authorities most kindly allowed me to consult in person during about a fortnight in 1955, while preparing for this volume.

The manuscript is written on vellum, in a neat hand in the Sahidic dialect of Upper Egypt: there were probably not more than two scribes, one of whom could hardly have been less than 80 years of age, and the other 60 or 65. It is a book of 346 pages and is all but complete; it was bought for the Museum from the heirs of Dr. Askew about 1784, but for a long time its importance was unrecognised. It is clearly a copy of the original translation from the Greek, which has evidently undergone several recensions, with a good deal of accretion. There is no single title for the book, but in the middle occurs as a sort of sub-title the name 'Pistis-Sophia', by which it is generally known; I have cited it throughout as (PS); near the end occurs the sub-title 'Extracts from the Books of the Saviour', and Harnack suggests that a part may have been styled 'The Questions of Mary'; in fact it is clear that we have a composite work.

Horner analysed the book into five separate parts: (*a*) a Valentinian source, perhaps by the master himself, from p. 1 to p. 114; this, he thinks, shows no sign of knowing St. John's Gospel; however it seems to me clear that the writer knew as much of early Christian literature as the writer of the Gospel of Bartholomew or the Epistle of the Apostles; (*b*) from p. 115 to p. 233, which he thinks is mostly by Valentinus and a direct disciple; it seems to me likely that it is a later overwriting of a book by Valentinus; the author is admitted to have known Mt. Then we have (*c*), from p. 233 to p. 318, from the 'Books of the Saviour', which Horner dates, at least in part, to the reign of Philip the Arabian (244-250); it quotes Rom. by name on p. 294 and hints at the persecution under Septimius Severus (193-211), he says; (*d*) from p. 318 to p. 336, which is quite independent of the doctrine of the earlier strata and largely magico-sacramental, like that of our 'Gnoses of the Invisible God', a good deal contaminated with pagan sorcery; this section Horner dates between A. D. 245 and 388. Lastly, we have (*e*) an appendix, equally late, which now treats the pagan gods as fiends. Horner's view that the whole, as we have it, is a legal selection made by the orthodox to condemn heresy in the 6th or 8th century does not seem to have anything to recommend it to the scholar. There is no such idea in the mind of Schmidt or Mead or Amélineau, all of whom take this, like the other Codices, as genuine Gnostic works intended for the study of Gnostic students.

Horner agrees that the story of Wisdom is very early and that it may be the 'book of Wisdom' written by Valentinus; the tedious and rather far-fetched parallels from the Psalms, and the Odes of Solomon, seem likely to have been added no earlier than the 4th century, when the memorising of such works was popular among Egyptian contemplatives and ascetics. Horner points to a few slight contradictions in detail here and there, which he believes suggest varying recensions current at the time; I doubt it.

After telling how Jesus was glorified at his Ascension, the book narrates how he found Wisdom waiting outside the Thirteenth Aeon and was after many labours and prayers enabled to restore her to her place in glory. In the meantime Jesus answers many questions of the disciples on spiritual matters, and these questions continue after the story of Wisdom ends rather abruptly; they cover all aspects of the moral and spiritual life. Much of the teaching is the same as that of Hermes; rebirth is assumed, but at the same time punishments in hell are insisted on, as though they were not thereby rendered superfluous. The absolute need for initiation in the Gnostic Mysteries is constantly stressed, and the qualifications of candidates are clearly laid down. While all are to know of this possibility, actual initiation is to be reserved for the few made worthy by lives of total renunciation of worldliness. The book has sometimes been called 'The Fifth, or Gnostic, Gospel'.

b. **The Bruce Codex** lies in the Bodleian Library, Oxford, having been deposited there by its discoverer, the famous African traveller. It is written on 78 leaves of papyrus in book form, in the Sahidic dialect, and it contains two main documents, with fragments of another. The leaves are in great confusion, the disarrangement having perhaps originally occurred in the Greek text from which they were translated, maybe in the latter part of the 4th century. I have followed the rearrangement made by Mead, which seems far more reasonable to me than Schmidt's, though I have retained his page-numbering.

The *Untitled Apocalypse*, to which the name 'The Gnosis of the Light' has been aptly given (cited as GL), is in fine handwriting and is of great sublimity both in matter and in style. Indeed it is one of the few works in Coptic which deserve the name of 'literature'. It seems to belong originally to the earliest stage of the Christian Gnosis, though later over-written, and has much in common with the recently found 'Gospel of the Truth' written by Valentinus (c. A.D. 140). It is hard to find a grander attempt to describe the Divinity than we have here; stage by stage Its unfoldment is pictured, and the mission of the 'Light-Spark' in the world is outlined. It is true that we have a characteristically late over-elaboration of detail while speaking of the Deeps, the Fatherhoods and other celestial Powers, but it is easy to dissect these away from an earlier core which must have come from one of the great and truly inspired geniuses of the age. Could it have been the unknown Phōsilampēs once named in our text, or the Nikotheos who is also spoken of as a true Gnostic—though the fragment of his Apocalypse published by Scott seems pretty poor stuff. The use of the name Sētheus for God in this book seems to point to an origin among 'Sethian' Gnostics, of whom we can say only that they were mainly Egyptians and thought of the Supreme as Light, co-operating with the Darkness in bringing the universe into being (GG 5 : 3-10). We owe much that is finest in our 'Gospel' to this little book, whose title is unhappily lost along with its first and last pages. A complete translation into English was attempted by Lamplugh, but this is at times inaccurate.

The *Gnoses of the Invisible God* (cited as GIG), which forms the major part of the Codex, is thus styled at its beginning, while at the end we have the sub-title 'The Book of the Great Word for Every Mystery'. For some unknown reason Schmidt dubbed it 'The Two Books of Ieou', which it most certainly is not.

The book seems to be one, though its parts are very confused now. After a statement of the nature of the Gnosis, Jesus promises to initiate his worthy disciples into every Mystery, even the highest, which will make them one with the All; they are to keep these Mysteries from all save those known to be worthy of initiation. He then admits them into the Baptisms of Water of Life, of Fire, and of the Holy Spirit, in each case after an invocation conferring on them the magic seal, mantram and prayer. Then after removing the 'Evil of the Rulers', *i.e.*, of their fallen human nature, he speaks of the might of the Absolution from all sins, which alone opens the inward path to Ieou, God Manifest, and so on beyond to the Unknowable and Unattainable. But before they actually take these final steps he confers on them the name, seal, number and mantram of each of the Fourteen Aeons in turn, and then initiates them into the mysteries of the Three Rulers who are under Ieou. Then we have a tedious account, with diagrams quite beyond my understanding, of the twenty-five Treasuries of the various Ieous, or Forms of God Manifest, leading on to the supreme Mystery-Name of God and to several Hymns, of greater or less sublimity but with a typically oriental love of repetition.

This book, as we have it, seems clearly later than the Apocalypse with which it is bound; it may have been written in Greek not earlier than A.D. 270, and the Coptic version may be about half a century later. It uses a more cursory script, including certain hieroglyphs in place of oft-repeated phrases; though there are here and there passages of great beauty, noted by Mead in his summary, the general literary level is such that it is unlikely anyone will publish a complete English translation of it. Schmidt's German version is fair, though it shows the usual Teutonic heaviness.

(*c*) **The Akhmim Codex.** This lies, I believe, in the Berlin Museum, and as long ago as 1896 Carl Schmidt promised to publish it in two years' time. Unhappily, this promise has not been fulfilled, and we have no means outside Berlin of consulting the important documents comprising it. The text was bought in Cairo, said to have come from Akhmim; it is written on 71 pages of papyrus, each of about 20 lines; the writing is said to be of great beauty and to date from the 5th century, so late a date being interesting as showing how long Gnosticism vigorously survived in Upper Egypt. It contains three separate treatises, the last being a small and uninteresting fragment of the *Acts of Peter*, which has been published separately and is available with me.

The first work is prefixed by the title '*The Gospel of Mary*' and ended with the title '*The Apocryphon of John*'; as Mead points out, it is very important because here we have the original Gnostic text which Irenaeus tried to summarise, and we can see what a sorry hash he made of the work; his prejudices made him quite unable to understand what he was attacking. After Jesus answers several questions from the disciples, we have an account of the 'Barbēlō-Gnosis', which proves in no way different from the Gnosis of our other main sources and to bear close resemblance to the 'Gnosis of the Light'. The book must have been written in Greek about A.D. 160, in Coptic perhaps by A.D. 300; its origin was clearly in Egypt, like most of our Coptic texts.

The Wisdom of Jesus the Christ would be of great interest to us, but unhappily it has not yet seen the light, so far as I can trace. Derived from Schmidt's preliminary notice, Mead gives a few words from its beginning; his suggestion that it may be the 'Wisdom' of Valentinus does not seem likely to me, but *we* have really no evidence whatever on the point.

Though I have used a few sentences from this Codex in the footnotes, I have not ventured to draw on it for the text of our ' Gospel '. It is really deplorable that scholars who have a sort of ' corner ' in texts of importance to all students should be able thus to block their free circulation. It is the first duty of anyone coming into possession of such early texts to make the *text* itself available without delay—the treatment of the Dead Sea Scrolls has been in this way excellent—translations, commentaries, and disputations may then follow at the leisure of the scholars interested, but the dog-in-the-manger policy of certain scholars who hold up for years material needed by their fellow-students is most unworthy. Unhappily it seems to be not rare nowadays.

(*d*) **The Jung Codex,** found at Nāg-Hammādi, Upper Egypt, in 1948, was in 1952 bought for the famous psychoanalyst; it consists of five treatises of the utmost importance. After an early promise to publish the text of all the five at once, so far Rascher Verlag, Zürich, has published one only, with superfluous translations actually into three languages: French, German and English—which seems to me personally an extraordinary and wasteful procedure. Meanwhile the two scholars who have been entrusted with the work, H. Ch. Puech and G. Quispel, issued in 1954 a valuable notice on the whole Codex, on which I have had to rely for my information. It seems uncertain now whether we shall ever have the texts of the other treatises made available as in the case of the Bruce Codex by Schmidt and the Askew Codex by Schwartz; publication is made to depend on the sale of the first costly volume of a part.

The first treatise is a Gnostic *Letter of James*, carrying an esoteric teaching from Jesus after the Resurrection to James and Peter alone; it may well be from a Greek original of mid-second century. After several questions have been answered, James tells of the Ascension, whereat Jesus blessed the disciples with uplifted right hand. The Letter is complete and covers 16 pages of the whole Codex, which is in the sub-Akhmimic dialect of Coptic.

The Gospel of Truth, which has now been published in full in a most magnificent way, is almost certainly that anciently attributed to Valentinus himself; from its style one would say he wrote it early in life, say about A.D. 140. It tells how Ignorance about God arose and created misery among Souls, and how to disperse its darkness God revealed the Perfect Man who died on earth for men, His 'Name', teaching all those whose names were in the Book of Life and so were ready to hear his words. Then they awake from the dreams of Illusion, which is like a drunken sleep, and in the daylight all their frightful fantasies vanish and they are aware of God's Light. Blessed is he who opens the eyes of the spiritually blind, who rescues the lost lamb wandering on the mountains! God knows His own; those whom He calls answer His voice and do His will on earth; for such there is no darkness, no death any more, for "His children are perfect and worthy of His Name, for they are children such as He the Father loves". The whole Gospel was on 27 pages of about 35 lines each; of these 5 pages are lost from the middle. The language is somewhat archaic, suggesting an early translation, perhaps by A.D. 220.

The Letter to Reginus, five pages of the Codex, deals mainly with the real nature of the Resurrection, not of this corruptible flesh, but of the spiritual body which never dies but awakens from its sleep and rises into the brightness of the Heavenly Light. This is fully Valentinian in character, and may well have been written by the master himself.

Of the *Treatise on the Three Natures*, much of it unhappily lost, I know almost nothing; the notice calls it "a mythical and theological account, very elaborate and of vast dimensions". It may have dealt with the three types of Souls: spiritual, psychic, material. Of 83 pages we lack the beginning and also 32 pages in the middle.

The Codex ends with a fragmentary *Prayer of the Apostle* (Peter?) on two pages, of which I can say nothing.

The whole Codex probably belonged to a Valentinian, the scholars think, who later joined a 'Sethian' community near Asyūt; it is neatly written in the archaic sub-Akhmimic, and shows clear proof of having been translated from Greek originals of the second century, while our manuscript will date from late in the fourth. It was evidently part of a Gnostic library, for with it were found the massive collection of the (Cairo) Codex.

(e) **The (Cairo) Codex,** found along with that owned by Prof. Jung and retained in Cairo, where it is now being studied. Almost nothing has yet reached us about it in India, though the above-mentioned notice refers to two *Apocalypses of James* as being included in its almost a thousand pages, along with a so-called *Gospel of Thomas*. The latter has been roughly described by R. C. Fuller in the London 'Tablet' of 22nd December 1956; it contains twenty pages of Logia of Jesus written down by Judas Thomas the Twin, each preceded by "Jesus said"; some are canonical sayings, some known from apocrypha, and some are quite new.

In this great Codex we are told there are twelve manuscripts in all, all of them dating from the second century; students will wait with ill-concealed eagerness for their publication in full—without needless delays over translations and commentation. Most scholars can manage any one of English, French or German, even if ignorant of Coptic; there is no need to delay publication in order to provide all three at once.

No doubt the future will give us many more such delightful discoveries; there seems no end to the treasures held by Egypt for us to unearth when the time is ripe. Unfortunately, just now men are too busy contemplating mass suicide and wholesale murder to have any time or interest for the humanities which civilised their parents.

2. The Gnostic Acts

In order to appeal to the masses there is little value in books on straight philosophy; the early Gnostic, and Christian, propagandists therefore circulated what comes close to the idea of historical novels, purporting to narrate the adventures of the first disciples of Jesus. Many of these 'Acts' were quite orthodox; they were concerned simply with the story and with popularising the name of Christianity by heroic adventures among the barbarians—the question of historical accuracy just did not arise in the matter. Others were specifically Gnostic, designed to spread abroad a knowledge of the main qualifications for initiation in the Mysteries —asceticism, chastity, or rather encratism, and a high moral standard. After some years the skill of the Gnostic writers made their works more popular than those of their rivals; the Catholics then pirated them, diluted or excised the 'heretical' or doubtful doctrines, and gave them out as their own work. But the intelligence of these 'revisers' was not quite equal to their task, and they missed much, which to our very good fortune remains for us to study.

The most important, and earliest, group of the Gnostic Acts were those attributed to one Leucius Charinus, said to be a direct disciple of St. John. Because of the coincidence of their special teachings with Manicheism, they later enjoyed great popularity among the members of that Faith, to which an age of later ignorance even came to ascribe their authorship. The characteristically Manichean number 'five' appears in this collection, for it consisted of the Acts of five of the Apostles: Peter, Andrew, John, Thomas and Philip.

(a) *Acts of Peter.* A Gk. manuscript of part of these Acts survives, evidently subjected to a certain amount of catholicising revision; there is a fragment in Coptic translation in the Akhmim Codex, of slight interest to us from the Gnostic point of view. Much appears in Latin in Bibl. Patr. Max. ii, and we find parts also in Hegesippus and in the Acts of Nereus and Achilleus. The book was condemned by Pope Gelasius, but a Catholic version, stressing the very ancient story of St Peter's residence as Bishop of Rome, was later amalgamated with an old Acts of Paul. Thilo published it in 1837-8. James has made a translation which contains several portions of deep and beautiful Gnostic meaning (GG 38-40).

(b) *Acts of Andrew.* A fragment of the original book condemned by Pope Gelasius about A.D. 490 is preserved in Euodius: de Fide contra Manichaeos, 38; the book was elaborately purged of 'heresy' in perhaps the 4th century, and is in good Greek. While publishing it in 1847, Thilo rejected an earlier view that it dated from the apostolic age; we have used the famous Address to the Cross in GG 39-40, the only part still free from orthodox meddling.

(c) *Acts of John*; perhaps our richest source of this type, since the discovery by James in a Vienna manuscript of 14th century of a long and uncontaminated fragment (Apocrypha Anecdota II, 1897), which after a docetic introduction gives us our GG 29-37; almost every word of this fragment is of inestimable value to the student of the Christian Gnosis. Thilo published in 1847 other fragments of the Acts known at Halle, and Fabricius published a Latin account of the Apostle's death claiming to derive from the original of Leucius. There are also several beautiful prayers in the Acts, which lay much stress on the value of virginity (*cf.* GG 94).

(*d*) *Acts of Thomas.* This book is nearly complete in Thilo's collection, so too in Tischendorf's. The story of the Apostle's martyrdom in India may be historical, or it may be confused with the much later 'Thomas' of Mani's Faith, or refer to the 'Twin'-Teacher who accompanied every missionary, for there are constant references to Jesus appearing in the Apostle's form. But these Acts have special value to us for the separate poems which they have enfolded —chiefly the 'Hymn of the Pearl' (GG 70-77), Wisdom's Wedding-Song (GG 92), and the Eucharistic Prayers of GG 93—though on almost every page of the Gk. version there are traces of the Gnostic origin. Pseudo-Abdias is said to have been the catholicizing reviser; but even for the orthodox of an earlier age it ranked high among the 'Antilegomena'.

(*e*) *Acts of Philip.* In their original form these have almost wholly perished; those published in the Ante-Nicene volume, only a portion of the catholicised version, are much later and of little interest. The original is among the books condemned in the Gelasian decree.

3. Gnostic Gospels

We have a number of these, most of them tattered ruins of the original works, but some are coherent for many consecutive pages. I may here just mention the well-known fragment of the old *Gospel of Peter* found in 1896 and narrating the Crucifixion and Resurrection of Jesus, from a docetic angle, and another fragment believed by James to be from perhaps the same Gospel, relating to the Nativity; he published this in the London 'Sphere' for Christmas 1928, in English translation, taken from the 13th century Latin manuscript found in Hereford Cathedral. The *Revelation of Bartholomew*, also called the *Book of the Resurrection of Jesus the Christ*, is a long Coptic work covering much the same ground as the well-known Gospel of Nicodemus; it takes great delight in the discomfiture of Death and Hades, and in the excessive glory of the Risen Christ among his Angels; Bartholomew is described as the gardener of the Tomb. It was published with English translation from the Coptic by Budge in 1913 (BMOr. 6804) from an 11th century manuscript, 24 leaves of thin parchment said to have come from near Edfu in Upper Egypt.

4. Summaries in the Heresiologists

especially Irenaeus and Hippolytus. The former in his first book gives a detailed account of an early Valentinian version of the Wisdom Myth, to which Hippolytus adds his own materials a generation later. The latter also gives us excellent materials from

Basilides (GG 20-28), the Sethians (GG 5: 3-10), the Simonians (GG 4), the Naassenes (GG 88 and App. I), and various other minor 'sects'—which have been combined in GG 3: 3-4, 5: 2 and 12: 2-3. There is no reason to doubt the substantial accuracy of these materials, though we must always remember that they come from avowed enemies of the Gnosis, bent on proving it a deceit, error and monstrous lie, the very spawn of Satan.

5. Magic and Late Gnostic papyri, with prayers, invocations, and the like, some of them nearly incoherent, but many preserving traces of a more dignified source in an earlier century; some of these are as late as the 6th century; others are earlier, but expanded in the degenerate days when the light of Gnosis had waned dim.

3. Great Organisers of the Gnosis

Gnosticism differs from many other Western religions in having no one personal Founder, more or less deified as the ages passed by; in this respect it resembles rather the traditional religions of Egypt (attributed to the God Thōut or Hermes) and of Hindu India (generally attributed in some degree to Veda-Vyāsa), neither of which looks to a divine-human Founder for authority, both of them claiming to be timeless, established from of old.

It is quite certain that there is little or no historical evidence for the existence of most of the 'founders' of

Gnostic 'sects', so elaborately listed by the orthodox refutators and memorised by theological students to this day. At the best, they are all extremely shadowy personages—like Cerinthus, the fabled Simon, Harpocrates, Satornilos, Marcos, Nicolaus, Ptolemy and the rest—and they play no part in real history, even if they ever lived. The way a non-existent 'Epiphanes' was invented out of the word *epiphanēs*, distinguished, together with the fixed idea that no sect could exist without a personal founder, give adequate proof of how the refutators' minds worked.

Marcion was less of a Gnostic than a 'higher critic', who dissected the usual scriptures into the credible and the incredible; Heracleon was noted as the first Christian commentator, who chose St John's Gospel, always a favourite with the Gnostically-minded, to elucidate. Only four great names stand out as of Gnostics who were certainly historical figures, and as it happens all four of these must have been great men. We shall now turn our eyes on these four, who played a great part in the development also of Christian thought.

(*a*) **Leucius Charinus** was traditionally the author of the Five Apostolic Acts we have already touched upon and which so long enjoyed wide popularity, being in fact a major factor in the spread of early Christianity, both in their original Gnostic form, and even when doctored in the interests of Catholic orthodoxy. These were the Acts of Peter, Andrew, John, Thomas and Philip; they survive to our day in varied degrees of completeness.

Zahn has shown that at first the whole collection was not regarded as heretical at all; this may well be because of their very early association with the Fourth canonical Gospel. Leucius Charinus—whose two names curiously recur together in the 'Gospel of Nicodemus' as witnesses of the resurrection, having themselves been raised at the same time (pp. 213, 222, Ante-Nicene volume)—was a disciple of St John, presumably the evangelist; where we have reason to believe we have his original intact, the style would bear this out. A very old manuscript of the Gospel reads: Verily, I say I am not of this world; but John shall be your Father till he shall go with me into Paradise. And he (Jesus) anointed them with the Holy Spirit. ... (Jesus said): "Weep not; I go to my Father and to Eternal Life. Behold thy son; he will keep my place" [Codex Apoc. N.T. (Thilo), p. 880]. This preserves an old tradition, perhaps at Ephesus, by which John, not Peter, was left in charge of the Church. And the Leucian Acts are in a style of Greek which resembles closely that of St John's Gospel, with the same intimacy and sweetness, simplicity and mystical depth.

I find no sort of difficulty in believing that the old Saint, who died about A.D. 95, could have had then a disciple aged 20, who could have written these Acts when in the full prime of maturity, about 55, by which time it would have been A.D. 130; the style is not that of a young man, but of one experienced in much suffering from the world, after deep contemplation of the real meaning of the Christian revelation, one who after long struggles to overcome the flesh has at last attained the victory. There is nothing in these Acts which would go against their having been written in or near Ephesus, where St John lived and died; there are many signs that the first writing was very early, as where in the 'Acts of John' a trivial multiplication of bread is mentioned as a great miracle, which it could hardly be after the far greater stories of the canonical Mk. 6: 35-44 and 8: 1-9, generally regarded by critics as a 'doublet' or parallel version of the same event, were well known.

(*b*) **Basilides.** This great man, whose philosophy has at times a distinctly Eastern (Kennedy says Buddhist) flavour, claimed to be a disciple of Glaucias, the disciple of St Peter—nor is this quite impossible if Glaucias was very young at St Peter's death in A.D. 67 and lived to a great age. But Epiphanius, by no means a reliable witness, alleges that he was a fellow-pupil of Maenander under Satornilos at Antioch; his known writings show no sign of such a pupilship. He taught in Alexandria from about A.D. 117 to 138, and Agrippa Castor tells us he came to be regarded as a heretic in A.D. 133. He wrote twenty-four 'books' of exegesis, a Gospel (probably our important chapter 5, derived from Hippolytus's summary), and a number of Odes. Irenaeus, who seems to have confused Basilides with some other man, gives an account of his teaching quite different from the more reliable story of Hippolytus; it is said he appealed to (the Odes of) Zoroaster, *i.e.*, the Chaldean Oracles (?). He may have died by about A.D. 145, but his 'sect' survived in Egypt west of the Delta till the end of the fourth century and was even carried to Spain by one Marcus of Memphis.

(c) **Valentinus** is said to have been a disciple of Theodas, friend of St Paul, whom some believe to be the Theodotus from whose writings extracts are given by Clement of Alexandria and are close to the later Valentinian systems. This last fact seems to rule out the possibility for me. He was born at Phebōtinē on the Egyptian coast, and from about A.D. 130 was teaching Greek science and literature in Alexandria. Perhaps under the influence of the wonderful Library there, he realised the need to synthesise the many various forms of the Gnosis then circulating round the Mediterranean area; probably it was here that he began to organise the Gnosis into a single religious system, with its own initiations, and possibly its own baptisms and passwords. This will have been soon after his conversion to a form of Christianity more or less Johannine in its colour.

At all events, his successors always looked on him as the great organiser, though not the founder, of Christian Gnosticism. It is likely that his famous 'Gospel of the Truth', recently found in Coptic translation and published as a part of the Codex Jung in 1956, which bears marks of a young author, was written in these early days, while the 'Letter to Reginus' seems to have come from an older man. He was naturally later drawn to Rome, the Imperial centre which was so fast becoming centre of the Christian

Church, and he is said to have arrived there under Pope Hyginus about A.D. 138. At that time there was still no question of his orthodoxy, and we learn that his name was even at one time proposed to fill St Peter's See. He lived there till about A.D. 160, and then, we are told, retired to Cyprus.

It is more than doubtful if during his lifetime his orthodoxy was ever questioned; the Church was then far more liberal in its theology, and it seems much more likely that it was the extravagances of the later elaborators of his doctrine, among whom we learn was one called Ptolemy, which led to his being smeared with the name of 'heretic' and his work anathematized by the Church. What we now possess of his own writing seems hardly more heretical than, say, Dionysius the Areopagite or much that was written by St John of the Cross, a doctor of the Church. Though the influence of St Paul is clearly marked, he leaned heavily, like most of the Christian Gnostics, on the Gospel of St John.

We know nothing of the dates of his birth and death; he may have lived till about A.D. 175, for Irenaeus writes of him as his own contemporary in A.D. 195.

(d) **Bardaisan** (Gk. Bardesanēs), whose name itself tells us that he was born on the banks of the River Daisan near Edessa in Syria; that was on 11th July A.D. 155. His parents, rich and noble, were Nuhama, and Nahashirama, and he received the best education of the day, being brought up along with the Crown Prince Abgar of the royal family. As a boy he was skilled in archery, and he was still young when converted to Gnostic Christianity, leaving the heathen faith of the priest of Mabug (Hierapolis). He seems to have succeeded in converting his fellow-pupil, the Prince, who early in the third century came to be known as the King's counsellor and a holy man; he gave up the practice of ritual mutilation in honour of the goddess Tharathe.

This Abgar was probably the 'Bar Manu' who reigned at Edessa from A.D. 202 to 217; in the second year of his reign the Church at Edessa was destroyed by a flood, and in 216 he was overthrown by Caracalla, who thus put an end to the first Christian State.

After this disaster Bardaisan left for Armenia, but failing to make disciples there, proceeded to Ani; at Harran, or somewhere in Mesopotamia, he is said to have studied Indian religion (probably actually a Hermeticism using the Chaldean Oracles), and he died in A.D. 223, only eight years after Mani was born; his son Harmonius is said to have succeeded him as teacher of the ' sect '.

Bardaisan was a distinguished leader of the Church in both Greek and Syriac, and his book of 150 hymns was used in the Edessa Church until replaced by Ephraem's book about 170 years later. There is no evidence that during his life he was considered a heretic; indeed he came near to being a martyr and actually ranks as a confessor for Christianity; one writer notes that he was famous for his " patience and courteous answers to every man ". Mani opposed certain of his teachings in his 'Book of the Laws of Countries'.

We probably owe to his genius the lovely Syriac poem of GG 70-77, which Mead even suggests may be based on Bardaisan's own spiritual experiences; and Ephraem preserves for us two of his little Odes: "Thou fountain of joy / whose gate by commandment / opens wide to the Mother—/ a place which Divine beings / have measured and founded, / which Father and Mother / in their union have sown, / with their steps have made fruitful" (558 B.C.), and "When shall it at length be ours / to look on Thy banquet, / to see the young Maiden, / the Daughter Thou dost set / on Thy knee and caress?"

4. How Gnosis Comes to Man

Plotinus, in his Enneads (5 : 3 : 17) writes: "This is the true end to the Soul, to come into touch with His Light, and through it to behold Him—not by the light of anything else, but to perceive that very Thing itself by means of which it sees. . . . How can this be done? By an ablation of all things." For this we who are Souls exist, and there is no other purpose in life than this; nor can it be attained while we cling to other, lesser aims.

Fallen into Matter, as it were drugged by the forgetfulness absorbed before incarnation, the Soul now knows nothing of who or what it is, whence it has come and why, what it is to do and where it is to go.

This state is universal to all Souls still wrapped in the clouds of the Ignorance—whether they be spiritual, psychic and educable, or fleshly and carnal. The difference between the three types of soul lies in their varying ability to escape from this Ignorance and to enter into Gnosis. The spiritual soul is ready for the revelation of the Truth, the psychic can be prepared for it even during this life, the fleshly can appreciate nothing of it even if it be shown him in the clearest terms.

This Ignorance is compared to a drunken sleep, to a drugged incoherence of the mind and senses, to a state of fathomless darkness and of death. The realisation of the Truth which is the Gnosis is like a flash of incomparable Light wherein all things are at once made clear to those who are not blind. The change is not a gradual one; it is instantaneous where the Soul has matured and is ready for illumination. At one moment there is darkness, inertia, sleep; at the next, there is light, understanding, activity, and an awareness beyond anything that can be told. Krishnamurti said many years ago that even the 'savage' can also see that truth, provided he opens his eyes and mind to its glory.

Like the Advaitins of India, Valentinus in his Gospel compares the dawn of the Gnosis to awakening from the fantastic and unreal dreams of sleep; he says (G.J. 28-30): "What does He wish him to think? That I have become like the shadows and phantoms of the night; but when the Light appears he realises that the fear he had been seized by is nothing. Thus were they (once) in ignorance of the Father whom they did not see. While Ignorance inspired them with terror and trouble, with shaking torn and tattered, there were many vain and empty illusions and absurd fictions haunting them, like sleepers in the grip of nightmares, . . . until the moment when those who are passing through all these things awake. Then those who have experienced all these (things) suddenly see nothing, for all such dreams are nothing. This is how they drive far from them the Ignorance, as the sleep which they count as nothing, any more than they consider these visions to be real things; they abandon them like a dream of the night, and the Gnosis of the Father is the Light for them. Thus it is that each one has acted as if asleep during the time he was ignorant; it is thus he comes to himself as if he were awakening. Joy to the one who returns to himself and is awake, and blessed is he who has opened the eyes of the blind!"

Much is said in this book of ours on the content of the Gnosis; I need here quote only one passage from the *Acts of Thomas:* "Thou hast shown me how to seek myself and to know what I was, and who and what I am now, in order that I may again become as I was." It is a process of Self-realisation, of Self-adjustment to the eternal Plan of things, of perceiving God as He is in relation to us men in the universe He has made for us. Plutarch, an initiate of the Egyptian Mysteries which lie behind so much of our Gnosis, writes in his famous essay on Osiris and Isis (73:2): "Nor can the souls of men here on the earth, swathed as they are in bodies and enfolded in passions, commune with God, save in so far as they can reach some dim sort of a dream of Him with the perception of a mind trained in philosophy." Yet Plotinus personally saw God in the mystical experience of true Gnosis (Enneads 4:8:1), and Sri Ramakrishna and many Western mystics made the same claim.

Of such a true spiritual Gnostic Valentinus tells us in his Gospel: "He who has the Gnosis is a being from on high; if he is called he hears, replies and turns to Him who has called him, in order to come back to Him; and he understands how he is called. Knowing (it), he carries out the will of Him who has called him, he wishes to do what pleases Him, he receives Repose[1].... He who thus has the Gnosis knows whence he has come and whither he goes, he understands like a man who becomes sober after being intoxicated, and having come to himself he reaffirms what is essentially his own" (22).

So the Gnosis is a personal awakening; each Soul must of itself be called, roused and guided by the Light, put on the Robe of Glory. Yet if there be none to call, how can the sleeper be awakened? So the tradition is there, the ancient wisdom handed down through many ages, that every Soul may have the chance to arise and put on its strength, so that the Christ may illumine it. Thus we have the enduring

This is the stillness which is experience of the divine.

schools of initiation, secret as to detail from the masses, yet their existence known to all. Thus we have certain mystical Scriptures, to make the existence of the Inner Way known to all, while stipulating the conditions for its treading. Some of these scriptures are now known to us, though their deeper meaning may still be largely hidden from our uninitiated minds. Some are lost to our age, and will remain lost until the Souls who can benefit from their use come into birth, and their teachers are ready to take them as pupils on the Path.

Such a scripture was the medley known to us now as the 'Pistis Sophia', though its original name has been lost in the mists of time. And it points to others, as yet unknown to us, such as the two mysterious 'Books of Ieou', of which it writes: " So you have no need of the rest of lower mysteries, but you will find them in the two Books of Ieou which Enoch wrote while I spoke with him out of the Tree of Knowledge and out of the Tree of Life in Adam's Paradise. . . . And I made him place them in the Rock of Ararat, and I set (over them) the Ruler Kalapa-tauroth who is over Chemmut (and) on whom are Ieou's feet; and it is he who surrounds all the Aeons and the Fates. I set that Ruler as watcher over the Books of Ieou because of the Flood, and so that none of the Rulers might envy them and destroy them" (PS 99, 134). Mead has shown the connection between Thōut (Hermes, the God of Wisdom), whose seat was at Chmūne (Chemmut?) and the two mysterious Pillars in the Seriadic Land (Egypt) described by Josephus (see TGH I, pp. 114-115). The Sons of Seth (cf. Sētheus in GG 11: 1, etc.) " made two monuments, one of brick and the other of stone, and on each of them engraved their discoveries, in order that if it should happen that the brick one should be done away with by the heavy downpour, the stone one might survive and let men know what was inscribed upon it, at the same time informing them that a brick one had also been made by them." To this Ammianus Marcellinus (c. A.D. 360) adds about the Pyramids, identified with these two 'Pillars': "There are certain underground galleries and passages full of windings which, it is said, the adepts in the ancient rites (knowing that the flood was coming, and fearing that the memory of the sacred ceremonies would be obliterated) constructed in various places distributed in the interior, which were mined out with great labour. And smoothing the walls, they engraved on them numerous kinds of birds and animals, and countless varieties of another world, which they called hieroglyphic characters "—obviously here referring to the same Pyramid Texts which are now known, and which carry so much of the true Egyptian Gnosis down to our own day for those able to understand (cf. our 'Gospel of the Pyramids').

On the antiquity and authority of this Egyptian Gnosis, we may further note that telling the myths of his own people, the Phoenicians, Sanchuniathon says clearly that they derive from the Books of Thaaut (*i.e.*, Thōut), and also that the very idea of a spiritual consort, so prominent in the Wisdom Myth and in later Valentinianism, is also Egyptian—each God having his own Consort (Skt. *Sakti*), as Shōw and Tfēnewet, Usire and Eset. Even Hippolytus says (Ref. 6:17): "The source whence Plato derived his theory in the 'Timaeus' is the wisdom of the Egyptians; for from this source ... Solon taught his entire system ... to the Greeks, who were young children and acquainted with no theological doctrine of greater antiquity." 'Young children' is the technical term in the Gnosis for disciples.

But we shall wander far from the spirit of the Gnosis if we overstress its Egyptian origins, carried as they probably were through the first Cretans to the Greek mainland long before Mycene's walls were raised. The Gnosis is a worldwide truth, shared by all who can understand the Light. We have admired St Paul's splendid catholicity in his Gal. 3:28; what then are we to say of Plutarch in his same essay (77:2-4): "Not different (Gods) for different peoples, no barbaric or Greek, no southern or northern; but just as sun and moon and earth and sea are common to all, though called by various names by various peoples, so of the Mind that orders all things and of the Providence which also directs powers ordained to serve under her for all (purposes) have different honours and titles been made by different (nations) according to their laws. And there are consecrated symbols, some obscure and others more plain, guiding the intelligence towards the Mysteries of the Gods (though) not without risk. For some going entirely astray have stepped into superstitions, while others shunning superstition as a quagmire have unwittingly fallen into atheism as down a precipice."

Such was the catholic spirit of the Gnosis; and like to its devotees were the 'Therapeuts' of whom Philo speaks: few in number, ascetic, contemplative, " by their mind becoming free of body ". Elsewhere he calls them Magi " who by their careful scrutiny of nature's works for purpose of the gnosis of the Truth, in quiet silence and by means of images of piercing clarity are made initiate into the mysteries of godlike virtues, and in their turn initiate (others) " (Quod Om. Prob. 11). This tolerance and wide-mindedness which can alone keep the mind in perfect peace was the first qualification for the Gnosis, and every careful reader will see the relevance of these few extracts from contemporary books to the Gnosis which we are going to study. One who knows that the Truth is One and there is none else can alone afford to be truly tolerant; behind fanaticism and dogmatic bigotry only Ignorance tries to hide. One able to see the One Truth in all has already reached the illumination of the Gnosis and is made one with that All.

5. What Came of Gnosticism

True Gnosis is possible only when the Soul can wholly renounce worldly things and devote itself heartily to the single-minded search for God. The day had to come when, with the swift decay of the old Mediterranean culture and the rise of the barbarism of the new peoples from the North, Souls could no longer be found to tread this path of self-abnegation, save a very few who retreated into monasteries. The real Schools of Initiation ceased to function in the outer world and were withdrawn behind the veil.

Already, early in the fourth century, men in Egypt were losing their minds in violent and insensate fanaticism over futile theologisms and personal rivalries over the bishoprics; in the storm the great Alexandria Library was burned, the School of Philosophy was closed for want alike of students and of competent teachers. In place of the grand Gnosticism of the past, men began to seek a childish magic—the cure for diseases of possession, power over the spirits to injure their rivals, love-charms and the like. The same was happening in Babylonia, in Rome itself. The few who still through philosophy sought the Real found it desirable to hide behind the mysterious phrases of alchemy, or took brief refuge in the dying Neoplatonism of the age, or were caught up in the sweet and mighty devotion to Mani and his Gnostic creed, or lost in the endless repetitions of David's Psalms and competing in a fearful asceticism in the lonely places of the western desert. In time they learned to adapt their minds, lulled to sleep by these incessant repetitions, to the narrow orthodoxies of the Church, and passed lives of quiet contemplation, gentle scholarship, and busy fingers in the early monasteries of the European world.

The Gnosis went underground. No longer was it safe for the so-called heretics openly to enrol recruits after the first mad wave of persecution burst upon the Spanish Priscillianists, despite the humane pleadings of St Martin of Tours. The ceaseless hunt for ' Manicheans ' wherever the Church held power made it impossible for the Gnosis to survive, in the old form. The Gnosis passed underground.

Not until the fresh breezes of the Renascence began to blow over Western Europe and there began to arise schools of Mysticism built upon the deep foundations laid by St John and Dionysius the Areopagite, did the real Gnosis once more appear to men in the West. Writers like the unknown author of ' The Cloud of Unknowing ', the St Victors, St John of the Cross, even the Quietists and Quakers—brought back again the essence of the Gnosis to the West.

In Egypt it never rose again. The wild partisanships of Monophysite and Orthodox, the noble though rather superficial notions of the Arab conquerors, overwhelmed spiritual yoga with a simple obedience to the Faith, a belief in the Prophet and the Book. These left no room for any esoteric schools of the Wisdom.

Only in Iran, where the Gnosis had one of its earliest sources, could it continue in the changed and Muslim form of Sufism; and in this form it has continued down to our very day. In the deep attraction of the cultured Arabs of the Baghdad Khilafat for the higher Iranian culture, many during the Middle Ages turned to the fountain of spirituality which still flowed there for all who cared to drink of it. Rabi'a and her successors taught the ancient truth of the at-oning of the Soul with God. In 1186, Suhrawardi in his 'Philosophy of Illumination' (pp. 264-269, quoted by Scott), freely acknowledged the Platonic and Gnostic sources of his own inspiration: "Those philosophers who freed themselves from their bodies and thereby liberated themselves from Matter saw the incorporeal Lights (*noēta*); this is true of the prophets and sages; . . . of most of these men it can be proved that they saw the spiritual world. Plotinus tells of himself that he stripped himself of the garment of darkness, *i.e.*, got rid of his connections with corporeality, and saw the spiritual world, and all the philosophers of India and Persia experienced such visions. . . . The writer of these lines, when he first occupied himself with philosophy, . . . denied these visions and the existence of the spirits (*noes*) and ideas (*noēta eidē*). . . . But afterwards he saw the proof of God, that is, the vision of the bodiless Lights, when by means of constant solitude and many ascetic practices, he had released himself from his connection with corporeality, and made clear to himself that all forms of being in this bodily world are images of pure Lights which exist in the spiritual world. But if anyone is not satisfied with this proof, he may devote himself to ascesis and to the service of the mystics; and perhaps he will thereby acquire a 'natural disposition', and will thereupon see the Light which radiates in the world of Divine Powers, and the substances of the celestial realm, and also the Lights which Plato and Hermes saw, and moreover the Lights of Paradise ... of which that virtuous Sage and perfect Imām Zaradusht of Azerbaijan speaks. ... The proof of these doctrines ... is ... the immediate certainty of the illumination itself."

Nor has that fountain of sweet waters in Iran yet run dry. The student can easily see in the writings of the Prophet 'Ali Muḥammed, known as the *Bāb* or Gate (killed in 1844), how the old inspiration yet survives; his disciple Behā'ullah, followed by the apostles of the Behā'i Faith, have spread a new wave of Gnostic idealism over the world.

With the recovery in our days of so many original Gnostic works, with the gradual awakening of a scientific spirit of unprejudiced study of them unswayed by the student's personal religious predilections, ever since Mead's good work there has been a growing sympathy and understanding for this vanished Faith, which arose among men along with Christianity and was later so largely merged into it. Let me close, then, with Mead's own words: "It is true that today we speak openly of many things that the Gnostics wrapped up in symbol and myth; nevertheless our real knowledge on such subjects is not so very far in advance of the great doctors of the Gnosis as we are inclined to imagine; now, as then, there are only a few who really know what they are writing about, while the rest copy, compare, adapt, and speculate. ... Who knows with the intellect enough to decide on all these high subjects for his fellows? Let each follow the Light as he sees it—there is enough for all; so that at last we may see 'all things turned into Light—sweet joyous Light' (FFF pp. 592, 606-7).

LIST OF ABBREVIATIONS

Agr.	Agrapha
An.	Andrew
Apoc.	Apocalypse
Apok.	Apocryphal sayings
App.	Appendix
Asc. Isa.	Ascension of Isaiah
1 Bar.	1st Book of Baruch
Bhāg.	Bhāgavata-purāṇa
BMOr.	British Museum Oriental ms.
de Cas. Ani.	de Castigatione Animarum
CJ.	Codex Jung (page number).
Conf.	Confessions
Copt.	Coptic
1 Cor.	1st Epistle to Corinthians
Dan.	Book of Daniel
DVC	Philo's de Vita Contemplativa
Ecclus.	Book of Ecclesasticus
1 Enoch	1st Book of Enoch
2 Enoch	Book of the Secrets of Enoch
Eph.	To the Ephesians
Ep. Ap.	Epistle of the Apostles
Ep. Barn.	Epistle of Barnabas
2 Esd.	2nd Book of Esdras

Epiph.	Epiphanius
FFF	Mead's Fragments of a Faith Forgotten
Gal	Epistle to the Galatians
Gen.	Book of Genesis
GG	Gospel of the Gnostics
GGS	Gospel of the Guru-Granth Saheb
GH	Gospel of Hermes
GIG	Gnoses of the Invisible God
Gk.	Greek
GL	Gnosis of the Light
GMC	Gospel of the Mystic Christ
Gosp. Eg.	Gospel of the Egyptians
Gosp. Eve	Gospel of Eve
Gosp. Phil.	Gospel of Philip
GP	Gospel of the Pyramids
GPM	Gospel of the Prophet Mani
GY	Gospel of Israel
GZ	Gospel of Zarathushtra
Haer.	Against the Heresies
Heb.	Hebrew
2 Herm.	Second Book of Hermas
Hip.	Hippolytus
Hom.	Homilies
H.P.B.	Mme. H. P. Blavatsky
HRG	Hymn of the Robe of Glory
Isa.	Book of Isaiah
JAOS	Journal of the American Oriental Society
Jer.	Book of Jeremiah
Jn.	Gospel of St. John
2 Jn.	2nd Epistle of John

Lk.	Gospel of St. Luke
LXX	Septuagint Version
M.	G. R. S. Mead
Mk.	Gospel of St. Mark
Mt.	Gospel of St. Matthew
N.T.	New Testament
Oxyrh. Frag.	Fragments from Oxyrhynchus
Pap. Lond.	London Papyrus
PG	Migne's version of Greek Fathers
Phil.	Epistle to the Philippians
Prov.	Book of Proverbs
PS	Book of Pistis Sophia
Ps.	Book of Psalms
q.	Quoted by
Ref.	Refutations
Rep.	Repose (of John), part of Acts.
Rev.	Book of Revelations
Rom.	Epistle to the Romans
Skt.	Sanskrit
Sol.	Solomon
Syr.	Syriac
TGH	Thrice-Greatest Hermes
Thom.	Thomas
Wisd.	Book of Wisdom

SYNOPSIS

Chapter One: THE PROMISE OF INITIATION. 1. The Gnosis comes to those who have altogether renounced the world, 2. and by the gift of it Christ makes men true sons of God.

Chapter Two: HOW IT ALL BEGAN. 3. This vast universe arose from the One infinite uncreated Source 4. through the first differentiation in God of Mind and Thought, 5. and the reaction of the eternal Opposites upon each other through the contacting medium of the Spirit, whereby the individual Soul arises and is redeemed.

Chapter Three: INFINITE GOD AND THE SOUL. 6. Beyond all inconceivable Sources there is ever the One Ineffable, 7. who manifests Himself as God in His boundless universe while Himself remaining the Unknowable but Infinite Attraction to all that exist. 8. All things are from Him and in Him; to Him they all trend with the individual characteristics each one has through endless time. 9. The individual Mind is God in Man, holy beyond all words and receptacle of every grace, 10. being endowed with all spiritual gifts, so that it may uplift even Matter into Spirit and fulfil God's creative work. 11. Having achieved this, the individual is then adorned with the ineffable glory of the Divine, whereby the Real is discerned from all that is impermanent, unreal.

Chapter Four: THE AEONS' STORY. 12. Urged by Love, its own very nature, the One ineffable Source reposing in utmost stillness thought, and out of this Thought arose all Divine Powers. 13. The Powers themselves imitated His creative activity, though unable to know the Fullness of His Being. 14. Wisdom, the last-born of these Powers, driven on by her loving eagerness for Him, left her own place; held back by the invisible barrier between all 'creatures' and God, she was caught in the outer darkness, and gave birth to a monstrosity. 15. To restore order, God sent forth Christ and the Holy Spirit; all the Powers united to bring forth Jesus as the fruit of all perfection. 16. Robbed of perfection in form and knowledge, the Soul suffered in the Chaos, yearning for the Divine Light which she had lost. 17. The Saviour enlightened her, so that being somewhat lifted from the depths, she was able to produce the Shaper and Ruler of the worlds. 18. Naturally unable to see beyond his Mother, Nature, this Shaper fancied himself the Supreme, even though the man he fashioned had no spirituality 19. until Jesus came down and assumed the lower, psychic, nature; when all men are enlightened by the Gnosis, they will unite with God, and then this universe of gross Matter will cease to exist.

Chapter Five: THE MYTH OF THE GOSPEL. 20. Out of absolutely nothing, God beyond Being playfully caused the seed of a universe to exist, 21. and in this Seed were all the beings of this infinite universe, unfolding from the matrix one by one. 22. There are three types of being—the spiritual, which at once unites with God; the psychic or partly spiritual, which the Spirit can raise to Him; and the gross or carnal, which can know nothing of the Truth. 23. Out of the world-source rose the Shaper, and believing himself supreme set about fashioning from these materials an ordered universe; 24. after him arose another great being to rule those of the middle state. 25. Neither of these, or any other being, can imagine a state above his own, lest discontentment should disturb the balance. 26. To raise those whom God has called, He sent the Gospel into the world, descending stage by stage through all the planes, 27. till at last it came to us men in the physical body as Jesus, Mary's Son; and now it wakens us from the sleep of Ignorance. 28. When all of the destined Race Above have entered into Gnosis, the purpose of creation has been achieved.

Chapter Six: THE HYMN OF JESUS. 29. Jesus teaches his disciples to join him in the Cosmic Dance which truly glorifies God. 30. In his Hymn, wherein they share, he teaches how the Gnostic at-ones all opposites, unites himself with the whole universe, and so becomes a Saviour to his fellows. 31. Suffering can be borne and understood when it is welcomed as part of the universal Dance at God's will, revealing wisdom to the Soul; 32. and it is by this bold acceptance of everything as it is that the disciple can truly glorify the Father.

Chapter Seven: THE MYSTIC CROSS. 33. To John alone is Jesus ready to explain the real meaning of Suffering and the holy Cross, 34. which unites the lowest to the heights, and brings evil and good together in one embrace of love. 35. There are those who know, and those who are ignorant and are slowly being led into the Gnosis; when these have come to wisdom, the work of the Christ is done, and his disciple becomes like the Lord. 36. Suffering cannot be understood save through the Word, the expression of God's will. 37. When John was told of the physical Crucifixion, it seemed of very little moment, merely a type of the reality behind. 38. Man himself is crucified in Nature, but head downwards because he does not seek the Heights; he must change his whole attitude to life. 39. How blessed is he who embraces that eternal Cross uniting Man with God and bringing all the graces down into human life! 40. What joy to behold the adorable Cross wherein are found all the rich fruits of Love Divine!

Chapter Eight: THE GLORIOUS ASCENSION. 41. Jesus is now about to teach his disciples all Heaven's Mysteries, 42. and they see him ascend in a cloud of ineffable light. 43. The wonder of that sight and of the earthquake terrify them lest the world's end has come, until they see him returning to the earth in peace. 44. He tells them he has now authority to tell them everything, and they need have no fear. 45. He tells them why it is they who have been chosen to hear the Mysteries, for they are not ordinary human souls but Powers drawn from the inner worlds like John the Baptist and Mary. 46. As they were watching, the Light-Robe of the last and greatest Mystery, Omnidentity, came on him and crowned him with divinity; 47. when he put it on, the Powers of Heaven were afraid of his glory. 48. Passing inward and upward from plane to plane, human frailty in vain opposed him, for he had put on God's strength, 49. and so he overcame the forces of human destiny and subordinated them to himself.

Chapter Nine: THE SOUL REDEEMED. 50. Just outside her own sphere, Jesus finds the fallen Wisdom longing to be restored, 51. having been lured from her place by the desire to attain God's Heights 52. and snared by the false light of egoism until she fell into the chaos of the material world. 53. She cries for help on the ground that she has fallen in good faith, believing all light to be from the One Light Above, 54. and prays that justice may be victorious and evil overthrown, even though God has willed her present suffering and allowed her to lose her spiritual powers; yet she will trust in Him. 55. Sure that God is good, she now seeks His saving aid, but when Jesus helps her a little from her misery she is again assailed by egoism, and implores that she be not forsaken in her need but that her enemies may be destroyed. 56. Jesus makes her a little more spiritual because she has fallen in good faith, and she rejoices at the sight of him. 57. Four times more, as egoism renews its assaults, she renews her appeal, completing one prayer for each of the planes she has transgressed. 59. The first Light-Baptism comes down on her, and she is washed free of all defilements; 60. then the second Baptism, as a Light-Stream, pours down on her, glorifying her and stripping her enemies of their power. 61. Yet again egoism arises in her heart, assailing her with four mighty evil thoughts, 62. and she has now also to deal with her innate human frailty. 63. Christ sends God's two Angels to crush her foes beneath her feet, 64. and acknowledging her debt she gives him thanks as to the Universal Light. 65. Jesus then places her in the region at the border of Heaven where he had found her in GG 50, and she rejoices greatly. 66. When new fears arise that she will be attacked again when

Jesus goes away, she is assured that this will happen only at the end of time, and then when she asks his help her foes will be finally destroyed. 67. During the earthly life of the Saviour this actually happens, 68. and Wisdom is once more terrified to see her foes preparing to destroy her; 69. but Jesus leads her into Heaven, and once more she takes her place, safe, among her equals there.

Chapter Ten: THE SONG OF THE PEARL. 70. The Soul is sent forth into the world to obtain the Gnosis, equipped with his Father's treasures; 71. he goes down into incarnation and assumes the flesh and habits of worldly men, forgetting his mission. 72. To arouse him to his work, God sends down the Gospel, 73. which reminds him of his nature and his duty; he overcomes his passions, obtains the Gnosis, throws off the filth of physical matter, and starts for home. 74. On the way the Gospel message guides and encourages him until he comes to the borders of his Homeland, 75. where two couriers meet him with the Robe of Glory that his labours have deserved, 76. and it is perfectly adapted to his own spiritual achievements; putting this on, 77. he proceeds through the Gate of Heaven to the Father's joyful presence.

Chapter Eleven: BITTER WATERS. 78. Men are sinful, and it is sin that keeps them from the Gnosis which can destroy all sin and every human weakness. 79. As a Soul comes into the world, it is either made to forget the past, or is constantly reminded of its nature and mission until it cannot help but strive for Gnosis and Liberation.

Chapter Twelve: THE GNOSTIC IN THE WORLD. 80. Christ comes into the world to draw men back to God and teach them the way to Liberation. 81. To tread the path of Gnosis, man must avoid all sin and cultivate all good qualities; then nothing can hold him back from God. 82. Having suffered in so many lives, it were foolish indeed to postpone this effort to some future birth, which may not take place; 83. rather must every effort be made to tread the path now, and to make known to all who are worthy how they may come to freedom; 84. but this involves the transcending of sex differences and the withdrawal of the self into the self. 85. Those who do this can easily attain to the glory of Cosmic Consciousness, which makes them altogether one with God 86. and His instruments, shining with all His glory. 87. Seeking within the source of the 'I', the Soul can find God beyond experiencing.

Chapter Thirteen: GNOSTIC HYMNS AND PRAYERS.
88. The Soul wanders miserably about the field of creation, vainly seeking freedom till the Christ comes forth to guide her into Gnosis. 89. The spiritual Christ orders all things well, upholds the universe, and awakens Gnosis in the human mind. 90. May all good spirits protect and enlighten me, 91. who cry for help to the Universal Pantheistic God in everything. 92. Lovely indeed is the Soul when made ready for the Bridal of the King of Light, who has overcome the influences of the stars and learned to gaze on the Sun of Righteousness alone! 93. May all the graces of the Divine Mother come down upon and bless us at our eucharistic feast, 94. and may the Crown of Life, who is all in all to us, make us worthy to be His children! 95. May every grace purify and perfect the candidate for the Gnosis and unite him with the Infinite beyond all being! 96. It is God alone from whom we all have come, whom we reach through His creation, who glorifies us with His Love; 97. may every creature be blessed with the true Gnosis of God for which He made us all, bringing Himself down to us, that we might know Him and so manifest the perfect Man of His conception!

CONTENTS

	PAGE
The Gospel of the Gnostics	vii
Preface	xi
'The Path of Fire'	xvii
Introduction: Background of the Gnosis—Sources of the Gnostic Gospel—Great Organisers of the Gnosis—How Gnosis Comes to Man—What Came of Gnosticism	xxi
List of Abbreviations	lxv
Synopsis	lxix
Contents	lxxv
FOREWORD	1

CHAPTER ONE: THE PROMISE OF INITIATION

1. The Disciples Seek Initiation, 2. And are Promised All the Mysteries . . . 3

CHAPTER TWO: HOW IT ALL BEGAN

3. From the One Alone; 4. From Two Opposing Forces; 5. It is Really from a Triad . 8

	PAGE
CHAPTER THREE: INFINITE GOD AND THE SOUL	
6. God Unmanifest, 7. Is Manifested, 8. The One Source of All, 9. Glory of the Indwelling Light, 10. Preparation of the Saviour, 11. Man and the Universe	24
CHAPTER FOUR: THE AEONS' STORY	
12. Emanation of the Eight, 13. The Fullness Appears, 14. The Fall of Wisdom, 15. The Saviour Comes Forth, 16. Wisdom is in Distress, 17. Forming the Human Being, 18. The Creator's Delusion, 19. The Consummation of All Things	44
CHAPTER FIVE: THE MYTH OF THE GOSPEL	
20. Before the Beginning, 21. The Seed of the World, 22. The Triple Sonship, 23. The First Great Ruler, 24. The Ruler of the Seven, 25. The Great Ignorance, 26. The Gospel is Revealed, 27. It Comes Down to Our World, 28. The Consummation	69
CHAPTER SIX: THE HYMN OF JESUS	
29. Prelude to the Mystic Dance, 30. The Universal Dance of At-Onement, 31. The Lesson of Suffering, 32. The End of the Dance	91

CHAPTER SEVEN: THE MYSTIC CROSS

33. At the Crucifixion, 34. The Real Eternal Cross, 35. The Two Multitudes, 36. The Mystery of Suffering, 37. John Understands, 38. A Reversal of Values, 39. The Universal Cross, 40. Address to the Cross . . 102

CHAPTER EIGHT: THE GLORIOUS ASCENSION

41. The Disciples Still Know Little, 42. Jesus is Bathed in Light, 43. Jesus Goes Up into Heaven, 44. He Promises to Speak Clearly, 45. The Origin of Saints, 46. The Glorious Light-Robe, 47. Jesus Puts on the Robe, 48. He Enters Plane after Plane, 49. And Hastens the Day of Liberation 121

CHAPTER NINE: THE SOUL REDEEMED

50. Jesus Finds the Faithful Wisdom, 51. How She Made Enemies, 52. The Lion-Faced Power, 53. Wisdom's First Appeals, 54. Four More Cries for Help, 55. Three More Appeals, 56. Jesus Comes to Help Her, 57. The Four Last Appeals, 58. Arrogant Tries to Prevent her Escape, 59. She is Crowned with Light, 60. The Light-Stream Flows Down, 61. Arrogant

PAGE

Attacks Again, 62. Adamas Joins In, 63. The Light Prevails, 64. Wisdom's Thanksgiving, 65. She Rejoices in her Ascent, 66. Her Doubts are Solved, 67. Evil Makes its Last Attack, 68. Wisdom Again Cries for Help, 69. She Returns Home 148

CHAPTER TEN: THE SONG OF THE PEARL

70. The Soul is Sent Forth, 71. He Descends to the World, 72. The Father Sends a Reminder, 73. He Fulfils His Mission, 74. The Homeward Way, 75. The Coming of the Light-Robe, 76. He Puts It On, 77. The Father's Welcome 197

CHAPTER ELEVEN: BITTER WATERS

78. Sin and the Mysteries, 79. Rebirth in this World 217

CHAPTER TWELVE: THE GNOSTIC IN THE WORLD

80. The Messenger of Light, 81. Who Can Be a Gnostic, 82. Seriousness of Purpose, 83. Receive and Give, 84. Gospel Fragments, 85. The Way to the Higher Mysteries, 86. The Greatness of the Initiate, 87. The Final Secret of the Self 227

PAGE

CHAPTER THIRTEEN: GNOSTIC HYMNS AND PRAYERS

88. The Naassene Psalm, 89. Valentinian Poems, 90. From a Turin Papyrus, 91. A Song of Praise to the Aeon, 92. Wisdom's Wedding-Song, 93. Invocations by St. Thomas, 94. Prayers of St. John, 95. Marcosian Prayers, 96. From the Bruce Codex, 97. The Mother's Prayer for Her Children 251

CLOSING PRAYER 284

Appendices: I. *The Myth of Man in the Mysteries:* 1. Introduction, 2. The First of Men, 3. The Love of Adonis and Attis, 4. Osiris, 5. Hermes, Leader of Souls, 6. The Threefold Source, 7. He of Many Names, 8. Is One Soul . . 238

II a. The Prodigal Son . . . 312
 b. The Story of Cyriacus . . . 314

III *From the Chaldean Oracles:* The Universal Source, The Universe Evolves, The Light-Spark Appears, The Soul Travels Home . . 317

Index 327
Bibliography 331
The World Gospel Series 335

I AM THE GNOSIS OF THE ALL (PS. 253);
I HAVE LOVED YOU AND LONGED TO GIVE
YOU LIFE.
JESUS THE LIVING IS THE KNOWER OF
THE TRUTH[1] (GIG 39).

THIS is the "Book of the Gnoses of the Invisible God"[2] according to the Hidden Mysteries which show the Way In for the Chosen Race[3] through the inner Quiet[4] to the Father's Life through the coming of the Saviour, the Rescuer of the souls who are to receive[5] this word of Life that transcends all

---

[1] These beautiful words, prefixing the so-called "Books of Ieu", read in the Coptic: "*Aimere-tēutn, aiwōs eti-nētn m̅pōnh; I(ēsou)s petonh pe psown n̅tme*".

[2] In the face of this definite title, it is impossible to understand why any scholar should have foisted another title on the book.

[3] *i.e.*, the Race from Above, the 'heavenly man', those who are spiritual, not fleshly or merely psychic.

[4] Copt.: *pemton ehoun*. The importance of inner stillness or calm (Skt. *śānti*) for the aspirant is also stressed in GG 81, as in most other scriptures, for mental storm leads only to mental shipwreck.

[5] This suggests predestination, but as hinted at in GG 79 : 3 the truth is that it is only those 'old souls' who are to become perfect in this age who are born with the longing for wisdom that gives freedom.

life, by means of the Gnosis of Jesus the Living who has come forth through the Father from the Light-Aeon in completing the Fullness [1] (GIG 39).[2]

---

[1] A technical term of the Gnosis, sometimes referring to the whole manifested universe, sometimes to the totality of spiritual souls freed from matter. The Codex Jung in the Valentinian Gospel of Truth (21 : 3-8) says: "Those who are to be taught—that is, the Living inscribed in the Book of the Living—receive the Teaching for themselves alone." These are the Plērōma, the Fullness.

[2] This Preface compares with that of the Valentinian Gospel (CJ 16-17): "Joy to those who have received from the Father of the Truth the grace to know Him by the power of the Word come from the Fullness that is in the Father's Thought and Mind—who is called Saviour because he is the Messenger destined to come to save those who knew not the Father." Such a Preface is analogous to those prefixing many Sanskrit books, declaring the purpose of the treatise and for whom it is intended.

CHAPTER ONE

THE PROMISE OF INITIATION

It is by the true Gnosis of God that man overcomes the world and becomes the Son of God. Men in the world must leave all else to find that knowledge of Perfection, and then they will find the one Initiator into all the Mysteries. So will they become his co-rulers in the Kingdom of the Light, having in their very being been transmuted into the light of pure spirit.

1. The Disciples Seek Initiation

1. Blessed is the man who has known these things and has brought down the Heaven and lifted up the Earth ... to Heaven, and has made the Midst into a nothing.[1] ... (Now) the Heaven is the Father's invisible Word, ... while to lift the Earth up to Heaven is the one who hears the word of the Gnosis, having

---

[1] *i.e.*, has annihilated all that separates him from God—which can be done only by one who listens to His Word and then turns from worldly things to become a citizen of Heaven.

ceased to be mind of worldly man and become heavenly man. . . . For this reason shall you be saved from the Ruler of this Aeon, and he shall become the Midst, for it is a nothing (GIG 41-42).

2. Blessed is he who has crucified the world, and has not let the world crucify him.[1] . . . (Now) he who has crucified the world is the one who has found my word and fulfilled it according to the will of Him who has sent me (GIG 40).

3. Tell it to us, Lord, that we may listen to thee; it is we who have followed thee with all our heart. We have left father, . . . mother, . . . property, . . . and followed thee,[2] that thou shouldst teach us the Life of thy Father who has sent thee (GIG 40). Mentally thou hast given us mind of the Light,[3] and

---

[1] A striking sentence, possibly quoted from some Gnostic Gospel like that of the Egyptians; Copt.: *naiatf m̄pentafaṣt pkosmos auō m̄pefka pkosmos eaṣtf.* We may note that the word used for the 'world' in this sense is almost always that used by St. John in his Gospel.

[2] This relates to the promise of Jesus given in Mk. 10: 29-30, whereon also the Manicheans placed much reliance. Cf. also GG 80 : 1 and GMP 92 : 3.

[3] *i.e.,* thou hast made us of the Race of the Mind, mentioned by Hermes in GH 44 : 2, and thus thou hast made us sensitive to the urges of the Light, that is, of Good (GG 81 : 1).

thou hast given us a feeling and a very lofty thought (PS 182).

Gnosis of the Truth unites the depth to the height, man to God, and it is a spiritualising of the mind which makes this possible. This can only be when the neophyte has renounced all earthly ties, has 'crucified' the lower self in himself—" when the feet of the soul are washed in the blood of the heart"—a mystic baptism which initiates man into a truly spiritual life. Cut off thus from lower ties and interests, the aspirant finds the way to a Teacher of Divine Life wide open before him, and in his mind the ability to understand its very essence will already be.

2. And are Promised All the Mysteries

1. Come round me,[1] ... and I shall tell you the great mysteries of the Treasure of the Light in the Invisible God,[2] which no one knows (GIG 99), so that you may be worthy of the mysteries of the Light and be saved from all the chastisings (PS 255).[3] I shall give you all the mysteries, so that I may perfect you in every mystery of the Kingdom of the Light,[4] ... and I shall give you even the Mystery of

[1] The disciples are to surround Jesus as the planets surround the enlightening Sun, and as in the cosmic dance of GG 29.
[2] *i.e.*, the infinite Source of Light, so bright as to be unseen by mortal eyes and so It becomes the 'Divine Dark' of Dionysius the Areopagite.
[3] The mysteries save from sin, and so from its painful results, and unite the soul with infinite perfection.
[4] Mani's phrase; he was certainly in touch with the Christian Gnosis in his early years.

Absolution[1] ... so that you may be children of the Light,[2] ... sons of the Fullness perfected in every mystery (GIG 105, 126, 105).

2. For the expanding of the universe is the Gnosis of it (PS 219).[3] This is the Life of my Father, that you derive your soul from the Race of the Mind and it ceases to be earthy and becomes intuitional,[4] ... and you are saved from the Ruler of this Aeon[5] and his endless snares ... and become well by means of a freedom wherein is no blemish (GIG 40-41), and are made pure light and ascend and inherit the Light of my Kingdom (PS 251).

3. This is the People of the Beloved, who are loved by and love Him (FFF 305). Now

---

[1] *lit.*: the forgiveness of sins—preliminary to entry on the spiritual path: "Beware lest thou should'st set a foot still soiled upon the ladder's lowest rung" (Voice of the Silence, p. 31).

[2] Copt.: *ṅṣēre ṅtepwoein*—the same phrase as in 1 Thes. 5 : 5.

[3] A hint that there is no end to the Gnosis; it grows ever greater with our knowledge of the universe. Who, facing the countless universes, can worship a local deity?

[4] Divorce from worldliness, followed by marriage to spirituality, is the essence of the Gnosis. The word *noeros* means far more than intelligence or intellectuality; it includes an intuitional understanding of the Truth: "To be allied to Wisdom is immortality" (Wisd. 8 : 17). The Orphic epitaph in TGH 1 : 95 says: "I am child of Earth and starry Heaven; my race is of the Heavens!" This knowledge liberates from the illusions of darkness.

[5] *i.e.*, the dark Lord of Matter, the ignorant Demiurge of GG 24-25, in whose prison the Soul now lies enchained.

in the dissolving of the world ... when ...
I become King in the midst of the Last Helper,[1]
... every man who shall receive mysteries in
the Ineffable [2] shall be fellow-King with me;[3]
... for this reason, then, I have not hesitated
or been ashamed to call you my brothers,[4]
... knowing that I shall give you the Mystery
of the Ineffable—which Mystery am I, and
I am that Mystery (PS 230-231).

Having made the initial sacrifice, the disciples are
called to hear a promise of full initiation in the Word
of Life which will make them perfect children of the
Light. First they are to be of the Spirit, not fleshly,
so as to be wholly freed from the laws of the lower
worlds and incorporated in the higher life of God,
which is perfect freedom. Souls thus transmuted by
the fires of wisdom are united with God in fullest
love and share the Kingship of the Ages in His Light.
They are more than disciples, they are friends and
brothers of the Divine Initiator and enter his very
Being—which is the universal being of the Cosmic
Consciousness that cannot be told in words.

---

[1] *Cf.* the " Last Statue " of Mani's system (GPM 83), the totality of the whole Body of the Church, Christ triumphing in his Elect.

[2] *i.e.*, who shall know the One beyond word and thought, more fully explained in GG 85 : 2-3.

[3] " In those days the Chosen shall sit on my throne " (1 Eno. 51 : 3).

[4] In Jn. 15 : 15 Jesus calls his disciples ' friends ' ; Mani calls his " my brothers, my beloved '. He who enters into the One becomes the Christ, who is that One.

CHAPTER TWO

HOW IT ALL BEGAN

No set dogma or formula can tell what lies beyond all words; the Infinite cannot be defined by all the cleverness of theologians, nor can the Ineffable be described in speech. No human mind can realise God's real nature or say how from One beyond being came all these beings that we know by mind and sense. So the Gnostics left each 'school', each individual teacher, to frame his own cosmogony; these differ, yet have a strong likeness among themselves. Here we have chosen several, to show the three main ideas whereon they built.

Some said that all come from One nameless and inconceivable First Cause, evolved from within by a creative urge; others held that there were from the first Two infinite Powers, reflected by the sexes and the pairs of opposites, and that by their interaction arose the 'Son', the universe; yet others told that to bring the Two into relation there must have been a Third, a spiritual and more subtle Force; else how could opposites blend with one another?

But we must not think there was conflict between the 'schools' of the Gnostics, as among the doctrines of orthodoxy; they all were part of a single Movement, wherein each individual had total freedom to seek out and express what he found of the Truth in his own way.

3. From the One Alone

1. Before all things there is a certain First Source, first inconceivable and ineffable and nameless, which I reckon Uniqueness; with this Uniqueness co-exists a Power which also I name Oneness.[1] That Oneness and the Uniqueness, being (together) the One, emanated without emitting [2] an intelligible Source over all things, both uncreated and unseen, which Source the world calls a Monad. With this Monad co-exists that consubstantial Power which also is the One. These (four) Powers ... emanated the other emanations of the Aeons (PG 7 : 565).

2. 'Man' is the All which is source of everything,[3] unborn, imperishable, eternal;

---

[1] The four words can hardly be distinguished in English; they are *monotēs*, *henotēs*, *monas* and *hen*. To Irenaeus this seems unintelligible babbling.

[2] The Source arose within, yet did not separate from, the Oneness; the Soul is distinct from God, yet in no way separable or independent of Him. Hermippus 1 : 18 : 135, quoted by Scott, reads: " Now the Monad among the numbers is a sort of Source and Root, and God among the intelligibles, from whom as out of a Fountain flow all things."

[3] Man is " in God's image ", so where is blasphemy in saying God is an infinitely perfect and eternal ' Man '? This is the Unmanifest, who becomes in the ' Son of Man ' the Manifest men name and worship; *cf.* App. 1 : 1.

while 'Son of Man' is born [1] and passible, timelessly brought into being without design or destiny [2]—for such is the power of that 'Man'. Being thus brought into being by his power, the 'Son' is swifter than Thought and Will. . . . Now this 'Man' is one Monad—non-complex, indivisible, (yet) complex (and) divisible, loving all things (and) altogether peaceable, (yet) in all ways quarrelsome (and) in all ways fighting himself, dissimilar (yet) similar, just like a certain musical harmony having all things in itself, . . . manifesting all (PG 26: 3358).[3]

3. Above is One Source and Father of everything, both unknown and unnamed (PG 41: 364). God is the First, as it were a Fig-Tree's Seed, altogether tiny in size but potentially boundless.[4] . . . Now of such and so great a Being, the small and sizeless God, the world has in this way come to be: When

---

[1] "Mind, the Father of all, . . . gave birth to Man, one like Himself" (GH 3 : 1).

[2] Gk. *aboulētos, aprooristos*.

[3] *i.e.*, he contains all opposites in himself, and merges them there into one.

[4] The expanding universe of modern science; all arose from a point which grew and grew ever greater, and still grows.

the twigs of the Fig-Tree became tender, leaves came out, ... and then the fruit, wherein is guarded, treasured, the boundless and incalculable Seed of a Fig-Tree—so three: ..., stem, ... leaves and fruit. Thus from the First Source of everything Three Aeons have come into being: Darkness, Gloom and Storm.[1] For God has added nothing to the three Aeons, but they have been and are altogether enough for all that have come to be; and God Himself remains far apart from the three Aeons (PG 16: 3348 ff).

4. There was the uncreated [2] One who alone is Father of all (PG 41: 309), unknown to all (PG 16: 3322). From This Mind was evolved, and from the Mind Word, and from the Word Purpose, and from the Purpose Power and Wisdom;[3] and from both the Power and Wisdom (came) Sources, Authorities, Angels (PG 41: 309). Now from certain

---

[1] These three names may stress that this universe is fundamentally 'evil', born of darkness, as opposed to the pure light of the Spirit. This was a common idea of the age.

[2] This word *agennētos*, and others from the same root, gives trouble in rendering in English; it sometimes means born, produced, come into being, as opposed to what is eternal, never arising or passing away.

[3] The Aeons named in this system are Nous, Logos, Phronēsis, Dunamis and Sophia.

seven Angels [1] ... far lower than the uncreated Father ..., came into being the world and all that are in it ..., made ... by a certain Power separate from the Authority over everything and unaware of the Supreme God.[2] ... So Man is a work of Angels (PG 16: 3322, 3338, 3342).

Unable to follow the subtlety of philosophic thought, poor Irenaeus bursts out in tearful mockery at the advaitic teaching of this first paragraph. Its essence, of course, is that the ONE which alone exists did not cease to be ONE when in It appeared a certain quality out of which the universe arose. Maintaining the ONE-ness of Reality, this unnamed 'distinguished' teacher had at the same time to account for the obvious Duality—a problem no less known to India. Yet taking a Whole from a Whole, the Whole still is Whole, as the Upanishad has it; even giving rise to a universe, the ONE remains unique and indivisible.

This ONE is called 'Man' by the Naassenes and other 'sects' so long as He is unmanifest and unportrayed, 'Son of Man' when manifested in being and thereby limited. The ONE contains in Himself at once all pairs of opposites and is thus beyond all thought and speech.

The 'Docetic' school described the ONE First Source as a sort of infinite Tree expanding from an infinitesimal Seed, wherein from all eternity the vast

---

[1] These are presumably the "Seven Angels before the Throne", in effect, the planetary lords, who produce and rule all on this lower plane.

[2] *Cf.* the ignorance of the Great Ruler in GG 18.

variety of manifestation is hid away in the 'Divine Dark' of the Unmanifest.

Our last paragraph traces the unfolding of the universe from that eternal Seed in several stages—Mind, Thought, Expression, Will, and last the creative Force and Plan which produced all through the mediation of heavenly powers and the celestials veiled behind the planetary Rulers of the seven planes.

4. From Two Opposing Forces

1. Of all the Aeons there are two Offshoots with neither beginning nor end, (coming) from One Root which is a Power: Silence [1] invisible, unattainable. Of these (two) the one shines from Above, which is a great Power, Cosmic Mind managing all things, male; while the other (shines) from Below, Great Thought, female, bringing all things into being. Whence, matching each other, they pair off and manifest the Space Between: unattainable [2] Air, having neither beginning nor end. Now in this (is) a Father who sustains all things with beginning and end; it is this one who Stands,

---

[1] As 'Silence' is the Power beyond all being, so 'Stillness' is the first qualification for those who would know God as He is.

[2] Gk.: *akatalēptos*; *lit.*: what cannot be grasped by hand or mind; thus, incomprehensible, or sometimes subtle or non-physical.

has Stood, and will Stand,[1] being a male-female [2] Power like the pre-existing boundless Power which has neither beginning nor end, being in Uniqueness. For, coming forth from This, the Thought in Uniqueness became Two.[3]

2. Now that (Father) was One, for having Her [4] in Himself He was alone, . . . but having appeared to Him a Second came into being from Himself. . . . As then He brought Himself forward by Himself, He manifested to Himself His own Thought, so too the manifested Thought did not make (Him) but, seeing Him, She hid the Father in Herself.[5] . . . Now She is a male-female: Power and

---

[1] *i.e.*, the Eternal, immovable, beyond all time. "He has stood above in unbegotten power; he stands below when begotten in an image in the stream of waters; he is to stand above beside the blessed undefined Power when he is fashioned into an image" (Hip. Ref. 6: 12).

[2] That God is Mother as well as Father is fundamental to the Gnosis; His '*śakti*' *is* Himself in activity. *Cf.* GG 10, 93.

[3] Not that Thought can be apart from the thinking Mind; it manifests its inherent power, and so, like *śakti*, is feminine.

[4] *i.e.*, Thought.

[5] Nor can Thought ever fully reveal the Thinker, only an infinitesimal part of all that makes up the Mind. In the "Gospel of Mary" we have: "Barbelo gazed fixedly into Him, . . . and she gave birth to a blessed Light-Spark; nor does it differ from her in greatness. . . . This is the Aloneborn who has manifested himself in the Father." The universe is that 'Thought', as Philo has: "The Word is God's likeness, by whom the whole universe was fashioned" (de Monarch. 2 : 5).

Thought, whence they match each other, for Power in no way differs from Thought, (they) being One (PG 16 : 3210 ff).

The 'Simonian' book of "The Great Announcement" tells us how in the eternal Silence beyond being arose two Forces—Mind above and Thought below. Their interplay gave cause for the intermediary 'Air' or Spirit, eternal Source of all that is, has been, and will ever be. Yet Mind and Thought are originally one, inseparable—there is neither Mind without Thought, nor Thought without Mind. It is only when expressed in *word*, in form, that Thought assumes a separate existence, and so becomes a universe, the 'Thought' of God. Yet even then they are only one, for the universe can no more exist without God than a thought without the mind.

5. It is Really From a Triad

1. The world is one, triply divided.[1] Now one part of the triple division is a certain One Source just like a great Fountain able to be mentally divided into countless segments.[2] The first and best segment is the Triad, and the one part is called Perfect Good, Paternal Greatness; the second part of **the** Triad is as it were a sort of infinite crowd of Powers

---

[1] Gk.: *ton kosmon einai hena trikhē diēirēmenon.*

[2] The united stream may be thought of as made up of many separate streams; so is the ONE complex as well as simple in its nature—a paradox, but so is all else that we may say of God.

produced from them; the third is material.[1] Now while the first is uncreated, which is good, and the second is good, self-produced, the third is generated. So (there are) three Gods, three Words, three Minds, three Men. . . . The whole is Father, Son, Matter; each of these three has boundless powers in itself. . . . Therefore, between Matter and the Father is seated the Son, the Word—the Serpent[2] ever moving towards the unmoving Father and the moving Matter (PS 16 : 3159 ff).

2. There are three definite Sources of the universe (PG 16 : 3180) uncreated: two male, one female (PG 16 : 3193); and each of the Sources has boundless Powers (PG 16 : 3180). Now of the male: the one is called Good, it alone (is) so called, and foreknowing the universe, while the other is Father of all things produced, not foreknowing, and unknown and

---

[1] *i.e.*, the powers of nature, ever mediating between God and inert but ever-heaving Matter.

[2] This image of a Serpent (Heb.: *nahaṣ*) led to the name of the Naassenes, so the Catholics invented 'Ophites' (Gk.: *ophis*) as the name for an imaginary sect of Gnostics, who knew no sects but only the stream of enlightened thought and mystical experience. They were said to worship the 'Serpent' of Eden, the devil, and must therefore have been guilty of every kind of wickedness; but had their foes known of the 'Serpent Fire' of *kuṇḍalini*, they had been nearer to the truth.

HOW IT ALL BEGAN

unseen; while the female is not foreknowing, passionate,[1] two-minded,[2] two-bodied.... These Sources of the universe are Roots and Fountains whence all things came, and there was no other (PG 16: 3193).

3. Now the essences of the Sources are Light and Darkness,[3] and between these is pure Spirit, ... as it were a certain fragrance, ... a subtle power pervading by something inconceivable,[4] an impulsive perfume better than can be expressed in speech.... Now the Light has to shine like a sunbeam from above into the Darkness below, and further the Spirit's fragrance, in between, is spread and carried everywhere, just as we detect everywhere the fragrance of the incenses carried in fire; at the same time the power of the Spirit

---

Gk.: *orgilē*.

[2] Perhaps this is why women are held to have the right to change their mind at will!

[3] The same Iranian dualism on which Mani built his system, but modified by a third mediative Power which he expressly denied (GPM p. clx). Epiphanius (25 : 5) quotes: "There was Darkness and Deep, and Water; and Spirit in the midst of them separated them." Pap. Lond. 46 : 476-7, quoted in Abraxas, p. 69, says: "The God who separated the Light from the Darkness is the great righteous Mind ever dwelling in the all, ... Adonai the Lord IAŌOUĒE."

[4] Gk.: *anepinoētos*.

and of the Light is in the Darkness lying below.[1]

4. Now the Darkness is a terrible Water into which the Light is absorbed and transformed into the same kind of nature as the Spirit.[2] But the Darkness . . . knows that where the Light has been withdrawn . . . **it** remains isolated, unseen, unlit, powerless, ineffective, weak.[3] Therefore . . . it is forced to cling to the lustre and the spark of the Light, together with the Spirit's fragrance. . . . So then . . . the Light and the Spirit lay claim to the power that is their own, and they hasten to lift [4] and recover for themselves their powers mixed with the dark and fearful Water below.

5. All the powers of the three Sources, . . . when they remain by themselves, are all at rest. But if power approaches power, the inequality of the contact brings about a certain movement and activity . . . due to the

---

[1] Light reflected in water may be said to be *in* the water, while really it remains above it.

[2] *i.e.*, the light has now become water, spirit is now materialised.

[3] Of itself Matter is always inert (Skt.: *jaḍa*), and it derives activity only from the light (Skt.: *prāṇa*, *ātma*) which may ensoul it.

[4] The nature of Spirit is to hasten up to God (GG 22 : 1); caught in the snare of Matter it soon seeks to escape again upwards.

contact of the powers coming together.¹ ...
Since then the powers of the three Sources
are limitless in number, and from the limitless
powers there are unlimited contacts, necessarily
images of unlimited impressions² have been
produced; these then are the forms of various
living things.

6. From the (first) great coming together
of the three Sources has come a certain great
Form, ... Heaven and Earth.³ Now the
Heaven and the Earth are shaped like a
Womb ... at the first concourse.⁴ ... Again
countless hosts of various creatures are produced on Earth from the countless impressions,
and into all this infinity ... the Spirit's
fragrance from above is diffused and distributed along with the Light.

7. Thus⁵ from the Water has come into
being a firstborn Source: violent and boisterous

---

[1] Spirit acting on Matter brings about a living creature filled with energy and movement; out of the limitless contacts of the infinite forces arise an infinity of creatures.

[2] *lit.*: seals.

[3] The universe itself is the greatest of all living beings, instinct with Life or Spirit and enformed by Matter.

[4] Thus, infinitely fertile.

[5] Our refutator seems to have missed some link in the thought here; he does not tell us how the Wind (of passion) first arose in the Water (of Matter).

Wind, cause of all birth; for, inducing a certain ferment in the Waters, ... it raises waves, and the motion of the waves is just like a sort of shock. ... Now when this Wave, raised by the Wind out of the Water and made pregnant in (its) nature, receives in itself a female's generative power, it holds on to the Light rayed down from above,[1] together with the fragrance of the Spirit, that is, Mind, ... which is a perfect God who, out of unborn Light from above and Spirit, is borne down into human nature as into a shrine by Nature's motive force and the Wind's movement, ... being mingled and blended with the bodies **and** hastening to be freed from the bodies but unable to find its own release and way out.[2]

8. For a certain tiny Spark ... like a star's ray from above has been mingled in the complex (waters) of many (personalities).[3] Therefore every thought and concern of the Light from above is how ... by the death of

---

[1] Made generative by passion, the 'wave' tries to retain Spirit in its power, though it is foreign to its darkness and from the Light above.

[2] The spiritual mind seeks release from its bondage; *cf.* GG 88 : 1.

[3] The text is broken here; I have in part accepted the restoration offered by MacMahon.

the evil and dark body Mind may be freed from the ... Wind, in agitation and confusion raising waves and producing a perfect Mind, its own Son—though not its very own in substance.[1] For he was a Ray from above, from that perfect Light, overwhelmed in the dark and fearful and bitter and foul Water (PG 16: 3180 ff); the very tiny Spark is subtly blended in the dark waters below, and united and become one paste [2] (PG 16: 3187).

9. But the wind ... rushing along is like the Serpent in (its) hissing;[3] first then from the wind, that is, from the Serpent, the source of generation ... has arisen. ... So when the Light and the Spirit have been taken into the impure, baneful and disorderly womb,[4] the Serpent, the wind of the Darkness (that is)

---

[1] The Soul tries to subdue the waves stirred up by the wind of desire and in the stillness to become the perfect, or heavenly Mind; but that Mind is really a Ray from Above, different in nature from the human mind that seeks it.

[2] Gk.: *sunēnōsthai kai gegonenai en heni phuramati.*

[3] This is the 'roaring' of the Serpent in GG 73 : 2, the 'piping' of App. I : 7 : 10; it is the source of the generation of men, as opposed to the birth of Gods, the 'flowing downwards' of the Ocean in App. I: 5 : 5. "The Serpent is the Moist Essence and nothing at all of existing things, immortal or mortal, living or non-living, can hold together without him," says the Naassene in Hip. Ref.

[4] The Acts of John, p. 113, speak of "the foul madness that is in the flesh, ... the bitter death, ... my soul's secret disease."

the firstborn of the waters, enters in and produces the Man [1]—nor does the impure womb either love or recognise any other form. Having been thus assimilated ... to the Serpent, the perfect word of the Light from above entered into the impure womb, ... to loosen the chains encircling the perfect Mind born in (the) impurity of the womb of the water's firstborn.[2] ...

10. This is the "form of the Servant",[3] and this the need of the word of God coming down into a Virgin's Womb. But it is not enough for the Perfect Man, the word, to have entered into a Virgin's womb and to have freed the pains that were in that Darkness. No, for after entering the foul mysteries in a womb he was washed and (then) drank the Cup of living bubbling

---

[1] Did these Gnostics ever see the sperm entering the ovum, as certain hieroglyphs suggest the earliest Egyptians did? In our vain conceit we fancy that we alone have learned of such things.

[2] The Mind entered the Womb along with the Serpent-Wind of desire, in order to free itself from bondage to dark Matter. This is a great mystery, whereon we have neither time nor space to dilate here; suffice it that through plunging into the sea the pure Pearl is gained. It is the mystery of incarnation.

[3] Alluding to Phil. 2 : 7. The incarnation of the Divine Word in a human womb, however virginal, was a difficulty to the Gnostics as to Mani.

water¹ which he must needs drink who is to strip off the servile form and to assume a heavenly Robe (PG 16 : 3180 ff).

It can also be said that there are really Three Sources—God, Matter, and the Spiritual Powers that link and bring these into contact—among which is the Soul, the 'Word' in an almost Johannine sense. The Sethians taught this clearly, naming the Three as Light, Darkness or terrible Water, and Spirit's subtle fragrance. These interact to produce the universe, a blend of 'Good' and 'Evil'—the Wind of Power raising waves of passion in the waters of dark Matter, and so ensnaring Spirit in a material body. To escape this bondage and go to its own natural freedom of the Light above, becomes the aim of the 'spark' or individual soul—which even in the very foulness of the womb of Matter may become the spiritual and perfect man, the true Gnostic. Then, as a human 'Christ', born of the virgin-ocean of life, he is freed of imperfection and clad in the celestial wedding-garment of the Liberated One.

---

[1] This Cup is referred to in GG 79 : 3 and App. I: 6 : 3. While ignorant of its origin from Above, how could the Soul shake off the drunken sleep of ignorance and Egypt's filthy rags (GG 73 : 2), to put on the glorious Robe of Light? This is the 'Basin' of GH 37 : 3, wherein soul-memory is restored.

CHAPTER THREE

INFINITE GOD AND THE SOUL

We turn now from the Gnosis as represented by its orthodox foes to some of the original Gnostic books, preserved for us by happy chance in Coptic under the sands of Egypt—especially the sublime ' Untitled Apocalypse ' of the Bruce Codex.

In words of great dignity and beauty, even where the profundity of the subject treated makes them hard to understand, we are told of the ONE REALITY, eternally abiding in the Silence, unknown and unknowable, until revealed as the Infinite Goodness that is the All-Father. From this Manifest God came all that is; to Him—or rather, to THAT—all in the perfection of time return; in and through Him they exist, and in each of them is a spark of His Divine Light and Life, dowered with perfect qualities which are God's very nature. Destined to discern the REAL among the veils of Unreality, the human Soul fulfils the purpose of creation when it returns to its parent ONENESS and is crowned with Divinity's nameless glories.

6. God Unmanifest

This is the First Father[1] of these universes, this is the First Being, this is the King of these

---

[1] The Coptic text does not distinguish very clearly between the Unmanifest and the Manifest in this place—in fact, they are *one*. We are told elsewhere in GIG (115) that the mystic number of the ' First Amen ' is ' 530 '.

Intangibles; it is He in whom these universes [1] roam about, it is He in whom He has given form to them. This is the self-existing and self-produced Space; He is the Abyss of these universes,[2] He is indeed the Great Deep.[3] It is He to whom the universe has come; they [4] were silent before Him and have not told of Him, for He is beyond speech, beyond thought.[5] So This is the First Fountain; it is He whose Voice [6] has penetrated in every place—this is the First Tone (vibrating) until the universe feels and understands.[7] This it is whose Members [8] form a myriad of myriads of Powers, emerging one by one (GL 226).

[1] The use of the plural is striking; the Gnostics knew as well as the writers of the Upanishads and our modern astronomers that there are many universes (*brahmāṇḍa*), whereof we live in one.

[2] Arnobius (ad Nat. 1: 31, q. Scott) says: "For Thou art the First Cause, the place and space of things, the foundation of all that are." All things are in Him; He, being omnipresent, is both in all and in no one of them spatially.

[3] Copt.: *pai pe pbathos ṅnipterf, pai pe pnoc ṅhapnoun name*.

[4] *i.e.*, all creatures in the universe.

[5] "Whose true form none of the Gods can see (*or* : know), which changed into the all invisible in the senses of sight, O Aeon of Aeons!", says the Eighth Book of Moses (Abraxas, p. 176).

[6] The Creative Word which awoke being out of non-being and started the great 'Game of God' on its way. It is the *Praṇava*, the *Ahunavairya*, the *Logos* of the Greeks.

[7] The vibrating Expression of His Will made the unconscious conscious.

[8] Copt.: *melos*. His 'Members' are the sparks of His Life scattered abroad until the great Day of 'Come unto Us'.

The infinite and incomprehensible Deep of Silence IS, and in That all the universes exist; in Him they came to be, and finally resolve again. Words cannot tell of Him, for He is ever beyond all speech and thought—yet it is He who in the dawn utters the creative Word that manifests His infinity.

7. Is Manifested

1. The Second Space[1] came into being, He who is to be called Maker and Father[2] and Word and Fountain and Mind and Man[3] and Eternal and Infinite[4] (GL 227). He who has come forth in the Ineffable and Immeasurable who is really true, this ONE in whom is that which really is; ... through Him (are) those which really exist and those which truly are not,[5] He for whom exist the hidden

---

[1] Copt. : *pmehsnau ñtopos*. The word *topos*, borrowed from Gk., seems to imply almost a state of being; all things are in Him, so He is the 'place' for all.

[2] The Gospel of the Truth (CJ 37-38) says: "He is the Father, He from whom the beginning came forth, and towards whom will return those who have issued from Him and have been manifested for the glory and joy of His Name. Now the 'Name' of the Father is the Son. ... Who then has been able to utter a name for Him, the Great Name?"

[3] The word 'Man' (Copt.: *rōme*) is here used for the Perfection in whose 'image' man has been fashioned; elsewhere he is called 'Son of Man'.

[4] Copt.: *aperantos*, *i.e.*, one who cannot be transcended or passed beyond.

[5] Copt.: *etbēētf netṣoop ontōs name, mnnete ṅseṣoop an name*; *i.e.*, the Real or eternal, and the Unreal or transitory.

Realities and the manifest Unrealities[1] (GL 237).

2. This is the Column,[2] this is the Overseer, and this is the Father of the universe (GL 227). He is the Father of every father, and the God of all gods, . . . and the Silence of all the silences is He. He is the Infinite of all the infinites, the Uncontainable[3] of all the uncontainables is He . . . He alone is the One Intelligent,[4] being Himself before every mind, . . . an Incomprehensible who (understands) all; He is a Formless who is before all forms,[5] . . . existing before all the heights. And it is He who is Wise beyond all the wisdoms, and Holier than all the holies, a Good one more than all the good—He is the origin of all the goods, He again is pregnant of them all—the Self-formed, or alone the Sprout that was before these universes which

---

[1] The Real is not immediately visible, while the eye sees unrealities all around. This sounds very like Advaita, which many Gnostics would find not alien to their own mode of thought.

[2] *i.e.*, the Support of all.

[3] Copt.: *akhōrētos*, another of those Gk. negatives hard to translate; it comes from *khōreō*, ' to make room, retire, have space for, contain '; thus the adjective means almost ' boundless ', ' unattainable '.

[4] Copt.: *noeros*.

[5] Copt.: *ouateine pe ethathē ñeine tērou.*

He alone has produced. Being all Time, He is a Self-born and an Everlasting; having no Name, yet all the names are His.[1] Preceding in knowledge of these universes while He contemplates these universes, gazing down upon these universes, listening to these universes, being mightier than all Powers—He in whose incomprehensible Face none can look[2] (GL 274-275).

3. It is He upon whom the Aeons are a Crown sending out rays;[3] the outline of His Face is Unknowing in the outer world[4] which seek always after His Face, longing to know it, for His Word has reached to them and

---

[1] The Epistle of the Apostles (3) has: "God the Son of God, ... who is named by all names". It is a Hermetic, a Hindu and a Platonic thought.

[2] The whole of this sublime description could have come from Sanskrit verses, and it would have been equally at home in the Hermetic writings. I do not know of any finer attempt to put the ineffable into human words. As Ecclus. 43: 27 sums up: "The end of the matter is: He is all."

[3] This is parallel to the Mithraic 'Sol Invictus' so familiar from Roman imperial coins, where God is symbolised by the Sun in its glory. In GL 234-5 we read: "Twelve other (fathers) also surround His head, whereon there is a Crown, and these throw out rays to the worlds around them from the Light of the Alone-born hidden therein, after whom they seek."

[4] Copt.: *pkōte ṁpefho te tmntatswōns hn ṅkosmos ethibol*. I can understand this word 'unknowing' only by its use in the medieval title of 'The Cloud of Unknowing'; it is by putting away all knowledge of the outer worlds we come to know God, the 'Inmost of the Inmost'.

they yearn to see Him.[1] Now the Light of His eyes pierces as far as the regions of the outer Fullness, and the Word that comes from His mouth penetrates those above and those below.[2] The hair of His head is the number of the hidden worlds[3] and the edge of His face is the reflection[4] of the Aeons; ... the spreading out of His hands is the revealing of the Cross,[5] (while) the extension of the Cross

---

[1] Plutarch (de Iside 78 : 3) has: "When freed (their souls) pass to the Formless and Unseen and Passionless and Pure, this God becomes their Guide and King, as though they hung on Him and gazed insatiate on His beauty and longed after it—which no man can declare or speak about." *They*, i.e., those in the outer world.

[2] So too in GL 239 : "The Light penetrated down as far as Matter below and to those who had neither form nor likeness;" *cf.* GG 16 : 1.

[3] An exact parallel with the Vaishnava Tripād-vibhūtī-mahā-nārāyaṇopaniṣad 2: 16: "Out of each one of His hair-follicles are born endless crores of universes veiling Himself." "He created the hairs of His body as the type of the worlds of the Fullness" (GL 268). Could this be a cultural contact, or a common spiritual vision? Indian influences abound in the Gnosis, while there is no evidence of the Western Gnosis reaching India—whose scriptures are unlikely to have borrowed from those of unclean foreigners! This may suggest a *terminus ad quem* for the Hindu book, as not later than the late 2nd century A.D.

[4] Copt.: *kathikōn*; the idea recurs in GG 30 : 4 etc.

[5] *Cf.* the Odes of Solomon 27 : 1-2: "The extending of my hands is His Sign, and my spreading out is the Uplifted Wood." Earlier than the Crucifix, the Christ used to be shown standing before a Cross with arms outspread in blessing; this comes nearer the idea of the Mystic Cross we speak of in GG 34-40, which is wherever God's support and blessing reach; *i.e.*, through all the universe.

is the Ennead that is to the Right, together with those that are on the Left [1] (GL 227).

4. This alone is the Blessed One, for these universes have need of Him as they all live for His sake,[2] He being the One who knows, ... who contemplates these universes in Him. Uncontainable is He,[3] while He Himself contains these universes, drawing them to Himself. Nor is there anything existing outside of Him, but these universes are in Him—He being Boundary for them all,[4] enclosing all of them while they are all in Him (GL 276).

5. Twelve faces[5] has the Mind of the universe, and the prayer of everyone is brought

---

[1] As in GG 39 : 2, the Cross marks off the evil, or left-hand path, from the good, or right hand; the Nine Divine Powers are naturally on the Right side. This division of mankind by the Cross is the 'judgment' of St. John's Gospel; Christ embraces both sides.

[2] *or* : on His account. Clement in his Stromata 6 : 5 : 39 gives from the old Preaching of Peter: " The Unseen who sees all things, Uncontainable who contains all, having need of nought (but) of whom all stand in need, and for whose sake they exist; Incomprehensible, Incorruptible, Uncreated, who made all things by the Word of His Power." This writer moved in the same Gnostic circles.

[3] Copt.: *ouakhōrētos pe ntof*.

[4] God is the only boundary we can ever meet; we cannot fall from the universe save into His hands. He is the 'Limit' or 'Boundary' that restrained the wandering 'Wisdom' in GG 14 : 2 and purified her for the return home to her lost perfection.

[5] Here we again meet the 'Twelve', symbolised by zodiacal signs, apostles, Israelite tribes, and in many other ways. The Twelve Deeps are given in GL as All-Source, All-Wise, All-Mystery,

to Him:¹ it is He on whose account the universe has rejoiced because He has appeared, and it is He whom the Individual² has striven to know,³ and it is He on whose account the Man has appeared.... Now to speak of Him by means of a tongue of flesh, how He is—this is an impossibility;... each one of the Perfect Men has seen Him, and they have told of Him, giving glory to Him as they could⁴ (GL 232, 235).

So He whom we call God was manifested forth, the One eternal Reality still unchanged yet now expressing His infinite perfection in an infinity of worlds

---

All-Gnosis, All-Pure, Silence, non-existing Door, Forefather, self-fathered All-Father, All-Power, First Invisible Truth, Image of the Father, Mother of all Aeons, Oneness, Eternal Father—but it is not clear which of these epithets are bracketed together.

[1] An exact parallel to Gita 9 : 15, 23. Copt.: *auō psopsp ńwon nim euji mmof eratf*. The true knower can never be sectarian or bigoted, for he *knows* there is but one God, to whom all prayers ascend, who is the source of all good and saintliness in every creed.

[2] *lit.*: indivisible (Copt.: *patpōṣ*), equivalent of Gk. *atom*. Every individual soul seeks for God, even when unconscious of the search. For this reason He has manifested as the Perfect Man, the Christ, that we may love Him and rejoice at His very sight.

[3] "To know Thee is perfect righteousness; yea, to know Thy power is the root of immortality," says Wisd. 15 : 3.

[4] Saints, Prophets and Sages have seen God and spoken in their own ways of Him, yet as Guru Nanak so beautifully sings in Japji Saheb He remains ineffable, for "God's Saints have not the power to recount the wondrous works of His might" (Ecclus. 42 : 17). Yet the Acts of Thomas (149) cries: "Believe in this Beautiful, whose beauty impels me to speak of Him what He is, though I be unable to tell it fully." Our text names Marsanēs, Nikotheos and Phōsilampēs as Gnostics who have tried to sing His glory.

filled with teeming life. He is the Source of all that is, the fount of every beauty and strength and skill, formless, yet containing in Himself all forms, as a Seed the innumerable progeny of countless generations. He is the Goal to which they all aspire, being the Perfection hidden in every one of them. He is the Means of their attainment, their Providence, their Awakener, and their Crown; indeed, His very Body is the universe itself, and all beings turn to Him as the Light of their own self dwelling in their heart.

8. The One Source of All

1. Now every name has derived from the Father [1]—whether Ineffable or Imperishable, whether Unknown or Invisible, whether Simple or Solitary, whether Power or Omnipotence,[2] or all names (uttered) in the Silence [3] —they have all come to be in the Father, this One whom all the outer worlds see like the stars of the sky in the night. As men desire to see the sun, so too do the outer worlds long to see Him because of His invisibility that surrounds Him.[4] It is He who at all times gives the Aeons life, and through His

---

[1] Because He first IS, everything else that is or can be named must have come from Him: *cf.* St. Paul in Eph. 1 : 21 and 3 : 15.

[2] Copt.: *pandunamis*.

[3] As names arise out of the silence, so have all things come from God.

[4] This is why He withdraws Himself from our sight, so that our longing for Him may be increased.

Word has the Individual come to know the Oneness[1] ... and ... the holy Fullness has come into being[2] (GL 229-230).

2. This is the Truth[3] which clothes them all, this is the Father's Image, this is the Truth[3] of the universe, this is the Mother of all the Aeons—she it is who surrounds all the Deeps—this is the Oneness that is unknown or unknowable,[4] this Qualityless[5] wherein are all the qualities, this which is blessed to the eternities. This is the Eternal Father, this is the Ineffable Father, inconceivable, unthinkable, intranscendable. This it is in whom the universe has ceased to be—and they rejoiced, exulted, produced myriads of myriads of Aeons in their joy.[6] ... These are the worlds from which the Cross has sprung, and out of these

---

[1] Copt.: *monas*. *Cf.* the use of this word in GG 3 : 1.

[2] Gnosis or Liberation comes only when God gives the word that the time is ripe (*cf.* GG 60 : 1). Then comes the fullness of spirituality, the completion of the Soul's mission in the lower, or outer, worlds, the wearing of the Robe of Light and the return home to the Father.

[3] *i.e.*, Reality.

[4] Copt. : *tai te tmonas eto ṅakatagnōstos, ē eto ṅatsown m̂mos.* Characteristically, the Coptic gives a native term also when using a hard Greek one of almost identical meaning.

[5] Copt.: *atkharaktēr; lit.*: without seal-impression.

[6] The end of separate existence on merging into God is indeed the cause of infinite joy, naturally expressed by universal creativeness.

bodiless Members has the Man come into being [1] (GL 229).

3. It is He who has caused the Monad to come out of Him like a ship laden with all the good things, and like a field filled or overgrown with every kind of tree, and like a city filled with every race of man and every royal image.[2] This is how the Monad has all things in itself (GL 236).

He is the One whom all beings love under many various names, for no word can truly name Him who is all; and from Him they derive their very life and being. He is the One sole Reality in all, truly reflecting the Unmanifest in a formless form devoid of any quality we could perceive or name. In Him all things exist, and in Him they transcend existence in the ineffable bliss of creative joy. In all of them He is the eternal mystic Cross of Light, uniting the depths with heights immeasurable; He is the individual Soul in each of them, replete with all good and destined to merge in Him at last.

9. Glory of the Indwelling Light

1. This is the Aloneborn[3] in the Monad, which dwells therein like a city,[4] . . . which

---

[1] Note how the perfect Man is here parallel with the Mystic Cross, as in GG 39 : 1.

[2] All things good are in the Spark, so by the creative power of its infinite Source it can create new universes without end.

[3] Copt.: *monogenēs*; as rightly shown by Mead this means not 'only-begotten', but 'begotten by the One alone', *i.e.*, self-created.

[4] GL begins with the words: "He stood up to make them strive towards the City wherein their image is, and it is this wherein

dwells in the temple like a King and as if he were God,¹ . . . having come out of the place which one cannot say where it is, . . . that was before these universes. . . . It is this that has been called the Light-Darkness; because of the excess of its light they alone have made darkness for themselves ² (GL 235-238).

2. This is the Creative Word;³ it is this that controls the universe to make them ⁴ work. This is the Creative Mind under the control of God the Father, this one to whom the creation prays as God and as . . . Saviour;

they live and move, and it is the Father's house, and the garment of the Son, and the Mother's power, and the image of the Fullness" (226). In GL 266 we also read: "The Father took their whole likeness and made it into a City or into a Man; He modelled these universes, *i.e.*, all these Powers, upon it. . . . Each of them knew Him in this City; each of them gave myriads of glories to the Man, or to the City, of the Father that is in the universe." Wherein is much to be meditated on.

[1] "The dwelling of our heart is a holy temple to the Lord" (Ep. Barn. 5); *cf.* 1 Cor. 3 : 16-17. The future Perfect Man rests in the individual Soul like the image of a God in its temple. Whence comes he? That we cannot know. But we know that his origin is lost in God's glory, too bright for us to penetrate.

[2] Sin, or darkness, is no part of God's universe, but the effect of immature, unprepared, seeking after God; the eye is dazzled by too much light, the soul sees only 'evil' when before too great divinity.

[3] Copt. : *plogos ndēmiourgos*—the latter word implying rather 'fashioning' or 'shaping' than true creation out of nothing. God WAS, and His Word, the Son, the individual Soul, moulded a universe according to His Will.

[4] *i.e.*, all creatures in the universe impelled to activity by Life within.

... this one at whom the universe wonders because of His honour and His beauty, this one on whom the universe—those of the within—are a Crown, while those outside are under His feet, and those between surrounding Him bless Him, saying: "Holy holy holy is He, this Aaaēēēeeeiiiooouuuōōō!"[1]—which means: "Thou livest in the living and art holy in the saints and art in those who are! ... Thou art the House, and thou art the Dweller in the House![2] ... Thou art, Thou art the Aloneborn, the Light and Life and Grace!" (GL 238).

God and the individual Soul are one; He dwells in the heart mysteriously as its inner Ruler whose real home is before the universes were. None can look into this inner Light, it is so bright the eyes are darkened by its glory; and this is why God is called the 'Divine Dark'. He within the individual is equally without, the spoken Word of Creation "Let it be!" which perfectly expresses the Divine Will. So He is the chalice of every loveliness; every beauty He has made serves to adorn His infinite perfection. The

---

[1] The later Gnostics made much use of mantrams formed like this from the seven vowels, thrice repeated, to certain notes handed on by oral tradition only. The interpretation given to such mantrams rarely bears any relation in length to the mantrams themselves.

[2] Another strikingly Indian expression; *cf.* the pairs in GG 30 : 3. The Coptic reads: *ṅtok pe pēi aūo ṅtok pe etwōh hmpēi.*

magic melody of the Seven Vowels thrice repeated is a name for Him, for it proclaims His all-pervading glory in almost human terms—the seven Voices or the Angels before the Throne, of another idiom.

10. Preparation of the Saviour

Then the All-Visible[1] came forth (with) a crown on her; she placed it upon those who had believed—the Mother, the Virgin, and the Power of the Aeons. Then she gave order[2] to her worlds at the command of the Inmost, and she placed the Light-Spark in herself after the fashion of the Monad, and she put the hidden one around her.[3] ... Then she gave him Love and Peace and Truth,[4] and myriads of Powers, so that he

---

[1] Copt.: *tpandēlos*, the Universal Mother, in a sense, Nature.

[2] Copt.: *taxis*, a word which means 'ranks', 'orders', and apparently sometimes in Gnostic books the *organised* 'saints' of the inner worlds.

[3] "God mated with His Wisdom, and she brought forth the sole and beloved sensible Son, this very world," says Philo in de Ebrietate 8: 30 (q. Scott). Philo also tells us: "God is ... Husband of Wisdom, sowing for the race of mankind the seed of blessedness into good virgin soil" (de Cherub. 14) "and Wisdom, who like a Mother brings forth the Self-taught Race, declares that God is the sower of it" (de Mut. Nom. 23 : q. Scott).

[4] The Valentinian Epistle to James (CJ 8) has: "The Word is, first and foremost, the origin of Faith, then of Love, last of Works; in these actually Life consists."

might gather together those that had been scattered [1] by the shaking which occurred at the time the 'Three-Powered'[2] came forth with joy.... Then she set up the Firstborn Son as the type [3] of the 'Three-Powered'[2], ... and he undertook the struggle that had been assigned to him.[4] Then he raised up all the pure (part) of Matter, and he made it a World and an Aeon and a City, ... and it is also called the 'New Earth'; it is both God-bearing and life-giving [5] (GL 248-249).

In each individual is the Spark, the Monad, placed there by the Manifest Deity with various powers and qualities, that it might discern the Real among unrealities, draw into itself the scattered rays of Mind long dispersed amid the objects of desire, purify itself of all material contaminations, and so build up the Kingdom of God in itself and realise its own infinite perfection.

---

[1] *Cf.* GG 84 : 3.

[2] Copt.: *tridunamos*. This term seems to refer to the human soul, gifted with the three powers of will, reason and memory. In GG 50 : 1 'Arrogant', man's self-willed egoism, is called one of the 'three-powered ones'.

[3] *i.e.*, as the model for men to imitate.

[4] The struggle is to refine Matter by spiritualising it in God's service, thus building His Kingdom on Earth, the Heavenly City, Perfect Man.

[5] *Cf.* Mani's account in GPM 32: 1.

11. Man and the Universe

1. Then Setheus [1] sent the Spark [2] down to the Individual, and it shone out and illumined the whole region of the holy Fullness. Then they saw the light of the Spark and rejoiced ... on seeing that all their images were in it.[3] ... This is the Crown which the Father of these universes has given the Individual,[4] ... which strengthens all the powers and ... for which all the Immortals pray; ... this is the Servant of the Aeons, and he serves the Fullness.... Its Ennead is qualityless, but in it are the qualities of the whole creation (GL 238-241).

---

[1] A name for God apparently derived from the old Egyptian 'Sĕtech', in Gk. Sĕth; from this name some of the Gnostics who used it were wrongly named 'Sethians' and suspected by their foes of worshipping the Christian Satan!

[2] "This is the Monad that is like a thought in Sĕtheus", says GL 238. The Spark of Divine Life is somehow distinct from the individual Soul; it brings it light and wisdom.

[3] Every one of us from all eternity exists in this Spark, the Son of God, manifesting as His creation. "God created man to be immortal and made him to be an image of His own eternity" (Wisd. 2 : 23). "The worlds came into being through His Word and through the Thought of His heart" (Odes Sol. 16 : 20).

[4] It is the Divine Life that crowns our humanity, gives it all power, contains the whole of its being, and yet is beyond, distinct from, mere being. "They shall receive a glorious Kingdom and a beautiful Crown from the hand of the Lord" (Wisd. 5 : 16).

2. Now in the midst of the measureless Deep there are five Powers[1] called by these ineffable names: The first is called Love, all love having come out of it; the second Hope, whereby they have relied on the aloneborn Son of God. The third is called Faith, whereby the mysteries of the Ineffable have been believed;[2] the fourth is called Gnosis, whereby has come to be known the First Father for whose sake they exist, and they have learned the Mystery of the Silence which speaks of everything that is hidden[3]—the First Oneness on whose account the universe has ceased to be; ... this is the Door of God. The fifth is called Peace, whereby peace is given to everyone within and without, for in it the universe has been founded [4] (GL 245).

3. This is the measureless Deep which surrounds outside the holy Fullness . . .

[1] Christians call three of these the Cardinal Virtues: Faith, Hope and Love; the Gnosis added the loving Knowledge of God and life's meaning, and its fruit which is unshakable Peace. "The five wise (Virgins) are Faith and Love and Grace and Peace and Hope", says the Epistle of the Apostles (43), a 2nd century work.

[2] First comes belief in the real nature of the universe; only after that can we attain true knowledge thereof.

[3] Gnosis arises when the 'Voice of the Silence' can be heard, and through it one goes to God; cf. App. I : 7 : 4.

[4] This Peace is God Himself, (the silence and Stillness wherein human nature came to be individual.)

wherein the 'Three-Powered', . . . in whom the Son is hidden, . . . was glorified until he reached the Indivisible and received the grace of this Unknowable, whereby he received so great a Sonship as the Fullness could not endure because of the excess of the light and the brightness that was in it[1] (GL 245-246).

4. Then indeed the First Monad sent him an ineffable Robe, which is all Light[2] and all Life and all Resurrection[3] and all Love and all Hope and all Faith and all Wisdom and all Gnosis and all Truth and all Peace. . . . And in it is the universe, and the (beings of the) universe have found themselves in it and known themselves in it, and it illumined them all with its ineffable light;[4] to it were

---

[1] *Cf.* GG 9 : 1. The Acts of John (3) says: "We beheld in him such a light as it is impossible for a man who uses corruptible speech to tell what it was like."

[2] This Robe of Light constantly appears in all our Gnostic texts, as in those of Mani, the Pyramids and the Mandeans, etc. Its glory crowns perfected manhood.

[3] Copt: *anastásis*. As the Valentinian Epistle to Reginus shows well, this is the rising again into our true spiritual state (GG 73 : 1), not, of course, as the ignorant fancy, the standing up again of dead bodies, restored to an unneeded physical life.

[4] *Cf.* GG 47. This Robe of perfection is the cosmic experience of omnidentity spoken of in our GA, for in it all that exists has its being, and in its omnipresence all beings are embraced.

added myriads of myriads of powers, so that it might establish the universe once for all. Then it gathered its fabrics to itself, having made them into the form of a Veil around it on every side; and it spread itself out over them all in order, and according to command and prudence.[1] Then did the Real separate from the unreal—and the 'unreal' is the evil which has appeared in Matter. The Robe-Power separated the Real from the unreal; and it called the Real 'the eternal', and it called the unreal 'Matter',[2] . . . and it appointed cleansing powers to cleanse and purify them (GL 220-251).

5. Now this is the Individual which has striven for the universe,[3] and on him were lavished all things, and the measureless Deep was bestowed on him. . . . Then he made a Light-body, and he pressed on among the aeons of the Indivisible until he reached the

---

[1] *Cf.* the activity of the same Robe in GG 76; the 'fabrics' are the lesser robes of more partial consciousness referred to in GG 46 : 3, which at times partially veil even that all-embracing experience of Oneness, which yet dominates them all.

[2] *lit* : the things which are and the things which are not—Copt: auō atdunamis ṅhbsō pōrj ebol ṅnetṣoop ṅnetenseṣoop an, auō asmoute enetṣoop je ṅaiōnios, auō asmoute enetenseṣoop an je hulē—a most striking passage, parallel to much of Hindu thought.

[3] *i.e.*, aimed at at-onement with the universe.

Aloneborn in that Oneness which dwells in stillness or in solitude [1] (GL 241-242).

The Spark of Mind throws light on the universe and reflects everything in itself—a glory set apart for each individual by the All-Father before the beginning as the ideal after which even the lowest creature naturally yearns. The Soul's five great Powers are these: Love, Hope, Faith, Gnosis the door to God, and the Peace found in Him alone; these glorify every individual who has attained to become a Son of Light. Then is he robed in the Divine Vesture of Light, which comprises everything that exists, for he has now become all things, having known the ONE that really IS. In that Robe the deified Soul is veiled, and by its wisdom he discerns the Real everywhere as the one eternal thing and sets all else aside as temporary and evanescent. All this greatness is destined for the individual Soul, and thereby he comes at last into the ONENESS dwelling eternally in moveless peace.

---

[1] When the Soul has plumbed the measureless Deep of God and realised the ONE, its very body is transformed into Light and rushes on inwards until it enters the eternal Silence, which is the unknown God.

CHAPTER FOUR

THE AEONS' STORY

Irenaeus gives us a long account of some Valentinian book which fell into his hands—and here in effect it is. It tells the favourite story of how the human Soul, Wisdom, God's youngest child, out of love for Him wandered into the universe and was ensnared in Matter till redeemed by the Christ and at last restored to her real heavenly home. It is the story of each one of us, repeated in slightly different forms in cc. 9 and 10, as also in GPM 1—12, etc.; it is indeed the story of most intimate and passionate interest for every one of us, for we " have all gone astray like sheep " and have to be carried home by the one Good Shepherd of souls.

12. Emanation of the Eight

1. In unseen and nameless heights there is a certain One perfect pre-existent Aeon,[1] ... First Source, First Father and Deep, ... uncontainable and invisible, both eternal and unproduced (PG 7 : 445). There is nothing at

---

[1] Gk.: *tina hen en aoratois kai akatonomastois hupsōmasi teleion aiōna proonta.* We catch an echo here of the archaic Stanzas of Dzyān.

all unproduced save the Father alone, having neither Space nor Time,[1] no Adviser, nor any other Being able in any way to understand. But He was alone, Himself resting alone in Himself (PG 16 : 3236). He was in stillness and great calm during infinite ages of time, and with Him [2] was also Thought, who **is also named** [3] Grace and Silence (PG 7 : 445)—a nameless Duad, whereof the One is called Ineffable and the Other, Silence (PG 7 : 561).

2. Now when He was creative,[4] it at once occurred to Him to produce and bring forth the best and most perfect that He had in Himself, for He was no lover of solitude. For He is all Love, and love is not love unless there be the beloved [5] (PG 16 : 3236). So this Deep

---

[1] Gk.: *ou topon ekhōn ou khronon*, beyond Space and Time.

[2] Serapion of Thmuis writes: "For the Will of the Father is His Word; ... when the Word rests in the Mind, then there is Silence."

[3] The text reads here: "they name", obviously a modification brought in by the refutator.

[4] Gk.: *gonimos*. The change between eternal stillness and the dawn of creative activity is beautifully described in the Stanzas of Dzyān.

[5] I cannot think of any better reason for creation. The 'play' theory of many Hindus is all right so far as it goes, but it does not seem to go deep enough—*why* picture the Absolute as a play-loving child? God is Love Himself, and Love demands a Second to love. Hence, Advaita can only be a partial truth, whereof the whole must explain the actual existence of Soul and World. To

once planned to emanate from Himself a source of all the things, and this **Thought** He deposited with the coexisting Silence as in a womb.[1] And she ... having become pregnant (PG 7: 445) emanated and produced ... Mind (PG 16: 3236), both like and equal to the Emanator and alone grasping the Father's greatness.[2]—now this Mind is also called Alone-born and Father and Source of all; and with him was also emanated Truth; and this is ... Root of all (PG 7: 445 ff)—that is, a duad which became Mistress and Source and Mother of all the Aeons numbered in the Fullness (PG 16: 3236 ff).

3. Now Mind and Truth having been emanated from the Father, a creative from a creative[3] (PG 16: 3236 ff), this Aloneborn having realised why he was emanated, himself

---

call these mere illusion only evades universally observed facts and suggests that the All-Perfect is Himself subject to illusion—which is obviously absurd.

[1] The thought of a universe to be loved was left to mature in the womb of Silence until it manifested first as Mind. This reverses the usual order where Mind produces all thoughts—but who first thought of a Mind itself?

[2] The Divine Mind, not the limited human shadow of it, can grasp God's real nature. He alone can fully know Himself.

[3] Mind itself is creative, as is the 'All-Father' who created it without the aid of any partner; from Mind arises Expression, and then the Activity which manifests Life.

also emanated Word and Life[1] (PG 7: 445 ff), and out of this Tetrad[2] fruit was born (PG 7: 561)—from the Word and Life were emanated in a pair Man and Church.[3] Now this is (the) original Ogdoad, root and support of all things, named with four names: Deep and Mind and Word and Man—for each of them is male-female (PG 7: 445 ff).

This section is compiled from Valentinian fragments in Irenaeus and Hippolytus. It tells how at the first there was only the ONE, reposing for endless eternities in solitude and silence, wrapped in the one Thought of infinite Mind. Then came a 'change' in that Changelessness; Love demands an object to be loved, so the Absolute One became as it were a Two-in-One; Silence became pregnant with Thought, and so became active as Creative Mind and passive as immutable Truth. Once begun, the process followed itself; Mind was expressed as word or Speech, the 'Logos', and Truth was realised as Life—for what lives is the only reality. The perfect expression of

---

[1] "The God of Truth gave out a Voice speaking thus: 'Ie Ie, Ie!' and when He gives out a voice, this voice has come forth which is the emanations . . . proceeding forth behind each other, treasure by treasure" (GIG 51).

[2] This Tetrad, or group of Four, is symbolised by the Divine Name among the Hebrews, represented by us with the Tetragrammaton יהוה (Yahweh) and paraphrased by the Gnostics as IEOU, which name is always written in Coptic with a line over it, showing it to be an abbreviation of the real ineffable Name.

[3] *i.e.*, the Perfect Man, made up on the lower planes out of all the Elect who form the true Church—no sectarian idea this, but the spiritual reality. The word translated 'Church' is Gk.: *ekklēsia*, *i.e.*, that which has been called out (from the world).

God's Word is in the Ideal Man, while His Life is manifested in the community of the Elect, the Knowers, His Church. These Eight whom we have named are the Divine Ogdoad, from whom all come and in whom all subsist.

13. The Fullness Appears

1. Now these Aeons, ... wishing ... to glorify the Father on their own, evolved emanations in pairs: the Word and the Life **put forth** ten other Aeons, ... while the Man also, along with the Church, emanated twelve Aeons, (the last of which were) Willed and Wisdom. . . . These are the Thirty Aeons,[1] . . . this the unseen and spiritual Fullness.

2. Now the First Father was known only to the Aloneborn sprung from Him, that is, the Mind;[2] to all the rest He is invisible and

---

[1] Everything derived from the Father, who is creative Love, must be creative. Here is the full list of the Thirty Aeons: The 'Ten': Deep, Complexity, Ageless and Union, Self-produced and Delight, Immovable and Blending, Alone-born and Blessed; the 'Twelve': Advocate and Faith, Paternal and Hope, Maternal and Love, Everflowing and Understanding, belonging to the Church, and Blissful, Willed and Wisdom. I cannot pretend to explain these names. Together, they make up the Fullness (*Plērōma*) of Divine Perfection, when added to the original Eight.

[2] Proclus says in Theol. Plat. 171-172: "By the gods this unmoving Deity is called the Silent, and is said to consent with the Mind, and to be known by the Souls through Mind alone."

unattainable.[1] The Mind alone delights in contemplating the Father, and rejoices to think of His unmeasured greatness; but he planned to communicate[2] the Father's greatness with the other Aeons—and how mighty He is and vast, and how He is both beginningless and incomprehensible and unattainable to sight. But Silence restrained him at the Father's will,[3] . . . and the other Aeons likewise somehow (were) in stillness (though) longing to see the Emanator of their seed and to ascertain the beginningless Root.

Now other Aeons, eternal Beings, differentiate off from this primal Root of Being, till there are thirty in all—the last pair being what is God's Will, and Wisdom, the 'Pistis Sophia' of our c. 9, and already foreshadowed in certain of the Jewish scriptures, canonical and otherwise. Now it is only the Divine Mind, closest to God's Self, which can realise Him or share His nature; being Good like the Father Himself, this Mind longs to share its infinite wealth with Heaven's other Powers; but the incomprehensibility of God, beyond all word and thought, veiled in impenetrable Silence, made this impossible.

[1] Gk. *akatalēptos*; lit: what cannot be seized, held in, detected.

[2] Gk. *anakoinōsasthai*, to share together with.

[3] Divine Mind would have all the Glories know the wonder of God's infinite perfection, but its very infinity imposed silence, and Mind alone was left to enjoy the Beatific Vision. The Aeon-doctrine has its parallels in the 'polytheism' of Māni and the Six Divine Aspects of Zarathushtra's faith, also the Ennead of oldest Egypt.

14. The Fall of Wisdom

1. But the last and youngest . . . Aeon, that is, Wisdom,[1] sprang far ahead and suffered passion without the approach of Willed's yoke.[2] . . . Now the passion was a search for the Father, for she would discover His greatness, yet could not, through aiming at an impossibility; so she came into a very great struggle because of the vastness of the Deep and the Father's unsearchability, with the love (she had) for Him.[3]

2. Ever straining forward, by His sweetness she would have been finally absorbed and merged into (His) whole Being,[4] had she not

---

[1] The 'wisdom' here spoken of is the finite mind's desire to know God: "The fear of God is the beginning of wisdom" (Prov. 1 : 7). During the Jewish pre-Christian centuries it was fast coming to be personified, and the Gnostic use of the name is already heralded by the Qumrān sect near the Dead Sea, which is closely linked with our Gnostics by their common use of the Odes of Solomon.

[2] Her sin, or error, was to try to fathom God's infinity without the cooperation of His will; it was a sacrilege, like that of a layman entering the Holy of Holies. Hippolytus (6 : 25) tells us how she wanted to emulate the Father by producing without a consort, whereas all the other Aeons paired off; this savours of pride, and suggests the 'Arrogant' of GG 50 : 1.

[3] Yet it was love that impelled the search, and her suffering arose from the inevitable baffling of that love (*cf.* GG 59 ff).

[4] She would have ceased to exist in God, had He not kept her apart from Him by the barrier of the Cross, which parts those above and those below. He willed a lover, and that will had been defeated, had the lover merged in Him.

come upon the Power which stands fast and guards everything outside the ineffable Greatness. Now this Power is also called 'Boundary',[1] by which she was checked and steadied.[2] Then, having returned to herself and been convinced that the Father is unattainable, she put away (her) earlier intention, together with the passion which had followed on that amazing wonder. . . .

3. Having attempted something impossible and unattainable, Wisdom brought forth a shapeless being;[3] . . . and when she was

---

[1] Philo says: "On His Reason the Father . . . has bestowed a special gift—that standing between them as a Boundary it may distinguish creature from Creator. He is ever Himself the suppliant to the Incorruptible on behalf of mortal kind in its distress, and is the King's ambassador to subject nature" (Quis Rer. div. her 42)

[2] Her mad rush was halted by the realisation that her love was for Infinity, and could never be satisfied without His cooperation; she found some peace or resignation then.

[3] Yet, being creative like the other Aeons, that frustrated love of Wisdom also produced—no beauty worthy of the Beloved, but an Abortion of which she was ashamed.

"In the Unborn all things simultaneously exist, but in the Begotten the female projects substance and the male forms the substance projected by the female. Wisdom therefore prepared to project only that of which she was capable, namely a formless and undigested substance" (Hip. Ref. 6 : 25). Plutarch adds to this: "Before this universe was manifested and Matter was perfected by Reason, Nature, proving of herself imperfect, brought forth her first birth. Therefore also they say that God was lame in the dark, and they call him the Elder Horus; for he was not cosmos, but a sort of image and phantasm of the world which was to be.

grieved at the creature's [1] imperfection and then feared lest she herself be incapable of perfection,[2] then was she distracted and desperate, seeking why and how to hide the birth. Coming so into sufferings, she turned round and tried to hasten back to the Father, but having ventured some way she lost strength and became the Father's suppliant;[3] and the other Aeons, especially the Mind, prayed with her.

4. Hence (the) first beginning arose from the Ignorance and Grief, and Fear and Consternation.[4] Now with a view to these things the Father emanates the aforesaid Boundary,[5]

But this Horus is their Son, defined and perfect" (de Iside, 54-55). It is very easy to trace the likeness between these versions.

[1] Gk. *geneseōs*; or: birth's.

[2] So it is rendered; Gk. *mēde auto to einai teleiōs ekhein*.

[3] Like all the wise, she was driven by suffering to seek the Father humbly, and in this all the other Powers of the Fullness helped her. *Cf.* the use of the word 'suppliant'—evidently a technical term—in GH 44 : 1.

[4] The Gnostic commentator on the older Wisdom-Myth here explains that from her passions arose this world apart from God, outside the Fullness that is in Him alone. He elaborates this greatly, but we need not follow him into what must seem to us, as to the Christian refutator, mere childishness. The four 'passions' are thus named in Gk. *agnoia, lupē, phobos, epiplēxis*.

[5] Irenaeus tells us that "because Wisdom had no rest, neither in heaven nor in earth, in her grief she called her Mother to her aid. And her Mother, the First Woman, had compassion on her daughter's penitence, and begged of the First Man that Christ be sent as a help to her". This comes near to the GPM story.

through the Aloneborn in His own image, unpaired, non-prolific. . . . And this Boundary is also called 'Cross'[1] and 'Co-Redeemer' . . . in that it divides and discerns; . . . it indeed also destroys all material things as fire does chaff, but purifies the saved as the fire the grain. . . .

5. Now by this Boundary Wisdom was purified . . . and restored to the pairing;[2] for, the intention having been taken away from her together with the resultant suffering, . . . she was isolated and stripped by the Boundary. Then coming to be outside the **Fullness**, she was indeed spiritual, having an Aeon's sort of natural vigour, but through

---

[1] Hippolytus tells us (Ref. 6 : 26): "This is styled 'Boundary' because it separates from the Fullness the Hysterema that is outside, and . . . 'Cross' because it is inflexibly and inexorably fixed, so that nothing of the Hysterema can come near the Aeons who are within the Fullness." *Cf.* GG. 38-39.

The Cross is in the Father's image, outspread in blessing, to keep the human Soul apart from Him until it learns by humility His inconceivable vastness and glory. Suffering and deprivation of God discern the truly spirirual from the sham. Hippolytus adds to this (Ref. 6 : 26): "This abortion of Wisdom . . . separates itself from the whole of the Aeons, lest the perfect Aeons seeing this be disturbed because of its shapelessness. So then . . . the Father also again projects additionally one Aeon, namely 'Cross'."

[2] *i.e.*, she was brought back into union with God's will.

having understood nothing she was formless and indeterminate.¹

The youngest of these Powers, the human Soul or Mind, was not content to be in ignorance of her all-glorious Father; out of love and yearning for Him, and that restless curiosity which is man's saving grace, she plunged into the fathomless Deep to seek Him out. But there is a limit beyond which none can pass, for the finite cannot know or grasp the Infinite; it must first change its whole nature and be made Divine. Realising then the futility of her effort, the Soul dropped her desire—which at once became a 'shapeless being', an 'abortion', as St. Paul calls it. In her shame and misery, the Soul tried to abandon her 'child' and to struggle back to her heavenly place. but could not; she then prayed for help (cf. GG 53-57), and thus was purified of her foolish transgression and restored to union with God's Will—though still in misery outside His Kingdom of Perfection.

15. The Saviour Comes Forth

1. Next to the Aloneborn, another Pair was emanated according to plan,² so that none of the Aeons might suffer like her—Christ and

---

¹ Gk. *kai ektos autou (plērōmatos) genomenēn, einai men pneumatikēn phusikēn tina Aiōnos hormēn tugkhanousan amorphon de kai aneidion dia to mēden katalabein.* It is the absence of Gnosis which has made us hideous and unformed; we become what we are meant to be, perfected beings, only when we enter into Gnosis.

² Apparently the text, here confused, originally said that Christ and a holy Spirit (there is no definite article) were emanated from the *Aloneborn*, *i.e.*, the Mind. At all events the work of the new Pair was largely mental. The present Gk. text reads: *ton de Monogenē palin heteran probalesthai suzugian kata promētheian.* In

Holy Spirit, to fix and establish the Fullness; by these the Aeons were set in order. For the Christ taught them the nature of pairing; knowing how to grasp the Unborn,[1] they are ready for the knowledge of the Father to be proclaimed in them—that He is beyond understanding and unattainable, and is neither to be seen nor heard, but is known through the Aloneborn only... whereas the one Holy Spirit taught them all equally to give thanks, and pointed out the true Rest. Thus were the Aeons fixed equal in form and purpose—all becoming Minds, and all Words, and all Men, and all Christs,[2] while the females likewise all (became) Truths, and all Lives, and Spirits and Churches.

2. Thereupon, the whole having been confirmed and perfectly pacified, they sang hymns with great joy to the Father, sharing much delight... With one will and purpose the entire Fullness of the Aeons—Christ and the

---

Ref. 6 : 26, Hippolytus says: "The Father, then, pitying Wisdom's tears and accepting the Aeons' prayer, ordered a further projection; for He did not Himself project, but Mind and Truth (emanated) Christ and Holy Spirit to restore Form and destroy the Abortion, and console and cease the groans of Wisdom."

[1] Gk. *agennētou katalēpsin ginōskontas*.

[2] *Cf.* the close parallel in GG 5 : 1.

Spirit being well pleased and their Father setting the seal thereon— ... each one of the Aeons contributing whatever he had in himself most beautiful and flower-like—. ... evolved emanations to (the) honour and glory of the Deep. (This is) the most perfect beauty and star of the Fullness, a perfect Fruit,[1] Jesus, who was also surnamed Saviour and Christ and Word and All, because he is from all. .... And they together emanated Angels of like nature.

To help Wisdom, God sent Christ and the Holy Spirit, who taught her in the whole of creation how unattainable God is and how true Peace can be found. Then all the eternal Powers joined together to produce the Perfect Man, flower of all divinity, Jesus, the universal Saviour; and at the same time they produced his younger brethren, the Angels, to help restore the human Soul to her lost heritage.

16. Wisdom is in Distress

1. The Intention[2] of the Wisdom above, which is also called Aḥamōth, was shut away from the Fullness with the passion, thrown

---

[1] As to Mani, Jesus is the perfect Flower of the Father, the essence of all beauty and perfection.

[2] Gk. *enthumēsis*; lit: consideration, esteem. We here distinguish between Wisdom the Mother, the human Soul in itself—and Aḥamōth, the Abortion expelled from the fullness of perfection where Wisdom ever dwells, the fallen human soul as we know it down here.

out perforce into shadows and regions of emptiness. For outside Light and Fullness it became formless and indistinct [1] like an abortion, through having understood nothing. Then Christ, pitying her and overshadowing (her) by means of the Cross,[2] with his own power fashioned (her in) a form, only that according to substance but not that according to knowledge.[3] Then having done this, he hastened back, withdrawing his power, and left (her), so that on feeling the suffering around her ... she might aim at different things, having a certain perfume of incorruption left in her by Christ and the Holy Spirit.[4] ...

[1] Gk. *aneidios*; lit: of no species, indistinguishable, vague.

[2] Suffering, the recognition by the Cross that the Soul is separated from God, first enables the Saviour to approach the Soul and to lift her a little from her miseries.

[3] First the Abortion is given human shape; recognition of her true place lets Christ fashion her anew in the Divine likeness, though as yet without that Gnosis or realisation of God which will set her free from the outer darkness of rebirth. Satornilos, in PG 16:3322, says: "When it came into being and the figure could not erect itself because of the Angels' incompetence but kept crawling like a worm, the Power Above, pitying him because he was produced in her likeness, sent a Spark of Life which raised and vivified the Man." Note also the two stages of redemption in GG 59 and 63.

[4] The memory and yearning for something higher stays in the Soul even after the spiritual outpouring is withdrawn, as in GG 60 : 4 and 66 : 5.

2. And she eagerly set herself to seek out the Light that had abandoned her, but was unable to grasp it because prevented by the Boundary.[1] . . . Being entangled in the passion and left outside alone, she sank down under every part of the passion, which was manifold and various. Then she suffered grief that she did not succeed, and fear lest like the Light so too the Life might leave her, and besides these, embarrassment—and everything in ignorance.[2] . . . For at times she wept and sorrowed at being left alone in the Darkness and the Void, and at times having come on a thought of the Light that had abandoned her, she relaxed and smiled, while at times again she was afraid, and at others was at a loss and amazed.[3]

Meanwhile the Soul, cut off from its Divine Source, has become deformed and darkened, being robbed of all its light. So first the Redeemer comes to her and overshadows her with the mystic Cross, discerning right from left (wrong), and things celestial from things infernal. So she becomes a Soul in proper form, though

---

[1] She cannot of her own strength cross the barrier between herself and Divinity; this power she has still to acquire through Gnosis.

[2] Her failure again plunges her into all the sufferings inherent in her state of *virāham*, passions of every kind sweeping over her in turn, as in the hymn in GG 88 : 1.

[3] Gk. *diēporei kai existato*.

still lacking the Gnosis which will finally restore her to the heights. Christ leaves her with the ideal, so that she may strive for this, and not for lesser things, worldly and unworthy. She indeed strove to reach the light of that ideal, but was frustrated by that same limitation on all finite efforts—we can approach but never attain the ideal till we put on divinity. This failure has plunged her, as we have already seen, into the four miseries—from which all vicissitudes of life on earth derive.

17. Forming the Human Being

1. Therefore the Mother ... turned to implore the Light that had abandoned her, that is, the Chrst,[1] who ... sent out her Advocate, that is, the Saviour ... with the Angels his comrades. Revering him, Ahamōth first out of modesty put on a veil,[2] but afterwards seeing him in all his fruitfulness ran up to him, taking strength from his brilliance. Then he shaped her a form according to

---

[1] As in GG 97, the Mother intervenes to invoke Christ's aid for her helpless child below; so in GPM 3:2 the Mother of Life evokes the Rescuer.

[2] She has begun to learn the essential humility before even an Emanation of the Most High: Gk. *tēn de Akhamōth entrapeisan auton prōton men kalumma epitheisthai di' aidō*. The Excerpts from Theodotus (44:1-2) give us: "And on seeing him, Wisdom recognised he was like the Light that had abandoned her, and she ran up and was evangelised and prostrated; but having noticed the male Angels sent with him felt shame and put on a veil." *Cf.* 1 Cor. 11:10.

Gnosis,[1] and wrought a healing of her passions, separating them from her, . . . and changing them from bodiless passion into the bodiless matter. Next he worked into them aptitude and nature, so as to come into compounds and bodies, until two substances came into being: one worthless for the passions, and one capable of conversion. And this is why the Saviour potentially created.

2. Now Aḥamōth, coming outside passion and joyfully taking up the contemplation of the Angels with him, and having yearned after them, was impregnated with fruits like the image, a spiritual progeny like those who had become the Saviour's bodyguards. . . . But the spiritual (part) she could not shape, since it was of the same substance with herself, but she undertook to shape the psychic being which arose out of the conversion, and set before her the lessons (derived) from the Saviour.[2] So first of all she fashioned from the

---

[1] The Excerpts run: "The Saviour then immediately conferred on her the form according to Gnosis and a healing of the passions" (45:1); the Light of Gnosis frees her from blind suffering and gross matter and admits her to the spiritual path.

[2] Her longing then shapes her like the Redeemer, so far as the lower personal self is concerned, and on that Image she builds

psychic substance the Father and King of all, ... for she shaped everything according to Him, unconsciously moved by the Mother. ... For, wishing to do all things to honour the Aeons, this Intention had made images of them—or rather, the Saviour through her. And she kept herself in (the) image of the invisible Father, but this one of the Aloneborn Son and the rest of the Aeons who had become both Archangels and Angels (formed) by them.

Her Higher Self or Mother, Wisdom Above, then implored Christ to save her from these troubles. He came in all glory of his eternal Light and so illumined her, initiating her in all mysteries of the Gnosis; so he clearly marked off her passion-suffering body from her ever-glorious self. Love for her Saviour caused her to assume his image within the soul, and so she became like him, fashioned in the eternal Father's likeness. Yet this image was only in her soul, not yet in the inner spirit; the liberated personal self soon fell into confusion and imagined it was identical with the Absolute.

a splendid Personality, essentially human, yet inspired with almost divine power. The Personality becomes the Demiurgic Ruler and Maker of the worlds. The Valentinian in PG 7: 563-564 says: "The Mother, being left behind with the shadow and emptiness of the spiritual substance, brought forth another Son, and this is the Creator and All-Ruler of those below; and with him was emanated an excellent Ruler."

18. The Creator's Delusion

1. Then he became Father and God of those outside the Fullness, being Maker of all things, both psychic and material. For, having parted the two mingled substances and made from incorporeals a body, he fashioned both the heavenly and the earthly things. . . . For he built seven heavens, over which is the Creator (Himself), and for this reason he is called 'Hebdomad,'[1] and the mother of Aḥamōth (is called) Ogdoad. . . .

2. Now the Creator imagined he was building these things by himself,[2] but he made them while Aḥamōth was emanating, . . . thus he did not know throughout the forms[3] of what he made, or the Mother herself, but imagined himself to be all. (The) cause of this fancy of his became the Mother, willing thus to lead him on (as) head and source of

---

[1] The Personal then, separating the subtler from the grosser kinds of matter, fashions the outer universe we know—with its seven heavens, from which he is called the 'Hebdomad', the sevenfold Being, the earth and sea and sky.

[2] Unaware of the Divine Silence brooding over all, knowing only how he himself rose from the cleansing and freeing of the human soul, this Ruler takes himself to be the only God.

[3] Gk. *idea*; *i.e.*, prototypes, natures, models.

her own substance and lord of the whole work. Now this Mother ... has the region of the Midst and is above the Creator but altogether below or outside the Fullness. ... For which reason he, being too weak to know any spiritual beings, thought himself alone to be God.[1]

3. Now the World-Ruler is a creature of the Creator, and the World-Ruler knows that what are over him are a spirit of evil, but the Creator, who is merely a psychic being, does not know (that). ... Having indeed created the world, he had also made the earthy man—not indeed from this dry mud, but from the unseen essence, taking of liquified and poured matter, and into this he breathed the psychic;[2] ... and from this his essence has been called 'Spirit of Life', being from a spiritual stream.

4. But the embryo of the Mother of the Seed, Aḥamōth, ... even the Creator himself

---

[1] In his blind vanity he even forgot that above the redeemed Aḥamōth whence he arose is the supernal Wisdom, the heavenly prototype of humanity; he was led on by this blindness to become the 'God' of exoteric religions, arrogating to himself what belongs to the Unknown and Unseen.

[2] This deluded Creator fashioned the earthly human being out of the hidden fluid of sex, into which he breathed a 'human soul', the psychic nature, totally distinct from the real Soul, which is ever wholly spiritual.

did not know, and it was placed in him unawares without his knowledge,[1] so that having been sown by him in the Soul and in this material body ... it might become fit to receive the Perfect. So then the Spiritual Man, sown altogether in the implanting of him by Wisdom with ineffable forethought, escaped the Creator's notice; for as he did not know the Mother, so too (he knew not) her Seed, ... Church.[2]

This delusion still prevails in the human mind. Sharing the Father's creative powers, it fashions worlds and every kind of creature—each different for every individual—and believes itself the real God and Source of all. Actually, its creation is guided by the desires and passions of the 'Abortion', the Soul divorced from its real Root; it sees the world of its own desires and fears, not the eternal Reality, being misled by the 'Mother' of humanity, the impulsive urge for knowledge. It is this Demiurge, this Fashioner, who made the man we see, body and living soul, though he knows little of the realities that eternally lie behind these manifesting forms. And so the 'psychic' man or ordinary man is dark to the Truth until this day; to

---

[1] Into this degraded parody of the real Man is however placed the hidden Seed of the Spiritual Man Above, so that in due time it may mature into perfection. Of this the lower man, even the material maker of the world, has no knowledge; Gk. *kai lelēthotōs katatetheisthai eis auton, mē eidotos autóu.*

[2] Unknown to his material maker, the seed of the Spiritual Man lives hidden, like the Child Horus in the marshes, till the time chosen for his manifestation.

enlighten him, Jesus the Messenger put on a body like his own in seeming and came down to live in his company.

19. The Consummation of All Things

1. Then the Saviour came to help this psychic (part), so that he might save it, since it too had free will.[1] For of those whom he would save he took their first fruits: from Aḥamōth the spiritual, while from the Creator he (took and) put on the psychic Christ,[2] and from the ordered world he put on around him a body having psychic substance and fashioned with ineffable skill, so as to be invisible and impalpable, yet able to suffer. But he took nothing whatever material, for matter is not capable of salvation.[3]

[1] Irenaeus (1 : 30 : 14) quotes: "The consummation will be when the whole of the spirit of Light wherewith things are imbued is gathered in and caught away into the Incorruptible Aeon." It is not only the higher spiritual part of man, but even the lower personal part, which is worthy of salvation.

[2] The Christ had no physical body, nothing lower than the psychic (*sūkshma*). This school of thought has clear docetic tendencies, as in the Acts of John and the fragments of the Gospel of Peter. Irenaeus quotes: "What suffered . . . was the psychic Christ and he who was mysteriously framed by the 'Economy', that by him his Mother might exhibit the pattern of the Christ who is above, of him who was extended on the Cross, and who gave Aḥamōth her essential form" (1 : 7 : 3).

[3] Clearly refuting the gross idea then growing that even the body of this flesh will rise again and share the eternal life of Spirit in the higher planes. The Valentinian Epistle to Reginus in the Jung Codex, as too GG 78 : 2, also rejects the pagan error.

2. Now the end will be when all the spiritual has been shaped and perfected by Gnosis, that is, the Spiritual Men who have the perfect knowledge about God and Aḥamōth, and these are initiated in mysteries [1] ... For action does not lead into Fullness,[2] but the seed that is sent out thence infantile is perfected here. And as soon as all the seed is perfected, then Aḥamōth **the** Mother is to pass from the region of the Midst and enter within into Fullness and receive her Spouse, the Saviour, the one produced out of all [3] ... Now this is the 'Bridegroom' and the 'Bride', and 'Bridechamber' is the whole Fullness.[4]

---

[1] When by Gnosis, *i.e.*, perfect experiential knowledge of God and Nature and Soul, all spiritual men have matured and entered on the inheritance of Light, this lower world, fashioned by the deluded Creator, will vanish away.

[2] Mere action, however virtuous, can never lead to salvation; nothing save the Gnosis avails; Gk. *ou gar praxis eis plērōma eisagei.* This can be only when the time is ripe and when through much suffering the soul has become mature.

[3] When the 'Church' of all Spiritual Men is complete, then fallen humanity itself is lifted from the lower planes of dark chaos into the Light and becomes the Bride of the Heavenly Bridegroom, Christ. So St John appeals to his followers: "Join yourselves together in an inseparate marriage holy and true, waiting for the one true incomparable Bridegroom from heaven, even Christ, the everlasting Spouse" (Acts, 105).

[4] Entering on the whole Fullness of Divine Life, the Soul becomes one with its Lord, Fruit of the whole Perfection.

3. Then the Spiritual, having put away the souls and become intuitional[1] spirits, entering without force and invisibly[2] within the Fullness, will be assigned as Brides to the Angels around the Saviour.[3] Now the Creator, he too, will pass into the region of Wisdom the Mother, that is, into the Midst, while the souls of the righteous will also take rest in the region of the Midst, for nothing psychic finds place within (the) Fullness.

4. And when (all) this has so happened, the fire lurking in the world bursts out and flares up and, destroying all Matter, will with it be spent away and come to exist no more.[4] Now the Creator knew nothing of these things, . . . but on the Saviour's coming he learned all from him and willingly drew near to him

---

[1] Gk. *noera*. The Excerpts (64) read: "They enter the Bride-chamber within the Boundary and come to the vision of the Father, having become intuitional Aeons, to the intuitional and eternal marriage of the Pairing."

[2] The last stage is sweet and unopposed; cf. "Calm and unmoved the pilgrim glideth up the stream that to Nirvana leads" (The Seven Portals).

[3] Each liberated Soul will be espoused to one of the Angels of nature kindred to the Christ (cf. GG 15 : 2).

[4] As in almost every other religion which speaks of eschatology at all, the end of things is by fire, the hidden purifying agent which destroys Matter and itself then ceases to exist.

with all his power [1] . . . But the spiritual (parts) . . . are educated and nurtured here (as) righteous souls because sent forth immature, and are later held worthy of perfection, to be assigned (as) Brides to the Angels of the Saviour (PG 7 : 445-520).

> Jesus took from the world such as could benefit by his use, so he had no body of gross physical matter —which of itself is senseless, dead, incapable of light. So he taught men the Gnosis, that their immature souls born into fleshly bodies might mature, shake off the carnal burden, and leap away into eternal Light. It is Knowledge that liberates, for all actions devoid of real knowledge only chain the soul deeper in this lower world. When every individual human soul has been enlightened, freed from attachment to the flesh and its concerns, Wisdom, the composite Human Soul, ascends from this middle state of conflict into the perfect Fullness of God's life and becomes the Spouse of Jesus, Flower of all the Aeons. This is the 'Mystical Marriage', sung in almost every world-faith, the ultimate human destiny, shared spiritually by every individual human soul when matured—until which time the merely righteous, uninitiated by God's grace, tread the long paths of rebirth in the lower worlds until they became able to receive the Gnosis.

---

[1] As in GG 26 : 2, we are told here that the material creator learned from the Gospel all things and submitted to his Divine Lord.

CHAPTER FIVE

THE MYTH OF THE GOSPEL

Here Hippolytus gives us, probably in the Gnostic teacher's exact words, the Basilidean story of how out of nothing whatever, which 'Non-Being' is the real Absolute, a Seed arose, threefold in nature, and so the whole complex universe. Body, soul, and spirit, typifying the three kinds of men, represent the Divine 'Persons' in the 'Sonship' of Manifested God. Their various destinies, the arising of the two great 'Rulers' and their eventual enlightenment with all their domains by the descending 'Gospel' of the Gnosis, are all related in their turn—the chapter ending like the preceding with the final perfection of the Ideal Man restored to his divine inheritance.

20. Before the Beginning

1. (There) was when nothing was—but the 'nothing' was not any of the things that are; but solely and unexpectedly, without any quibbling, it was absolutely nothing at all.[1]

[1] I doubt whether even an Indian philosopher could have put more uncompromisingly this attempt to carry the mind back before its own existence. I quote the actual phrasing: " *ēn hote ēn ouden, all' oude to ouden ēn ti tōn ontōn, alla psilōs kai anuponoētōs dikha pantos*

70 THE GOSPEL OF THE GNOSTICS

Now when I say the 'was,' I do not say that it (actually) was,[1] but to signify what I wish to show I say that there was absolutely nothing.

2. Since then there was nothing—neither matter nor essence,[2] nor non-being, neither simple nor complex, neither imperceptible nor insensitive—no man, no angel, no god, nor in short anything that can be named or perceived by senses or mind; but even more precisely, all things having been totally excluded—Non-Being God,[3] inconceivably, imperceptibly, involuntarily, without forethought or passion or desire,[4] willed[5] to make a world. Now I say the 'willed' to indicate involuntarily and inconceivably and imperceptibly; and by 'world'

---

sophismatos ēn holōs oude hen." Clement (Hom. 5 : 3) has: "There was when naught was but Chaos and an indistinguishable mixture of unordered elements still jumbled all together."

[1] Even the verb 'was' implies a subject of the verb, but here there was no subject—simply the 'was'.

[2] or : being (Gk. *ousia*).

[3] Gk. *ouk-ōn theos*, a phrase fairly consistently used by our Gnostic, who will not allow even the absolute existence of a God before the beginning.

[4] This extraordinary series of adverbs reads in Gk. *anoētōs anaisthētōs aboulōs aproairētōs apathōs anepithumētōs*. It absolutely divorces God from any motive for creation, which is more negative even than the Vedānta.

[5] The word 'willed' after 'involuntarily' shows the paradox behind all spiritual truth. Creation arises spontaneously in God, without any purpose to be achieved by Him thereby.

(I mean) not what was later produced and stood apart with breadth and length, but the 'seed' of a world.

Like the writer of GG 3:1, Basilides tries to picture in human words a state beyond all words, before mind was. Even the word 'nothing' to the unwary calls up and negates the picture of a thing; but even that nihilism falls short of the real truth. What *was* did not ex-ist, for there was nothing 'out of' which It could have been. The Absolute could only, as by the Upanishads, be spoken of in terms of absolute negation. Nor could that 'non-being' have had a desire, a plan, a vision of what was 'going to be'; yet out of 'that' arose the source of a 'world' which itself also does not really exist, for it could not be outside of, apart from, the 'non-being' Source.

21. The Seed of the World

1. Thus Non-Being God made a non-being world out of the non-existing,[1] throwing down and depositing a certain one Seed having everything in itself—the All-Seeding of the world; ... just as an egg of a certain

---

[1] Gk. *houtōs ouk-ōn theos epoiēse kosmon ouk-onta ex ouk-ontōn.* How can existing things arise from non-existence? So one must admit the unreality of this seeming universe, illusory in its very nature. Lincoln Barnett (The Universe and Dr. Einstein, p. 21) writes: "Since every object is simply the sum of its qualities, and since qualities exist only in the mind, ... the whole objective universe ... does not exist except as a construction of the consciousness." Such total nihilism is a commonplace of modern thought, as it was long ago in India.

variegated and many-coloured bird,[1] ... being really one, has in itself many polymorphous and many-coloured and highly complex things; so has the non-being Seed of the world deposited by the Non-Being God many forms as well as many substances, **each** in its own way growing in size at the proper seasons,[2] ... much as for a newborn child we see teeth and paternal substance [3] later develop.

2. Now it were absurd to say that a sort of emanation of the non-existent God arose, some non-existence, ... for of what sort of emanation is there need, or of what kind of matter could one presume that God would construct a world [4]—as the spider the cobwebs, or (as) a mortal man takes copper or wood or some one of the forms [5] of matter? [6] But He said, and it came into being, and this is what

---

[1] This simile seems to me very apt; it may be compared with that of the fig-tree seed in GG 3 : 3.

[2] Here we have room for the evolutionary doctrine, long familiar to Greek thought in a simple form.

[3] Gk. *patrikē ousia*.

[4] How could a non-existent God create non-existent things out of something which already exists? Therefore creation is out of nothing but God's will.

[5] *lit*: parts.

[6] God does not draw the material for creation out of Himself, as a spider its web; nor from outside Him, as an artisan the wood for his carpentry.

was said by Moses: '"Let there be light?" and there was light'.¹ Whence came the light? From nothing; for it is not written whence, but only this—out of the Speaker's voice. Now the Speaker was not, nor was what came into being.²

3. Out of non-beings came into being the Seed of the World; ... this is the Seed which has the whole of the All-Seeding³ in itself... The Cosmic Seed having therefore become the basis, ... what I say came into being after this, do not ask whence. For in itself it held all the seeds, stored up and latent,⁴ such as the non-being things destined to be produced by the Non-Being God.

So appeared the 'seed' of the 'unreal' world which, like the seed of a plant contains, hidden away invisibly in itself, the future stem and leaves and flowers and seeds—together with all the later plants which are to come from the future seeds. So too are all the

---

[1] Quoting Gen. 1 : 3, the first act in creation, whence all later acts arose. This was the utterance of the Creative Word; implicit therein is the whole of creation, with the laws of nature and the moral laws of God.

[2] The Utterer of that Word is still the 'Non-Being God', *i.e.*, the Unmanifest, who by that involuntary expression of His essence becomes manifest.

[3] Gk. *panspermia*; *i.e.*, the source from which all things grew.

[4] Out of this 'seed' came into being all things held latent within it.

feathers and limbs, with their various colours, and the wonderful interior organs of a bird comprised in the single egg; so too the convolutions of the human brain are treasured up in the ultra-microscopic genes.

But the universe was not made by God unfolding latent elements from Himself, as a spider spins its web, but the spontaneous expression of His creative will, His very nature, brought it into being. He spoke the Word, and there was Light, and thereafter every other thing at His command. Yet it was enough for Him to will a 'world', and the world itself evolved from the 'seed' He thus called into being.

22. The Triple Sonship

1. In the same Seed there was a threefold Sonship,[1] in every way consubstantial with the Non-Being God, (but) arisen from non-beings. Of this triply divided Sonship, the one (part) was refined, another coarse, and another requiring purification.[2] First then, along with the Seed's coming into being and (its) first deposit by the Non-Being God, the refined (part) immediately thrilled and

---

[1] From the unmanifest Absolute things came into being, and first among these was a triple 'division' or differentiation within the Seed of the universe. Basilides uses this word (Gk. *huiotēs*) in a highly technical sense; the differentiations are derived from, sons of, the Absolute, and threefold in nature. This is how he understands the long-pre-Christian doctrine of the Trinity in God.

[2] Hippolytus seems to have failed here to follow Basilides correctly; one would have expected the three to be: pure, impure, and mixed.

THE MYTH OF THE GOSPEL

ascended, rushing up from below upwards[1]...
like wing or thought, and attained the Non-Being. For every nature of that (part) aspired through excess of beauty and youthful bloom,[2] each differently.

2. Now the coarser (part) still remaining in the Seed, being somewhat imitative, was unable to rush up ... (and) was left behind. So the coarser Sonship winged itself **with** a holy Spirit, having put on which, the Sonship benefits and is (also) benefited ... For, carried up by the Spirit as on a wing, the Sonship (also) lifts up ... the spirit,[3] but, coming nearer to the refined Sonship and the Non-Being God and creating out of non-beings, it could not retain it with itself.[4] For it was not consubstantial, nor had a nature like the (refined) Sonship; but as ... pure and dry air is fatal to the fishes, so was that

[1] The 'pure' part naturally rushes up to its kindred perfect purity in the Absolute.
[2] Gk. *di' huperbolēn kallous kai hōraiotētos*. Spiritual souls are drawn to God by His perfection of beauty or by His omnipotence.
[3] The partially pure or psychic soul raises itself to God by the help of His grace, the holy Spirit, and in turn—an idea remote from Christian thought—actually raises the Spirit also nearer to Absolute Perfection.
[4] Yet such a soul cannot merge in God, being inferior to the spiritual and unable to exist in that total subtlety of being beyond being, any more than a fish can live on dry land.

region of both the Non-Being God and the (refined) Sonship—more ineffable than ineffables, and higher than all names—contrary to nature for the holy Spirit.

3. Therefore the Sonship left it near that Blessed Place which can neither be conceived nor represented by any word—not wholly alone, nor separated from the Sonship; no, for as a most fragrant ointment is kept in a jar, even if it be emptied with the utmost care, yet a certain scent of the ointment still remains [1] . . . So has the holy Spirit remained, without a share of the Sonship and separate, yet it has in itself the power (of the Sonship) almost as a scent of an ointment . . . . Whence the Sonship began to ascend, as it were on an eagle's wings . . . sustained.[2] For all things hasten up from below, from the lower to the better, and nothing is so stupid among the better as to go down below.[3]

[1] So the redeeming Christ (*cf.* GG 65 : 1) leaves the aspiring soul a little below its ideal, where however she is always breathing the sweet fragrance of Divinity and ever remembers the perfect Light she has seen from afar.

[2] Then the higher part of even the psychic soul slowly ascends nearer and nearer to God's perfection.

[3] This refutes the idea that Christ actually came *down* to earth; all noble things rise continually, and there is no downward path (*cf.* GG 26 : 1).

4. But the Third Sonship, that needing purifying, has remained with the great bulk of the All-Seeding, doing good and being benefited (in turn).[1]

This 'Seed' was trinitarian: part pure spirit, part pure matter, part of the two mingled. Nothing could hold pure Spirit away from God; it merged in Him at once, drawn by beauty and energy; the blend of spirit and lower things, by good deeds and efforts aided by the Holy Spirit, rises gradually to the limit it can attain, being incapable of existing in the infinite subtlety of the highest spiritual plane; here then it remains, inspired by a memory of perfection and slowly climbing towards that. The lowest part of the 'Seed' stays in the lower worlds, suffering and enjoying, reaping the good and evil fruits of its deeds and slowly being purified.

23. The First Great Ruler

1. Between the supramundanes and the world a Firmament[2] was set up, ... which is above the heaven. The Great Ruler thrilled and came into being from the Cosmic Seed and the bulk of the All-Seeding, (as) the head

---

[1] It is here Hippolytus seems in error; the 'Third Sonship' must surely correspond with Matter (*khoikē psukhē*), which cannot possibly be 'saved' (GG 19 : 1). For the earthy type of soul there is nothing higher than mere ethics and good deeds; to her the door to Gnosis remains unopened.

[2] This 'Firmament' (Gk. *stereōma*), dividing the spiritual from the earthy, seems parallel with the 'Boundary' (*horos*) and 'Cross' (*stauros*) of other Gnostic systems.

of the world, a certain beauty and greatness unable to be destroyed.[1] For he is more ineffable than ineffables and mightier than powers and wiser than wise ones and better than all the beauties you could tell. Having come into being, this one lifted himself and soared and was wholly raised up as far as the Firmament, but supposing the Firmament to be the end of the uprush and of the height, and fancying there was nothing at all afterwards, he became wiser, mightier, comelier, brighter than all below . . . save only the Sonship still left in the All-Seeding—for he did not know that there is one wiser and mightier and better than himself.[2]

2. So considering himself to be Lord and Master and wise Architect, he turned to the creation of the world in detail.[3] First he thought fit not to be alone,[4] but made for

---

[1] As in GG 17 : 2, here too the Ruler (Gk. *Arkhōn*) arises from the lower part of the cosmic Seed, from the 'Abortion'; he is in fact the 'God' of exoteric religions—far below the Reality, though in himself of vast power and beauty and wisdom.

[2] Checked by the eternal 'Boundary' between the Real and the unreals, even this 'God' is led to think he has attained the heights and is supreme.

[3] Gk. *kath' hekasta*, one by one.

[4] The motive alleged by Valentinus in GG 12 : 2 reappears here at the far lower level of the Demiurge, or mere Maker of the world.

himself and produced out of those below a Son far better and wiser than himself; for the Non-Being God had forewilled all these things when He threw down the All-Seeding.[1] Seeing the Son, then, he wondered and loved and was amazed [2]—for some such beauty of the Son appeared to the Great Ruler . . . . This is the Ogdoad [3] where the Great Ruler is seated. All the heavenly creation, therefore, . . . the same Creator, the great Wise One, fashioned; but the Son who was born of him, being far wiser than the said Creator, works and suggests in him.[4]

From the higher planes of the Seed came into being the Ruler of all below the heavenly Firmament, great in wisdom, power and beauty. Seeing none better than himself, he thought himself the Supreme and created a world below himself that he might rule, the Ogdoad. From this he called forth a Son, wiser than himself, who rules through him, being in affinity with the Sonship.

[1] All beings are already implicit in the first act of the Non-Being God.

[2] We may compare this wonder and delight with that shown in GH 3 : 2 when the beauty of Nature is first seen.

[3] The word is otherwise used than in GG 12 : 3; it is not here a matter of the Divine Powers but of the seven planetary lords and their ruler, the Arkhōn.

[4] It is Nature who really guides the Maker in his work, though he may fancy it is only his own wisdom.

24. The Ruler of the Seven

1. So when all ethereal things were arranged, yet another Ruler went up from the All-Seeding, greater than all those below save only the Sonship left behind, but far inferior to the First Ruler,[1] though this one too is called ineffable, and **his** region is called (the) Hebdomad. Now this one is manager and fashioner of all those below, and he too has made for himself a Son out of the All-Seeding—who also is more prudent and wiser than himself.

2. Now what is down here ... and the All-Seeding and what is produced, come into being according to nature, as has already been decided by the Planner of what is to be[2]—when and how they should be, and of what kind. And of these no one is chief or thinker or creator, for that plan which the Non-Being thought out when He made (them) is enough for them.[3]

---

[1] This second Great Ruler seems to represent the individual human soul that rules over the seven bodies and planes and produces a 'Son' higher than itself, the aspiring human being.

[2] All in the lower planes obey the laws of nature laid down as implicit in the utterance of the First Decree: "Let it be!"

[3] Gk. *arkei gar autois ho logismos ekeinos hon ho ouk-ōn hote epoiei elogizeto.* There is really no need for any lower Ruler, for all things move according to the original perfect Plan from before the beginning.

3. When therefore the whole world was finished and the supramundanes, and nothing was lacking, the Third Sonship left behind in the All-Seeding remained.[1] . . . Then the Sonship left behind had to be revealed and reinstated above, set over the bordering Spirit near the refined and imitative Sonship and the Non-Being—as it is written: " Now the very creation groans and labours together, awaiting the revelation of the sons of God." [2] Now we, the Spiritual, are (the) sons,[3] having been left down here thoroughly to adorn and rectify and perfect the souls [4] who have a nature to remain below in this quarter.[5]

4. Therefore " until Moses from Adam sin reigned ",[6] as it is written, for the Great Ruler reigned who has his realm as far as the

---

[1] Immersed in Matter, the Third Sonship has now to be freed and raised into perfection.

[2] From St. Paul's Rom. 8 : 23, a passage beloved by all the Christian Gnostics.

[3] *Cf.* the somewhat self-complacent remark of the Naassene in App. I : 7 : 8.

[4] The Gnostic is down here on earth, not for his own self-purification but that he may uplift the psychic and natural man entrapped in the snares of Matter. This idea could easily generate false pride and arouse hatred.

[5] Gk. *en toutōi tōi diastēmati*; *i.e.*, in this physical world of ours.

[6] Quoting Rom. 5 : 14, which suggests that the Law of Moses helped to undo the sin of Adam.

Firmament, thinking that he alone is God and there is nothing over him,[1] for all things had been guarded with hidden silence. This is the " mystery which was not made known to the former generations ", but in those times the Great Ruler, the Ogdoad was King and Lord, as it seemed, of the universe, while the Hebdomad was King and Lord of this quarter. Now whereas the Ogdoad is ineffable, the Hebdomad is effable; this is the Ruler of the Hebdomad . . . therefore all the Prophets who were before the Saviour spoke thence.[2]

The heavenly planes having been thus formed, a Second Ruler arose from the Cosmic Seed; he rules the Hebdomad, the sphere under the seven planetary lords. He too created lower planes, and in his turn called forth a Son, representing down here the manifest God. Now all this was involved in the First Thought of the new-manifesting Deity, though in his turn this Ruler of the Seven also fancied himself planner and creator of all. The purpose of all this is the release of the spiritual part held in matter, and this is done largely by the ministry of spiritual men among the

---

[1] The egoistic Great Ruler is here identified with 'Sin'; elsewhere he is called Ialdabaoth (*cf.* GG 52:4), most intimately associated with 'Arrogant' or 'Self-Willed'. In fact, egoism is the real enemy to spiritual Gnosis, for it continually sets up false gods to worship in place of the One Supreme.

[2] As in Mani, the source of the prophecies, of all inspiration, is here roundly denounced as being this lower deity, who is, in effect, the egoism implicit in individuality.

more worldly of their brothers. So the Prophets came from among these, not from the Real, the Absolute, as Jesus said: " All who were before me were thieves and liars."

25. The Great Ignorance

1. God will bring the Great Ignorance [1] on the whole earth, so that all things may remain according to nature, and nothing may desire contrary to nature. Moreover, all the souls of this quarter, as many as have nature to stay in this alone, remain knowing nothing different or better than this quarter. Nor will there be any rumour of things above or (of) Gnosis in those below, lest the lower souls be tormented by longing for impossibilities [2] just like a fish desiring to be grazed on the mountains along with the sheep; such a desire would be their destruction. So all things remain safe [3] in (their own) land but perish if they wish to wander and move over from the things natural (to them).

---

[1] Gk. *hē megalē agnoia*.

[2] Basilides shows that spiritual ignorance (Skt. *ajñāna*) is the result of God's very love for us, lest we be made miserable to see glories we cannot reach. Could we know the joys and beauties of the far future, how many of us could endure the squalor and injustices of life down here?

[3] *lit.* incorruptible.

2. Thus the Ruler of the Hebdomad will know nothing of those above, for the Great Ignorance will seize even upon him, so that grief and pain and wailing may depart from him [1]—for he will desire nothing impossible, nor will he be grieved. But in the same way that Ignorance will also lay hold upon the Great Ruler of the Ogdoad, and equally all the creatures below him—so that nothing may in any respect long for what is against the nature of anyone.

One is not allowed to see what lies above, lest the sight of what is out of reach produce discontent and misery. So the Rulers, and those they rule, see only themselves and what lies below and remain ignorant of the higher planes; so too we are blind to the glories behind death. This is a kindly providence, for each soul can function only in its own plane and in those below it (*cf.* GG 85 : 1), or it would seek destruction in trying to escape its proper element, like a fish trying to live ashore.

I have displaced this section, which Hippolytus puts after §27, to where it fits more naturally. From the whole of this chapter I have deleted many laboured similes and quotations, with much that seems to me tautological.

---

[1] Even the highest beings in the universe are under that same ignorance or delusion, so that in their estate they may find some sort of happiness. God alone is wholly above Illusion.

26. The Gospel is Revealed

1. Since then we had to be revealed as the children of God,[1] ... the Gospel[2] has come into the world and passed through every Rulership and Authority and Lordship and every name that is named. Now it really came, even though nothing came down from above,[3] nor did the blessed Sonship separate from that unimaginable and blessed Non-Being God, but rather as the Indian camphor, lighted only from a far distance, attracts fire.[4] ...

2. Therefore the Gospel came first from the Sonship, through the Son seated beside the Ruler (of the Ogdoad) to the Ruler (himself);[5] then the Ruler learned that he was

[1] *Cf.* GG 2:1 and 24:3; for God is the Light. The Codex Jung (32:38) has it: "You are the children of the inner Knowledge."

[2] GG 27:1 defines the 'Gospel' as "the Gnosis of supramundane things", and Valentinus (CJ 37:35) says it is "the act whereby one grasps and knows Him who is hidden", which is the true Gnosis, the attainment of God.

[3] Nothing spiritual falls; no Book fell on earth from the skies, yet the knowledge of God was manifested from one plane to another.

[4] Christ never left the Father's side, as St. Thomas also sings; yet the fire of Truth was kindled on earth as camphor takes flame from a distance.

[5] Note that it is the 'son', not the 'father', in each case who first contacts the truth flashed down by the 'Son of God', the Christ, who is himself the Gospel, the 'Word'.

not God of the universe, but was produced and had over him the deposited treasure of the ineffable and unnameable Non-Being and the Sonship.[1] And he turned and was afraid, realising in what ignorance he was, . . . for he began to be made wise when taught by the Christ seated near [2]—learning who is the Non-Being, who the Sonship, what the holy Spirit, what is the order of the universe, and how this will be restored.[3]

3. Having been thus instructed and taught and frightened, the Ruler began confessing the sin he had committed in magnifying himself. . . . Since then the Great Ruler had been instructed . . . and the whole creation of the Ogdoad taught, the mystery became known also to the celestials; the Gospel had finally to come also to the Hebdomad, so that the Ruler

---

[1] So the Ruler learns that he is not over all, but far below the Real Lord.

[2] Gk. *ērxato gar sophizesthai katēkhoumenos hupo tou parakathēmenou Khristou*. Here the 'Son' of the 'Ruler' is frankly styled the Christ; so he is, for that lower plane, though he is only a pale reflection of the Real Christ Above, from whom the 'Gospel' comes.

[3] In fact, this is the essence of the Gnosis: God, the creative Word, uplifting Grace, the Universe, and how it returns to God. What more need we know?

of the Hebdomad also might be taught and evangelized in the same way.[1]

4. The Son of the Great Ruler kindled the light in the Son of the Ruler of the Hebdomad, having himself been set on fire from above by the Sonship.[2] Then the Son of the Ruler of the Hebdomad was illumined, and he proclaimed the Gospel to the Ruler of the Hebdomad, and in the same way he too feared and confessed. . . . As then it was shown to him that the contacting Spirit is also holy, and the Sonship, and God the Cause of all, the Non-Being, he rejoiced and exulted at the things said, that is, (at) the Gospel.

The Gospel or Gnosis was revealed from above in order to enlighten spiritual souls in the world, coming down stage by stage—first to the Ogdoad through its 'Son' and its 'Ruler', and then to the Hebdomad through its 'Son' and its 'Ruler'. The Light passed from 'Son' to 'Son', and each enlightened the 'Ruler' as to the truth of God, and so won his repentance for his foolish egoistic conceit and taught all in his sphere.

---

[1] So the Good News about God came to the still lower plane of the Seven, our world of fate ruled by the planets.

[2] Here too it is the 'Son' who passes it on, by virtue of being a reflection of the Christ Above, the perfect Sonship.

27. It Comes Down to Our World

1. When then everything in the Hebdomad had been illumined and taught the Gospel, ... the Gnosis of supramundane things,[1] ... the formlessness in us[2] had also to be illumined, and the Mystery to be revealed to he Sonship left behind just like an abortion in the formlessness.

2. Therefore the Light came down from the Hebdomad ... upon Jesus the Son of Mary,[3] and he was illumined when shone upon by the Light which rayed on him[4] ...

---

[1] These few words have been inserted from a passage at the end of the excerpts by Hippolytus. Puech-Quispel write: " Our book is an appeal to resapiscence and to life, to this ' conversion ' to oneself and to God which is the Gnosis, discovery and restoration of our true Self, along with knowledge of God and return to Him, in whom our true being has both its source and its end " (p. 35). The Excerpts of Theodotus read: " The Gnosis (is) who we are, what we have become, whence we have come, where we have been thrown, whither we hasten, whence we are redeemed, what is birth, what rebirth " (78 : 2).

[2] This word (Gk. *amorphia kath' hēmas*) links with the ' Abortion ' or ' Formlessness ' of GG 14 : 3; it well describes the spiritual state of those whose Divine image has been lost in the slime of materiality and selfishness. Yet, however foul it be, that ' Abortion ' is a part of God's own ' Word ', the ' Sonship ' destined to be freed and raised on high to Him.

[3] Our first mention of the human Jesus, whom the Gnostics carefully distinguished, to the fury of the orthodox, from the immortal Son of God, impassible, divine.

[4] The Gospel of the Hebrews describes the event when at the Baptism Light shone forth from the water—hinted at in the canonical Gospels by the approving Voice from heaven and the appearance of the Holy Spirit as a Dove.

The whole Sonship, that was left behind to benefit the souls in formlessness, . . . having been transformed, followed Jesus, hastened up, and came fully purified;[1] now it becomes most subtle, so as to be able thereby to rush up like the First—for it has all the power naturally associated with the Light which shone down from above.

3. So as soon as all Sonship comes to be above the contacting Spirit, then the creation will receive grace, for until now it groans and is tormented and awaits the revealing of God's sons, so that all the men of the Sonship may come up from thence.[2]

Finally the Gnosis came down to this lowest physical plane of men, incarnating in Jesus, the human Son of Mary: it awakened all who have the capacity for spiritual truth to self-purification and a mystical resurrection into the higher life. This is the " revealing of God's sons " for which creation longs so ardently.

---

[1] The Spiritual embraced the new Faith taught by Jesus in the inner schools of the Gnosis, and swiftly received the Mysteries of the Light, which drew them on into the Inheritance of the Light-Treasure Above. Being akin to the Christ-Spirit, those initiated rose unopposed into the heights (*cf.* GG 78 : 5) and merged into oneness with the Saviour (*cf.* GG 85 : 3).

[2] When the Spiritual have transcended the field of Grace and entered the perfection of the Christ, even the lower creation will be blessed and in some measure redeemed from the suffering of material life.

28. The Consummation

And thus will be the restoration of all who are founded by nature in the Cosmic Seed at the beginning and destined to be restored in due time.[1] . . . This is the inner Spiritual Man in the psychic [2]—which is Sonship that has left the soul there, not mortal but remaining according to its nature; much as the First Sonship has left the contacting holy Spirit above in a suitable region—having then thrown round itself a fitting Soul [3] (PG 3302-3319:16).

So, with the liberation of all Spirit from entanglement in the darkness of Matter, history comes to its destined close—the ideal Perfect Man is revealed in union with God and manifesting in a purified soul, freed from all its fleshly bonds.

---

[1] A clear teaching of predestination; not every soul is to attain this perfect end, but only those who are gifted with real spirituality, called to be Sons of God, Limbs of His endless glory.

[2] Together these glorified souls compose the Perfect Man, hidden now in the psychic nature which we contact through personality.

[3] Assuming a new and higher personality suited to the Spirit's manifested glory, each spiritual soul will be in God, having left His Grace below to aid those who could not attain to such perfection.

CHAPTER SIX

THE HYMN OF JESUS

This lovely fragment of deep mystical import [1] comes from the Gnostic Acts of John—a work dating probably from not much later than A.D. 130, so that it could well be from a direct disciple of the Evangelist. We are fortunate to possess the original Greek in a text which, though preserved in a late Vienna MS., seems to be very little corrupted. There are portions of a Latin text made in the course of refuting the Priscillianists, who seem to have used it as a drama of initiation.

In his "The Hymn of Jesus", G. R. S. Mead made a very valuable study of it, and it has been set to lovely music by Gustav Holst. A few emendments of the text by various scholars have been accepted here. However, after much thought over many years, I cannot agree with Mead's interpretation of it as a dialogue; to me it seems quite clear that the Speaker is throughout the Divine Christ, the Initiator, who expresses the union of the opposites realised in all

---

[1] In our MS. this beautiful Hymn is prefixed by: "The Hymn of the Lord, which he sang in secret to the holy Apostles, his disciples.... This Hymn is not put in the Canon because of those who think according to themselves and not according to the Spirit and Truth of God, and that it is written: 'It is good to hide the King's sacrament, but it is honourable to reveal God's works.'" This alleged quotation from Scripture is not otherwise known. The comment made above suggests a new reason for the exclusion of certain 'apocrypha'; they were deliberately withheld by those who loved and believed in them.

true initiation; the disciples or neophytes are limited to the circular dance and the repeating of the 'Amen', whereby they follow the mystic teaching of at-one-ment with the universal Life—we are told as much in GG 29 : 1-2.

After the initial doxology in a veiled Trinitarian form, the Teacher declares that all are one—the slayer and the slain, the teacher and the taught—" Food I, Food-Eater I ", as one of the Upanishads put it—and then points to the consolation this teaching will bring the disciples who are about to be severed from their beloved Lord. In the middle of this is interposed a short paragraph drawing attention to the universality of this law : it is through oneness alone true Gnosis or knowledge can be attained. This realisation is shown also to explain the mystery of Suffering and Endurance, found in their Master. Finally the passage ends with a second doxology and a few words of deep mystical import.

29. Prelude to the Mystic Dance

1. Now before **Jesus** was taken by the lawless Jews and those governed by a lawless Serpent,[1] gathering (us) all together, he said: "Before I am handed over to them, let us hymn the Father, and so go out to what is waiting." Having bidden us therefore to make as it were a ring, holding each other's hands [2]

---

[1] *i.e.*, the Evil One; certainly not here the Serpent of Wisdom (*nahaṣ*) revered by the Naassenes or Ophite Gnostics.

[2] Symbolising their unity, and allowing the 'magnetic currents' to flow through them unchecked. The disciples represent the Christ's Powers dancing to the rhythm of Grace Above, suggests Mead.

and himself coming in the middle,[1] he said: "Reply with the Amen!"[2]

2. So he began to sing a Hymn[3] and to say: "Glory to Thee, Father!" and we, going round in a circle, said the Amen. "Glory to Thee, Word! Glory to Thee, Grace!" Amen. "Glory to Thee, Spirit, Holy One! Glory to to Thy Glory!" Amen. "We praise Thee, Father, we give Thee thanks, O Light in whom no darkness dwells!" Amen.

This is taken as the 'Hymn' sung by Jesus and the disciples after the Last Supper, with its touching emphasis on their oneness as a loving family (Mk. 14: 26). The dance in a ring likens the disciples to the planets circling the earth—or, as we would now say, the Sun; to each Person of the Trinity are assigned two sentences: the Father is perfect Light, the Word is Grace, the Spirit is Glory—have these last two been in error interchanged? Grace seems more naturally to belong to the Spirit, and St. John's Gospel speaks much of the Glory belonging to the Son before the world was.

---

[1] The Cosmic Dance, whereby at-onement with the universe is achieved. God is the centre of the universe, the Teacher is the centre of his disciples.

[2] By repeating this 'Fiat' to every sentence, the candidates for initiation at-one themselves with the One who for them is passing through its gates afresh.

[3] Exoterically, the 'Hymn' referred to by St. Mark would have been one of the Psalms, or a Hymn concluding the Passover Rite such as Jews sing now at the close of the Seder.

30. The Universal Dance of At-Onement

1. And for this reason we give thanks: I say: "I will to be saved,[1] and I will to save!" Amen. "I will to be freed,[2] and I will to free!" Amen. "I will to be wounded,[3] and I will to wound!" Amen. "I will to be born,[4] and I will to bear!" Amen. "I will to devour, and I will to be eaten!"[5] Amen. "I will to hear,[6] and I will to be heard!" Amen. ("I will to understand),[7] and I will to be understood—

---

[1] *i.e.*, from the labyrinth of rebirths and ignorance, as in GG 88:1, and from the vortex of passions and desires.

[2] or: loosed—from the bonds of fate. Gk. *luthēnai thelō kai lusai thelō*.

[3] or: pierced—by the Ray penetrating the heart, as St Teresa was mystically pierced by the Angel. The Latin version read: "I would be dissolved (by love)."

[4] The new birth as a Christ-Child, or as Horus in the secret marshes of the North. This is the true, mystical rebirth only symbolised by baptismal waters.

[5] Gk. *phagein thelō kai brōthēnai thelō*. Mead rightly says this is the consuming of the ego in us by its eating the 'Superstantial Bread', the 'Flesh' of Christ—spoken of in St John's Gospel. The candidate takes in the Divine Food and gives himself for others in total self-sacrificing surrender.

[6] "Before the Soul can hear, the image has to become as deaf to roarings as to whispers" (Voice of the Silence); "before the ear can hear it must have lost its sensitiveness" (Light on the Path). Only after self-surrender can the neophyte hear the true Word of God.

[7] These words have obviously dropped from our text.

being all Mind!"[1] Amen. "I will to be washed,[2] and I will to wash!" Amen.

2. "Grace dances;[3] I will to play on the pipe[4]—dance, all (of you)!" Amen. "I will to mourn—lament, all (of you)!" "Amen. "One Ogdoad sings with us!"[5] Amen. The Dodecad Above dances in time!"[6] Amen. "Whereon the whole begins to dance!"[7] Amen. "He who does not dance knows not what is going on!"[8] Amen.

---

[1] As Mead says, these words may be a gloss; being Mind, the soul can receive the Gnosis; *cf.* GG 13:2.

[2] *i.e.*, in the great Ocean of Oneness, the baptism in the Chalice of GH 37.

[3] Divine Wisdom breathed in the soul leads it on the way of initiation. I do not think with Mead that these words are a rubric; they seem to lead naturally to the next set of parallel phrases.

[4] *i.e.*, Pan's seven pipes, the 'Seven Voices' of GG 41:2, the "music of the spheres" referred to in App. I: 7:10. It seems to refer to the mysterious gnomon in Mt. 11:17, which may come from some earlier source.

[5] We keep time to the Divine Powers ruling our universe.

[6] Gk. *ho dodekatos ruthmōs anō khoreuei.* Freed from the realm of the planetary lords of destiny, the Soul enters the higher sphere of the Twelve Zodiacal Signs. It is gratuitous to suppose with some that the Decad has been missed out here; we are not moving in the sphere of the Valentinian Thirty Aeons.

[7] The Soul is now aware of the united activity of the whole universe, with which he is being made one.

[8] To reach Gnosis, first the lower self must be surrendered and the Cross taken up; then the Soul follows and keeps in tune with the great powers behind life, and so alone can share the Cosmic Life of the One in all (*cf.* Jn 4:17, 9:31). Otherwise he is blind, asleep, deaf to the song of the worlds.

3. " I will to flee,[1] and I will to stay!" Amen. " I will to adorn, and I will to be adorned!"[2] Amen. " I will to be made one and I will to make one!"[3] Amen. " I have no house, and I have houses!" Amen. " I have no place, and I have places!" Amen. " I have no shrine, and I have shrines!" Amen.[4]

4. " I am a Lamp for you who look at me!"[5] Amen. " I am a Mirror for you who think of me!"[6] Amen. "I am a Door to you who knock at me!" Amen. " I am a Way for you, a wayfarer!" Amen.

The earlier stages of Initiation are run through. Jesus comes to save the Soul from the miseries of

---

[1] *i.e.*, from the lower life, and to abide in the higher.

[2] Gk. *kosmein thelō kai kosmeisthai thelō*; *i.e.*, to be set in order as the whole cosmos is in order, following the Divine laws of rhythm. The Bride is now to be adorned ready for her Spouse.

[3] Now comes the yearning for oneness with the Beloved; and thereby to share His saving work in all; separateness vanishes. Gk. *henōthēnai thelō kai henōsai thelō*.

[4] And now the Soul, possessing no things, possesses all, for she holds them as the All; every barrier between her and other children of the One vanishes, and she is infinitely rich, and infinitely poor, with no place even to lay her head, like the 'Son of Man' on earth, yet possessing all things.

[5] He leads others on the Path and is a light to them.

[6] In himself he reflects the inner nature of everyone; Gk. *esoptron eimi soi tōi noounti me*. Agraphon 93 reads: " See me in yourselves, just as anyone of you sees himself in water or in a mirror;" and the Odes of Solomon (13: 1): " The Lord is our mirror; open the eyes and see in Him, and learn what your face is like."

ignorance, and to free her from the bondage of the 'world', *i.e.*, Matter. But this salvation demands a painful effort; the Saviour must suffer for the lost sheep, and at the same time must give pain in rousing the prisoner to break his chains. Through this pain comes a new spiritual birth typified by baptism, and then the neophyte is ready for a sacramental union—the Eucharist—with the Initiator, wherein he himself becomes the offering on the altar which he himself consumes. Having thus been made one with the Teacher, he can hear the silent Voice, understand its utterance, and be thoroughly purified by the inner communion. In all these stages, pupil and teacher simultaneously perform both rôles, as the repeated 'Fiat' shows.

Joy and Sorrow are one, both to be accepted gladly as the will of God, which appoints music and mourning in turn. Thus the neophyte shares in the universal 'dance' of Nature; the heavenly Ogdoad and the twelve Zodiacal Powers (GG 45 : 2), represented down here by the Apostolic ring, dance at God's will. The whole universe obeys His signal, and without such obedience, such surrender, there cannot be true Gnosis or understanding of the universe and God.

Further opposites to be unified follow. The lower self dreads the implications of such surrender and would flee from it, but the higher self welcomes and embraces the coming Passion. Then the victor-soul is adorned with the Robe and Crown of Light (GG 10, 11 : 4, 47, 59 : 1, 75-76, etc.), which is immediately followed by the soul's total union with her Saviour. Now she knows that blissful state of having all while having nothing for herself; the whole universe is now her home and temple, for like her Lord she has become omnipresent.

By her light others can now see the truth in her, find themselves reflected, through her can enter on the path to union with God, and becoming one with that Path can tread it to the end: "Thou canst not tread that Path until thou hast become the Path itself."

31. The Lesson of Suffering

1. "Now respond to my dancing; see thyself in me as I speak,[1] and seeing what I do keep silence on my mysteries.[2] He who dances understands what I am doing, for thine is this passion of the Man [3] which I am about to suffer. For thou couldst not wholly realise what I suffer, had not I, a Word, come to thee from the Father.[4] Seeing what I suffer, thou hast seen (me) as suffering, and seeing, thou didst not stand (firm) but wast altogether moved, (being shaken to grow wise?).[5] Hadst

---

[1] Now is the Soul essentially one with the Christ and needs but to be at-oned in consciousness, understanding the Passion. Mead believes that at this point came the dance-drama, representing the passion; it is not sure.

[2] The Soul is invited to identify herself with every stage, and warned not to chatter about the mysteries afterwards to those unfit to hear; cf. GG 83 : 3.

[3] "Feel with me in your suffering, that you may take knowledge of what I suffer, and (so) escape suffering", says the Acts of Andrew, p. 353. Every soul must tread the path of suffering, even in its higher forms, before it can be wholly one with God and so transcend all pain.

[4] Seeking with the mind cannot find out truth; it is realised through a revelation to the Mind of spiritual men.

[5] Not yet is the Soul wholly free from storms of emotion; it can still be shaken where the affections are involved. Gk. *kai idōn ouk estēs all' ekinēthēs holos kinētheis sophizein.* I have accepted James' restoration of the text.

thou known how to suffer, thou wouldst have been able not to suffer;[1] then know how to suffer, and thou wilt be able not to suffer. What thou knowest not, I myself shall teach thee.[2]

2. "Thou hast me (as) a Couch, rest upon me.[3] Who am I? Thou shalt know when I go away.[4] What I now seem, that I am not, but what I am thou shalt see as soon as thou comest.[5] I am thy God, not the betrayer's;[6] I will to be harmonized with holy souls; know thou in me the Word of Wisdom.[7]

---

[1] A tremendous truth, bearing great strength to all who know it; suffering is swallowed up in joy when borne for the Beloved and His cause.

[2] Gk. *ho su mē oidas autos se didaxō.*

[3] *Cf.* Mead FFF 3 : 275. The Divine now utters 'comfortable words' after the storm of suffering is past; the initiated Soul becomes a support to others.

[4] Strength comes when the neophyte is left to stand on his own legs! Then he knows the greatness of the Teacher who has strengthened him.

[5] The Christ can be really known only after at-onement with him.

[6] *i.e.*, the "lawless Serpent" of GG 29 : 1; only in the most exoteric sense can Judas be referred to. Not he who rejects or betrays can ever know the Christ as God, but the devotee nourished on His divine Being.

[7] Christ himself yearns for souls to approach him and be made one with him, so that they may share his work, and it may grow and grow.

Having thus outlined his own system of yoga, the inspired writer returns in some detail to the Passion hitherto only hinted at. The human soul naturally shrinks from pain, so she is given a Divine Exemplar to encourage her in facing it. One who joins the Cosmic Dance of acceptance of God's will learns the real meaning of suffering and gains the power to bear it; it is the Word of God, expressed by the living Saviour's example, which brings the Soul this understanding and this courage to welcome what all must experience. Suffering is like a nettle, it loses its sting when firmly grasped; then it changes to what cannot be distinguished from joy—so happy is the lover with whatever gift the Beloved choose to send. Then does the Example become indeed a Couch and the Repose of the soul immersed in happy suffering; then she begins to realise it is God Himself with whom she has so familiarly ' danced '—as Arjun played unknowingly with the universal Lord, Sri Krishna. But she can only have full knowledge of His divinity when the human teacher has withdrawn his well-loved intimate form ("It is good for you that I go away", Jn. 16 : 7): and that knowledge can never come save to the lover or devotee; the enemy, the unclean soul, can never understand or enter into union with it.

32. End of the Dance

"Say with me again: 'Glory to Thee, Father! Glory to Thee, Word! Glory to Thee, Holy Spirit!' You have willed to know my Word: once for all I rushed on everything and was in no way put to shame—I leapt forward.¹ But thou, understand the all ² and, having understood, say: 'Glory to Thee, Father!'" Amen.

Here a shorter doxology is followed by a strange and obscure sentence. Jesus tells his disciples that they have earnestly desired to know His Word, the 'Word of Wisdom' of GG 31:2, which experiences the passion in GG 36:3, *i.e.*, how to become one with God through him, the yoga of true Gnosis. Then he adds that he himself attained that 'Kingdom' by storm (Mt. 11:12) and was not foiled or disappointed. They too must storm the gates of that Kingdom rather than wait for others to open to them: they too will not be put to shame, but will make rapid progress into union. When they have thus realised the whole 'Dance of Life', nothing more remains than to utter joyous thanks to God, the Giver of all good things.

---

¹ The Kingdom of God is won by storm; the Christ himself won that glory by his own supreme effort long ago. A difficult passage; Ak. *hapax epaïxa panta kai ouk epēskhunthēn holōs; egō e kirtēsa.*

² A breath of Hermetic teaching here; it is the one who can carry all in himself (*cf.* GH 42:3) who is worthy of the Gnosis. Gk. *su de noei to pan kai noēsas lege.*

CHAPTER SEVEN

THE MYSTIC CROSS

In the Greek Acts of John, this chapter follows immediately upon the preceding; in neither case have I omitted any word from this precious relic of an early Johannine mystic school. The last three sections are from the similar Acts of Peter and Andrew, which have undergone rather radical revision by orthodox Catholics, to suit them for an orthodox audience, yet have retained much of the old colour of the Gnostic author(s).

The Seer, doubtless remembering Mk. 14: 26, goes to the Mount of Olives during the tragic Passion of his Lord; there he sees the real eternal Cross which separates and unites various kinds of men and is a symbol of the Christ himself—distinct from the wooden Cross whereon men fancied they could nail the Christ. When all spiritual souls are taken up in this mystic Cross, they will become initiates like John, while he himself will be like his Master. The apparent bodily sufferings of Jesus have no reality; the actual pains of the Christ are beyond imagination—the strain of uplifting all mankind. The Cross changes every measure we have known, inverts all our values, and turns the lowly into the transcendentally high. Only by embracing this Cross can man enter the Kingdom of eternal Life, for it alone leads from the pit, like Jacob's Ladder, to the skies. With what joy, then, does the aspirant draw near to such a crucifixion which is to make of him little less than a God!

33. At the Crucifixion

1. Having danced these things with us,[1] the Lord went out; and we as though misled (or even a little asleep)[2] fled in all directions.[3] Now then I, knowing him, could not bear his passion while he suffered,[4] but fled to the Mount of Olives[5] weeping over the catastrophe; and when he was hung to the bush of the Cross,[6] darkness came on over all the land.

[1] A striking way of putting it; this was no mere verbal teaching but a living drama, wherein all took part.

[2] These words have been restored: *ē kai apokoimēthentes*; they refer to the 'drunken sleep' of ignorance.

[3] In the canonical Gospels this flight is placed in the Garden at the foot of the Mount, immediately after the Agony and before the actual Passion began. It is easy to see, then, why it comes here.

[4] A very human touch; the disciple knew the human Jesus, so his Passion was terrible to watch; *cf.* GG 31 : 1. Such phrases in the canonical Gospels are often claimed as proof of their historicity; they prove only a skilled writer.

[5] The usual place for Gnostic revelations; of course, as Mead says, it is the 'Heights of Contemplation'.

[6] Gk. *tēi staurou batōi*. This is the fiery Bush of Life whence God spoke to Moses in the desert, a link between Light and Darkness, the Way Up and Down of souls, parting deficiency from the Fullness, the Boundary dividing Being from non-being, causing all opposites and sharing in them all. This is the mystical Point of Balance, the centre of all things, the heart and life of the universe. The Valentinian James says (CJ 5 : 31 ff): "Remember my

2. Then our Lord, standing in the midst of the Cave[1] and lighting it up,[2] said: "John, to the crowd below in Jerusalem[3] I am being crucified, and pierced with lances and reeds, and given both gall and vinegar to drink.[4] But to thee I speak, and hear what I say: It was I who induced thee to come up into this mountain, so that thou mightest hear what a disciple should learn from a teacher and a man from God.[5]

3. Having said this, he then showed me a Cross of Light set up, and around the Cross a great crowd, and therein was one form and one appearance;[6] while in the Cross was another sort of crowd not having one form.[7]

Cross and my death, and you will live; ... none shall be saved who has no faith in my Cross. It is those who have faith in my Cross whose is the Kingdom of God." So this is the Road to the Heavens, and Christ himself is that Gate, that Path.

[1] In this 'cave of the heart' the mystic birth takes place; it is the grotto of Bethlehem, as equally the Holy Sepulchre in the spiritual Jerusalem.

[2] So in the early Gnostic Gospels a great Light shone and illumined the Cave at the moment of the birth of the Divine Child (*cf.* GMC 7 : 3-4).

[3] *i.e.*, the unillumined lower mind, says Mead.

[4] The writer of these Acts, perhaps about A.D. 130, seems to have known all the four canonical Gospels.

[5] *i.e.*, the Gnosis.

[6] Gk. *ēn morphē mia kai idea mia*.

[7] *i.e.*, partly conformed to the divine symbol of the Cross.

And above the Cross I saw the Lord himself, having no shape but a kind of Voice [1]—only not such a voice as we are used to, but somewhat sweet and gracious and truly of God—saying to me: "John, there must be one to hear this from me, for I am in need of one who is ready to hear.[2]

When this 'Cosmic Dance' of the Initiator and his neophytes is done, Jesus goes to his 'Passion', and John to the Mount of Vision, to mourn his Master in the calamitous darkness. But there in the Cave of his own heart he sees the Lord, shining with great light and calling him to a secret revelation of the Cross of Light wherein and around were great crowds —the former still under the limitation of the 'Boundary' (GG 14 : 2) and differing all from one another, a vast confusion; while the latter were liberated into glorious unity. A Voice, sweeter than any human voice, spoke in the heart an appeal for an understanding listener.

34. The Real Eternal Cross

1. "For your sakes this Cross is at times [3] called by me Word, sometimes Mind, at times

---

[1] John hears only a *bat-qōl* (Skt. *ākāśa-vāṇī*), a Voice from Above, for the Light prevents him from seeing anything; *cf.* App. I : 7 : 1. Origen quotes the lost Gnostic Acts of Paul, saying: "I am about to be crucified from Above."

[2] If the disciple needs the teacher, so equally the teacher a true disciple—or where is his teaching? That John was channel for the Gnosis is often hinted at in the canonical Gospels; also "But John shall be your father, until he comes with me into Paradise. And he touched them in the holy Spirit" (Agr. 120).

[3] We have such lists of Names of the Cross in several places; *e.g.*, in GG 94 : 2, and in the Acts of Peter, 20, where it reads: "The Door, the Light, the Way, the Bread, the Water, the Life,

Jesus, then Anointed, sometimes Door,[1] then Way,[2] at times Bread,[3] then Seed,[4] then Resurrection,[5] sometimes Son, sometimes Father, sometimes Spirit, at times Life, then Truth, then Faith, then Grace—and in relation to men it is those things.[6]

2. "But what it really is, its own meaning to itself and when spoken to you—it is a defining of all things, and a lifting and a basis of things fixed out of things unstable, and a harmony of Wisdom.[7] Now being Wisdom in the Resurrection, the Refreshment, the Feast, the Treasure, the Seed, the Harvest, the Mustard-Seed, the Vine, the Plough, the Grace, the Faith, the Word; he is all things, and there is none greater than he." It is possible to trace the line of thought through this labyrinth of names.

[1] *i.e.*, of equilibrium leading to the inner consciousness.

[2] *i.e.*, of no travel, which enters into itself, the Means or 'method', leading from below upwards, says Mead.

[3] Substance of Divine Life.

[4] The self-initiating power of infinite growth.

[5] *i.e.*, rising from the death of materiality into the eternal life of the Spirit.

[6] Uniting all opposites in itself; from above it leads grace down to the depth. As it contains all things, above and below, it is eternally stable and sure.

[7] Gk. *ho de ontōs estin, autos pros hauton nooumenos kai eis humas legomenos, diorismos pantōn estin, kai tōn pepēgmenōn ex anedrastōn anagōgē kai basis kai harmonia sophias.* It is in fact the harmony or articulation of all wisdom, which is the expression of destiny (*cf.* GH 25 : 2).

THE MYSTIC CROSS

harmony, to Right and Left [1] there are Powers, Authorities, Sources and Spirits, Energies, Threats, Angers, Accusers, Satan—and the Lower Root from which has come forth the nature of things brought into being. So this is the Cross which has differentiated all things by a Word,[2] and marked off what is from genesis and even lower down, and then joined all things together into one.

3. "But this is not the wooden Cross [3] which thou shalt see on going down from here, nor am I the one on the Cross whom now thou seest not but hearest only a Voice."[4]

---

[1] The upright of the Cross is the personality, viewing things as good or evil, right or left, angels or demons: in GL 261 there is talk of two 'lands': Right, Life, Light, Repose; and Left, Death, Darkness, Trouble. This personality is deeply rooted in the ancient past, and it expresses latencies as it soars upwards to the sky. Irenæus (1 : 6 : 1) says: "The material, . . . that on the left hand, necessarily . . . perishes, as being incapable of receiving any breath of incorruption; but the psychic principle, . . . that on the right hand . . . departs in that direction to which it makes itself incline. As to the spiritual part, . . . it is sent forth in order that being here joined to the psychic it may be moulded, sharing its discipline in its relations here."

[2] Ever uniting and dividing, male-female, good-evil; it is ever the Word (Logos) which discerns between these, separating the spiritual from the earthy; as in App. I : 5 : 5 the Ocean flows up to form Gods and down to form men.

[3] Exoterically Jesus was crucified on a wooden Cross, esoterically the Christ "hangs from every tree", being eternally crucified by the downpouring of Divinity.

[4] How could that pantheistic omnipresent Jesus be 'seen'? I is only through the Sound of the eternal 'Word' he can be known

I was thought what I am not, not being what to many others I was; but they will say of me something else base and unworthy of me.[1] As then the Place of Rest [2] is neither seen nor spoken of, much more shall I the Lord of it be neither seen nor spoken of.

This Voice explained that the Cross John saw was itself the Word, the expressed Will, and Christ of God —all things needed by the human soul; but at the same time it is more than that. For it is the very framework of creation, the trunk of the Cosmic Tree, linking the lowest with the heights, and separating to either hand the good and evil. This Cross is indeed the 'Way Up' for souls (GH 6 : 1), at no time to be confused with the gross material instrument of torture it appears upon the lower planes. Men took Jesus for a man (GPM 10 : 2) and spoke unworthy things of him, such as that he was born of a woman; he was never really that, for he is the Lord of all, standing in the depths, head in heaven and arms outspread in blessing over all that is.

35. The Two Multitudes

" Now the uniform crowd around the Cross is the Lower Nature, but those whom thou seest in the Cross, if they have not also one

---

[1] Mani shared this firm belief that Christ was beyond our understanding and we err in thinking him a man.

[2] This " Place of Rest " is at the point of balance in the centre of the Cross, where in suffering the Soul is at perfect peace, being attuned to the Divine Will.

form (it is because) every Limb of the One who came down has not yet been gathered together.[1] But as soon as the Higher Nature and Race,[2] coming to me in obedience to my Voice, is taken up,[3] (then) what does not hear me now will become as thou art[4] and shall no longer be what it is now, but over them even as I am now.[5] For until thou callest thyself mine, I am not that which I am, but if thou hearest me attentively, thou too shalt be as I am, while I shall be what I was, as soon as I have beside myself thee as I am. For from this thou art.[6]

---

[1] They are not yet perfect, though united to the will of God, which is the Cross (*cf.* GG 84 : 3). These may be the Five Limbs of Mind in the Acts of Thomas (GG 93 : 1): *nous, ennoia, phronēsis, enthumēsis* and *logismos*; or the scattering of the self's powers after various desires, or into various bodies, as Mead thinks. *Cf.* GPM 19-23.

[2] *i.e.*, those risen from the death of 'genesis' or *saṁsāra-sāgaram*, whom the Naassenes call the 'Kingless Race', 'the ineffable Race of the perfect men' (App. I: 6 : 2). Philo calls them the 'self-taught, incorruptible and perfect' (q. TGH 1 : 220) and Hermes, the 'Race' of the Mind; *cf.* GG 2 : 3.

[3] The "Higher Nature" obeys the Word and becomes divine (*cf.* Jn. 10 : 4).

[4] Gk. *to ou nun akouon me hōs su touto genēsetai.*

[5] When man becomes a devotee and the slave of Christ, the Divine comes into being in him.

[6] The Gk. of this passage reads: *ean de me akouseis akouōn, kai su men esēi hōs k'ago; egō de ho emēn esomai hotan se ekhō hōs egō par' emautōi; para gar toutou ei.* It would take pages to elucidate this fully.

The undifferentiated mob on the lower plane is the flock of psychic men; those seen in the Cross are not yet wholly unified in God because their spiritual Resurrection, reuniting their scattered 'limbs' (GG 84 : 3; GP 23 : 5) into the One, is yet to take place. But when the Cross of Light has lifted up these Spiritual Men into surrender to God, then all will be initiated in the Gnosis; John will then himself become another Christ, while Christ himself will re-enter on his primal glory of the Godhead, from whom John too derives (GG 45 : 2).

36. The Mystery of Suffering

1. " Pay no heed then to the many,[1] and think little of those outside the mystery;[2] for know that I am wholly with the Father, and the Father with me.[3] Therefore I have suffered nothing of what they are going to say about me; nay, even that suffering which I showed thee and the rest while dancing I will to be called a mystery. For what thou seest, this have I shown to thee; but what I am, this I alone know, no other.[4] Let me then

[1] In order to concentrate on the One, the 'many' must be ignored (cf. GH 49 : 2).

[2] The Crucifixion was a mere shadow of a vital reality in every Gnostic's life; this was typified by the 'dance' teaching freedom from suffering in the very midst of it.

[3] This passage shows well the simplicity of the Gk. in these Acts; it reminds us of the style of St. John's Gospel.

[4] Gk. *ho de eimi, touto egō monos oida, allos oudeis.*

keep what is mine, and see what is thine through me.[1] But see me truly, not what I said I am, but what thou, being akin (to me), canst realise.

2. "Thou hearest of me suffering, yet I have not suffered; not suffering, yet have I suffered; pierced, yet was I not smitten; hanged, but was not hanged; blood flowing from me, yet it did not flow. And in a word, what they say of me, these things I did not have: while what they do not say, those I have suffered. Now will I shadow forth for thee what they are, for I know that thou wilt understand.[2]

3. "Understand me then (as the) slaying of a Word,[3] piercing of a Word, blood of a Word, wound of a Word, hanging of a Word, suffering of a Word, fastening of a Word,

---

[1] *i.e.*, as in a mirror: *cf.* GG 30 : 4. Our realisation is partial.

[2] When John realises this, he like his Master will be conqueror of woe, knowing intense bliss in the midst of deepest pain, and joy and sorrow as one.

[3] *i.e.*, the immediate intelligible Utterance of God, pure Reason, the Divine Monad which expresses His will. The non-physical nature of Jesus's body is well told by these same Acts (7): "Sometimes when I took hold of him I met with a material and solid body, and at other times . . . the substance was immaterial (*aülon*) and bodiless (*asōmaton*) and as in no way existing." Clement (Strom. 6 : 9 : 71) has: "Now he was in brief without suffering (*apathēs*), into whom no movement of pain or pleasure or grief slipped in."

death of a Word—and, so defining, I mean a Man. First, then, understand the Word, then shalt thou understand a Lord, and third the Man and whatever he has suffered."[1]

Misled by appearances, the ignorant think the Lord is suffering on a wooden Cross outside Jerusalem. How can this be, when he is one with the omnipresent God, and God is one with him? No time or space can limit him who is one with the All. Even the suffering shadowed forth in the cosmic 'dance' is only a part-truth; the reality can never be told another—each can see only his own experience in the radiant mirror (GG 30 : 4) of the Saviour's soul. Suffering there is, yes; but it is not what men can see or think about. Nails, thorns, spear gave no real pain to God; the real agony was the labouring to give birth to souls, to lift them from the depths. It is the Word, the salvific Will of God, that really suffers; realising this, John will share with his Master what it is to be the Divine Man of the Mysteries, sacrificed and glorified.

37. John Understands

Having said to me these things, with others which I do not know how to speak as he would wish,[2] he was taken up, none of the

---

[1] Knowing pain as God's Will, the Gnostic understands the real nature of the Heavenly Man, the Christ or Word. This Man is the eternal Cross, blessing through self-sacrifice, establishing and redeeming all things. Pope Xystus, in his 2nd. c. " Ring ", says: " Know God, in order that thou mayest know thyself; the greatest honour paid to God is knowledge of Him in silence " (567-568).

[2] Man cannot explain all things; he can speak only to the limit of his own power (*cf.* GG 7 : 5).

crowds seeing him. Then when I went down and they all told me what they had done with him, I laughed at them, holding this only in myself that the Lord had carried out everything symbolically and as planned for the conversion and saving of men.[1] (Acts. John)

John hears much else that cannot be put in words, then goes down to face the more worldly of the disciples. In their grief they told of all the pains and indignities their beloved Lord had endured, but in himself he thought their sorrow foolish, knowing that all things were but a drama enacted for the uplifting of mankind.

38. A Reversal of Values

1. Learn the mystery of all nature and the beginning of all things, what it was. For the First Man,[2] whose Race I represent by my position with head downwards, symbolises a birth into non-being—for it was dead and had no movement.[3] But of His own compassion the Power Above came down upon the earth

---

[1] Gk. *hoti sumbolikōs panta ho Kurios epragmeteusato kai oikonomikōs eis anthrōpous pros epistrophēn kai sōtērian.*

[2] *i.e.*, fallen man, the 'old man' of St. Paul.

[3] Mani also stresses the lifelessness of man as first created, before God breathed into him the 'breath of life' (*cf.* GPM 10: 1).

and fixed this whole arrangement of things, being hanged up as an image of creation.[1] For which reason he made the things of the Right Hand into the Left, and those of the Left into the Right, and reversed all the signs of their nature, so that he thought what was ugly to be fair and what was really evil to be good.

2. Unless you make your Below into the Above,[2] and the Above into the Below, and the Right into the Left, and the Left into the Right,[3] and what is Before as Behind, you shall not know God's Kingdom[4] (Acts. Peter 38).

---

[1] The Acts of Philip, p. 71, reads: "And having turned, the Saviour stretched up his hand and marked a Cross in the air, coming down from Above, and it was full of light and had its form after the likeness of a Ladder. And all the multitude that had gone down from the City into the Abyss came up on the Ladder of the Cross of Light."

[2] "What is Below is like what is Above, for all is Above, nothing is Below; it seems separate to those in whom there is no Gnosis," say the Odes of Solomon (34: 5); thus the midst is annihilated, as in GG 1.1, and all is known to be but *one*.

[3] The Acts of John, p. 114, read: "Let the places of the Right Hand stand fast; let not those of the Left Hand remain!"

"I have made the Inner into the Outer, and the Outer into the Inner; may Thy will be done in all my limbs" (Acts of Thomas, q. Ropes, p. 103).

[4] The second part of this sentence is found in Latin: "*et quae sursum sicut deorsum, et quae ante sicut retro, non cognoscetis regnum Dei.*" So it is the adult must become as a little child, be born again, to enter the Light.

The earliest traditions tell how Peter was crucified at Rome under Nero, head downwards because he protested his unworthiness to die like his Lord. In these Acts he tells the watching crowd how his position shows the Fall of Man, a spiritual power fallen from heavenly estate into slavery to Matter. Only when Christ mounted on the Cross, head upwards, shadowing the eternal machinery of salvation, the Way Up from earth to heaven, the upward Path was opened. He thus discerned the right-hand from the left-hand path, those ascending from those still going down. Now every man must change his values, from material become spiritual, from wicked good, putting his former selfish aims behind him. He will thus become a Son of Light and enter the inheritance of its Kingdom.

39. The Universal Cross

1. It is right to mount upon the Cross of Christ, who is the one and only Word stretched out, of whom the Spirit says: "For what else is Christ but the Word, the Sound of God?"[1] So that the Word is the upright beam whereon I am crucified, and the Sound is that which crosses it, the nature of Man, while the nail which holds the cross-beam[2] to

---

[1] Here too we have the equation of the mystic Cross with the Christ, the Source whence creation arose; I do not know whence this quotation comes, probably a lost Gnostic gospel.

[2] "These are not the Father's plants, for if they were they would seem to be the branches of the Cross," writes Ignatius to the Trallians, 11.

the upright in its centre is the conversion and repentance of Man (Acts. Peter, 38).

2. I[1] come rejoicing to thee, O living Cross whom I know (to be) my own! I am aware of thy mystery for which thou wast planted in the world to make the unstable things firm. For thy head is stretched up towards heaven[2] so as to signify the heavenly Word, but thy middle parts are unfolded like hands both right and left to repel the envious and hostile Power of Evil and gather into one the things scattered abroad,[3] whereas the part near thy feet has been fastened to the earth, fixed in the deep, so that thou mayest join with the celestials those under the earth and those held back among the infernals[4] (Acts. An. 359).

[1] The Gk. version of this Address is more original than the Syriac, which we also have.

[2] The same Acts of Andrew elsewhere has: " O blessed Cross! without the longing for thee no one enters into that place." *Cf.* the quotation from CJ given in the footnote to GG 33 : 1. The Gospel of Nicodemus, 24: " I again raise you all up through the wood of the Cross." Such ideas passed straight into orthodox teaching, and many Catholic Saints have paralleled them.

[3] This full description of the Gnostic Cross is of great interest when compared with that in the Acts of John, perhaps from the same author in the first place, though more heavily revised. Gk. *kai ta dieskorpismena sunagageis eis hen.*

[4] Philo has such thoughts also: " The ladder . . . is . . . the Soul, the foot of which is as it were its earthly part, sensation, while its head is as it were its heavenly part, the purest mind " (de Som. 23).

3. The bar of the Cross is the invincible [1] Man.[2] This is the Father, this is the Fountain that wells out the Silence; it is He who is sought after everywhere. This is also the Father in whom the Monad has evolved like a Light-Spark (before) which all the worlds are as nothing, . . . this it is has moved all things by its shining. So they have received Gnosis and Life and Hope and Repose and Love and Resurrection and Faith and Rebirth and the Seal. This is the Ennead, and it is this that has come forth from the Father of the beginningless ones, who alone is Father and Mother to Himself, whose Fullness surrounds the Twelve Deeps (GL 227-228). But how long do I delay saying these things, and do not embrace the Cross (Acts. An. 359)?

The Cross is the Christ; he who embraces the Cross embraces the Christ, the living Word of God uniting in one the upright, which is the Divine, and the crossbar, the human nature. God and Man meet in that Cross, in the conversion, the transformation, of the lower nature into spiritual reality.

[1] The coincidence of this account of the Crossbar with that in para. 1 will strike any reader, and it proves that even in their doctored form these Acts are still essentially Gnostic. Copt. *nata-mahte m̂mof*.

[2] *i.e.*, the Heavenly Man, in whom abides the Ennead of all perfection which comes from God Himself.

What joy must fill God's lover as he draws near this fearful engine of pain, our daily sufferings, in and by which he is united with his Beloved! Pain thus welcomed with open arms repels all demon powers and unites the scattered souls with God. The suffering devotee then remains on earth to draw the lowly up to God, even while his head is lost in heavenly glories. From this Cross every blessing comes; it merges the individual soul with the eternal Father from whom it came; it flowers forth in all the higher graces, the Nine Divine Qualities of the spiritual life. With what joy, then, Andrew rushes to embrace the Cross!

40. Address to the Cross [1]

1. O Word of Life, now called Tree [2] by me (Acts. Peter, 39), thou ever upright, ever raised on high, eternally above (FFF 445-446)! O Cross, most skillfully devised Engine of Salvation, given me by the Highest! O Cross, invincible Trophy of Christ's conquest of his foes! O Cross, life-giving Tree, roots planted in earth, fruits treasured up in heaven! [3] O Cross, most venerable sweetness and sweet

---

[1] Pointing to the skies, this Royal Banner of Christ raises the soul to God through a suffering which blesses all the worlds.

[2] Even by the orthodox the Cross is often called the 'Tree of Life'; as Widengren shows, it is in several religions a title for the Saviour.

[3] The Tree of Life is the Vine, with a cluster of grapes at the top and branches spreading everywhere below.

Name!... O Cross most worshipful,... who through Gnosis bringest the worthy to God, and through repentance callest sinners home [1] (Acts. An. 359)!

2. O name of the Cross, hidden mystery! O ineffable grace that is expressed in the name of the Cross! O nature of Man that cannot be separated from God![2] O Love ineffable, inseparable, that cannot be declared by unclean lips![3] ... I will declare thee what thou art; I will not keep silence on the mystery of the Cross which of old was ... hidden from my soul. ... Let not the Cross be to you this which appears,[4] for it is another thing, ... even this Passion that is like Christ's[5] (Acts. Peter, 37).

This section is drawn from two more of the Gnostic Acts, wherein the two crucified Apostles burst into lyric fervour of delight when they contemplate the glorious

---

[1] Two kinds of souls come to God: the spiritual who receive the Gnosis, and the sinners or merely psychic who repent and are lifted by His grace.

[2] A sublime thought like St Paul's ecstatic cry in Rom. 8 : 35, 39.

[3] Perhaps a reference to Isa. 6 : 5.

[4] *Cf.* Note 3 to GG 34 : 3.

[5] Suffering which is welcomed, as Christ welcomed his, becomes a blessing to all that lives.

Cross that lifts man from the squalid things of earth to the matchless wonders of eternity. In words of real beauty they hail no mere Cross of wood to slay the body of earthly matter, but the Cross of Light, the saving tool of God's all-loving grace.

The Christian's adoration of the Cross was always a wonder, even a scandal, to the non-believer, who could see in it only the shameful instrument of punishment for those condemned for the most fearful crimes, while the Christian saw it as the instrument of his liberation from sin and glorious exaltation to the skies of heavenly perfection. The astrologer realises a little of this higher aspect of the Cross in his doctrine of the ascendant and the zenith of the horoscope, and the esoteric significances of the conjunction and opposition of the major planets.

CHAPTER EIGHT

THE GLORIOUS ASCENSION

For twenty-nine sections we now pass to the Coptic book known since its discovery as the "Pistis Sophia", we have no idea of its real title, though it may in fact have been all drawn from a Gnostic collection called "The Books of the Saviour", referred to on p. 252 of the ms., which has almost certainly been translated from a Gk. text of about A.D. 170, perhaps slightly interpolated a little later. It seems generally of a Valentinian colour.

We have seen Jesus in his Ministry (GG 29-32) and in his Passion (GG 33-40); we now follow him to those glorious days when he taught the disciples after his Resurrection and until his Ascent to Heaven. At first we learn that he has so far given little real knowledge to them; when they see him transfigured in a cloud of light ascending, and then coming down again, he begins to initiate them in the higher mysteries. Explaining how it is they have been chosen for this privilege, he tells first of the great Mystery of the Light which rewards the saint with cosmic powers, and how after assuming this Robe he penetrated the highest planes and overthrew the agelong rule of the planetary lords of the horoscope.

41. The Disciples Still Know Little

1. Now after Jesus had risen from the dead,[1] it happened that he passed eleven years

---

[1] The book starts rather abruptly in this way, without even a title. Of course, the inner meaning is, as always, the 'spiritually' dead.

speaking with his disciples and teaching them only as far as the regions . . . of the First Mystery that is within the Veil[1] . . . which is before every mystery, the Father in Dove-form[2] (PS 1).

2. Jesus was saying to his disciples: "I have come out of that First Mystery,[3] which is the Last Mystery, namely the twenty-fourth." Now the disciples had not known . . . there is anything within that Mystery, but were thinking . . . that it is the Perfection of all perfections; . . . moreover Jesus had not told his disciples the full extent of all the regions [4] of the Great Unseen,[5] . . . with their Rulers and Authorities. . . . Nor had Jesus told . . . them their Saviours for every plane, how each one is; nor . . . which Guard is at the gate of each (region) of the Treasure of the Light;

---

[1] The 'Veil' is the barrier between mortal and immortal, the 'Boundary'.

[2] Christians speak of the Holy Spirit as in this form.

[3] Here not what is mentioned above; it is the 'first' counting from within outwards, whereas above it is the first from outside inwards.

[4] Copt. *topos*, *i.e.*, the space occupied by an object, and so the area belonging to it. I have conventionally used the word 'region' for this word, while preferring 'plane' for Gk. *taxis*.

[5] The Gnostics give endless details about the inner planes; we can neither accept nor reject these, in our total ignorance of how they are arranged and governed.

nor had he even told them the region of the Twin-Saviour [1] who is the Child of the Child,[2] and ... the region of the Three Amens,[3] ... and ... the Five Trees;[4] ... nor the Seven Amens which are the Seven Vowels,[5] what is their region and how they are spread out in it. Nor even had Jesus told his disciples of what type are the Five Helpers,[6] or in what region they are brought, nor ... that the Great Light has spread abroad (PS 1-3).

3. But in a word he had only spoken with them to teach them that they exist. ... For Jesus used to say to his disciples: " It is that

---

[1] Copt. *sōtēr ṅhatre*, probably the 'Twin' Mani tells us of (*cf.* GPM). It must be the 'Higher Self' which guides the Soul to its own glory.

[2] Copt. *euete ṅtof pe ṁpalou ṁpalou*: not the 'grandchild', but the 'very little child', by imitating whose simplicity we enter the Kingdom; it is also the 'Little Child', the newborn initiate in the Bethlehem Grotto.

[3] Probably the three vowels of the great Name IAO.

[4] Mani tells us much of these 'Five Trees'; they correspond with the Five Limbs of the Mind, the Soul's five powers.

[5] *lit*: voices. In Gk. and Copt. there are seven vowels: a e ē i o ō and u, though the order varied. The correct enunciation of these is a powerful mantram, the secret Name of God; GIG 106 gives their 'Number' as 9879. The magic Name of Abraxas consists of these 'seven poles', *i.e.*, the year of 365 days or the Aeon, a Lion-headed god born at Epiphany; as Epiphanius (Haer. 51 : 22) says: "Today at this hour the Maiden, that is, the Virgin, has given birth to the Aeon"; he is called the 'Aloneborn', and is the Monad or Plērōma.

[6] Presumably the higher counterparts of the Five Trees.

Mystery[1] which surrounds these universes whereof I have told all of you from the day I met you even up to this very day." So this is why the disciples were thinking that there is nothing within that Mystery (PS 3-4).

This book does not tell us how long after the Resurrection this esoteric teaching went on altogether; some sources say it was forty (*i.e.*, many) years in all. The presence of the risen Christ guiding them was a living reality in their lives, and comforted them for the 'tragedy' of Calvary. Up to this time he had not explained the mysteries of each plane inward in the Divine world, but had only taught that such a world exists. Only the higher grades of initiation could reveal more.

42. Jesus is Bathed in Light

1. So it came to pass while the disciples sat together on the Mount of Olives,[2] . . . rejoicing with great joy, . . . they were saying to one another: "It is we[3] who are more

---

[1] The Gnostics had many meanings for the word 'mystery', some of them defying our interpretation.

[2] *Cf.* the Gospel of Bartholomew: "When they came up to the top of the mount and the Master was a little space withdrawn from them . . ."; also GG 33: 1.

[3] Strongly emphasised: Copt: *anon henmakarios anon para ṅrōme tērou ethijṁ pkah*; out of all people in the world Jesus has chosen these few, and he tells them why in GG 45. The Acts of Andrew (p. 351) has: "Blessed is our Race! . . . We are not the offspring of Time later dissolved by Time; we are no product of Motion afterwards destroyed by itself, nor of earthly birth ending therein

blessed than all men on the earth, because the Saviour has revealed these things to us and we have received the fullness and the whole completeness,"¹ ... while Jesus sat at a little distance from them (PS 4).

2. So it happened, on the fifteenth day of the month Tōbe,² which is the day the moon is full, ... when the sun came forth on its way, a great Light-Power came forth after it, shining most exceedingly; ... for it had come from the Light of lights, ... the Last Mystery, ... the twenty-fourth mystery from within outwards. ... Now it, that Light-Power, came down upon Jesus and wholly surrounded him as he sat apart from his disciples, and it shone most brilliantly, there being no limit to the light that was in it³ (PS 4-5).

again. We belong then to a Greatness to which we aspire, ... to the One by whom we have turned away from the Many; to the heavenly by whom we have learned the earthly; to the abiding by whom we have seen the transitory."

[1] *i.e.*, everything there is to know. They anticipate the full initiation.

[2] To me, Mead's idea that this is the source of Luke's statement that Jesus was baptised in the 15th year of *Tibe*rius seems far-fetched and quite untenable. The Coptic month of Tōbe was from November to December, the first of 'spring', naturally associated with the Gnostic Resurrection and the glorifying of the Initiate.

[3] These phrases are often repeated in the original, and I have usually deleted them.

3. Then the disciples did not see Jesus because of the great Light he was in, or that was in him, for their eyes were darkened [1] because of the great Light, ... but they were seeing only the Light shooting out many light-rays. ... Now ... the Light was of various kinds, ... one excelling the other ... in a great glory of light immeasurable; it was reaching from below the earth right up to the skies.[2] So when the disciples saw that light they fell into great fear and a great trembling (PS 5).

As usual, the initiation occurs on the 'mount of contemplation', withdrawn from the confusion of the lower world (cf. Mk 9: 2-4, 25-26), and the way for it is opened by thankfulness for earlier graces. At dawn on the full-moon day, when occult forces are near the highest, they see a great Light overshadow and enfold the Master, and so bright was this they could no longer see him and were afraid. This is the Ladder which, like Jacob's, leads from earth to heaven.

43. Jesus Goes Up into Heaven

1. So it was when that Light-Power came down on Jesus it gradually[3] surrounded him

---

[1] *i.e.*, dazzled; *cf.* GG 9: 1.

[2] *Cf.* the Light-Stream of GG 60, which leads Wisdom to the heavens.

[3] Copt: ṣēm-ṣēm; *lit*: little (by) little.

THE GLORIOUS ASCENSION

altogether. Then Jesus ascended ... on high, shining most exceedingly with an unmeasured light; and the disciples were gazing after him, not one of them speaking until he went up to Heaven, but they were all in a great silence.[1] ... When Jesus went up to Heaven, after three hours all the Powers of the Heavens trembled, ... and the whole earth with those who dwell thereon shook[2] ... until the ninth (hour) of the next day.[3] Then ... were all the Powers of the Height singing hymns to the Inmost of the Inmosts,[4] so that the whole world heard their ceaseless voices[5] (PS 6-7).

2. But the disciples sat close together, being afraid ... because of the great earthquake that took place; and they wept together, saying: "Now what is going to happen?

---

[1] This stillness is the first qualification for candidates; *cf.* GG 81:2.

[2] Mt. 27-28 tells of earthquakes at the Crucifixion and Resurrection.

[3] *i.e.*, till 3 p.m. on the second day, a total of 33 hours, one for each of the 33 Aeons of the Valentinians. In such coincidences the Gnostics delighted, as when they attributed the 33 years of the Master's life to the same cause.

[4] Copt: *epsanhoun nte-nisanhoun*, a phrase hard of literal translation.

[5] Such tales are not to be taken literally (*cf.* the darkness 'over the whole earth' during the Crucifixion); they are subjective experiences.

Perhaps the Saviour is going to destroy all the regions!"[1] . . . The heavens opened, and they saw Jesus coming down, shining most exceedingly, . . . for he shone more than at the time he had gone up to the Heavens, so that no man of earth can speak of the light that was on him. . . . It was of three kinds, each infinitely excelling the other, . . . and the first glory that was below them all [2] was equal to the light that had come down on Jesus before he had ascended to the Heavens, and in its light was like itself alone.[3] (PS 7-8).

Jesus is drawn up by the glory of his perfection in all the graces; the disciples are rapt in that mystic silence wherein alone true Gnosis can arise. The ascent of the risen Master shakes all the Powers till they sing his glory, but this tremendous Vision terrifies the disciples into fear lest it portend the expected end of the world. Presently they see Jesus again, more glorious than before because of his direct contact with the inmost Reality.

44. He Promises to Speak Clearly

1. When the disciples saw these things, . . . they were very frightened and trembled.

---

[1] This shows as little imagination as we have in Acts 1: 6, and little idea of the meaning of the word 'Saviour'!

[2] *i.e.*, the least of the glories.

[3] *i.e.*, cannot be compared with anything else.

So Jesus, the kind and tender of heart,[1] ....
spoke to them, saying: "Take courage; it
is I, do not fear!"[2] Then ... they said:
"Lord, if it is thou, withdraw thy light of
glory into thyself, that we may be able to
stand;[3] otherwise our eyes have gone dark
and we have trembled, and the whole world
too has trembled, because of the great light
that is in thee" (PS 8).

2. Then Jesus withdrew into himself the
glory of his light, and when this was done all
the disciples took courage; they came up to
Jesus and all prostrated at once and worshipped him, rejoicing in great joy. They
said to him: "Master,[4] where didst thou go,
or what was thy mission whereon thou didst
go" (PS 8)?

3. So Jesus the kind said to them: "Rejoice, (all of) you, exult from this hour on,
for I went to the regions from which I had

---

[1] Copt: *pnaēt auō phalc ṅhēt*; no love for Jesus was greater than that held by the Gnostics and Manicheans.

[2] Almost identical wording with Mk. 6 : 50.

[3] This may be compared with Arjuna's prayer to Sri Krishna after the terrific vision of the Viśwarūp in *Gita* 11 : 45-46. Man cannot bear the Beatific Vision yet.

[4] Copt: *hrabbei*, *i.e.*, Rabbi.

come forth. So from today onwards I shall speak openly with you from the beginning of the truth until its end, and I shall talk with you face to face without metaphor[1]. . . . For authority has been given to me by the Ineffable [2] . . . to speak with you from in out, and from out in.[3] Listen, then, and I will tell you everything " (PS 8-9).

Jesus at once frees them from a fear which would make their enlightenment impossible, and at their request hides his glory so that they may approach him more freely. He tells them he has been to the highest Heaven and has now permission to tell them freely of all the mysteries in the inner world, resorting to no ' parable ' or metaphor henceforward.

45. The Origin of Saints

1. While I was sitting it happened . . . that I thought of the sections [4] of the mission whereon I had been sent, that it was finished,

---

[1] Copt: *ajn-parabole*, the word so common in the canonical Gospels *e.g.*, Jn. 16 : 25. " According to the ability of each one of you I will share with you what you are able to bear," says the Acts of John, § 1.

[2] Copt: *hitm-piatsaje erof*; *i.e.*, the one about whom, or to whom, one cannot speak. The phrase generally refers to Cosmic Consciousness.

[3] Copt: *jin-houn sa-bol auō jin-bol sa-houn*; everything in full detail.

[4] Copt: *taxis*; *i.e.*, the points in order.

THE GLORIOUS ASCENSION 131

but the Last Mystery[1] ... had not yet sent me my Robe;[2] ... it was while the sun rose in the east. So thereon, through this First Mystery[3] who was from the beginning and for whose sake the universe has come into being,[4] from whom also I have now come—not in the time before I was crucified, but now[5]—, ... my Light-Robe was sent to me, which He had given me from the beginning and which I had left in the Last Mystery[6] ... until the time should be completed for me to put it on me and to begin speaking with the human race and to reveal all to them. ... Rejoice then, ... for it is you to whom it is given that I should speak first with you; ... this indeed is why I have chosen you from the first[7] (PS 9-10).

[1] *i.e.*, God, to whom we return at the last.

[2] The Robe of Glory, whereof Mani too has so much to say; it is the glorified body we earn by our righteous labours and spiritual advance.

[3] *i.e.*, the first to manifest, the 'Second God,' 'Man, Son of Man,' in other ways of expressing it.

[4] Copt: *pai enta-ptērf ṣōpe etbēētf*; we exist for Him and not for ourselves.

[5] *i.e.*, not when born on earth but after his resurrection.

[6] *Cf.* GG 73:2, also the thought behind Jn. 17:5 and Phil. 2:7 —the '*kenōsis*' whereof theologians have said so much.

[7] *Cf.* Jn. 15:16 and Agraphon 100: "I have chosen you before the world became"; here we have the seed of predestination.

2. So rejoice and exult that when I set out for the world I brought with me from the first Twelve Powers, . . . whom I took from the Twelve Saviours of the Light-Treasure at the First Mystery's command. These then I inserted[1] into your mothers' womb as I was coming to the world; . . . for it is you who are to save the whole world,[2] and that you might be able to endure the troubles of the world.[3] . . . For (for) every man in the world (a) soul has been taken out of the Rulers of the Aeons; but the Power that is in you is from me, and you, your souls belong on high.[4] . . . And when I set out for this world I came among the Rulers of the Sphere, and I took the likeness of Gabriel, the Messenger[5] of the Aeons; then the Rulers of the Aeons did

---

[1] *lit*: threw.

[2] As the Twelve Saviours in the higher planes, so the Apostles down here.

[3] Ordinary souls are ruled by the stars; those chosen to save the world are free from their dictation.

[4] Copt: *ṅtōtn de ere tetnpsukhē ēp epjise*. The Saint, of the Chosen Race, naturally flies upwards like the 'First Sonship' of GG 22: 1; he belongs Above.

[5] Copt: *aggelos*. At the Annunciation Gabriel came to Mary (Lk. 1 : 26); it is easy to think of him as the one then incarnated— as Sri Krishna when incarnating through Devaki appeared in the real form as Vishnu (Bhāg. 10 : 1 : 40).

not recognise me but were thinking that I was Gabriel the Messenger[1] (PS 10-12).

3. At the First Mystery's command I looked down to the world of men and found Elisabeth; .... in her I sowed a Power which I had received from the Little IAŌ[2] the Good, who is in the Midst,[3] that he should be able to proclaim before me and to (prepare) my way, and baptize with water of absolution. . . . So that Power was in John's body. Moreover, instead of the soul of the Rulers he was to receive, I found the soul of Elijah the Prophet in the Aeons of the Sphere;[4] . . . then I took his soul also and brought it to the Maiden of the Light,[5] and she gave it to her

---

[1] The common idea that the Powers could not recognise Jesus as he came down to earth; cf. Ep. Ap. 13: "I passed by the archangels and the angels in their likeness, just as if I were one of them, among the princedoms and powers," and in the Asc. Isa.

[2] IAŌ, the Three Amens of GG 41:2, is said in the Epiphanian system to be Lord of the First Heaven.

[3] i.e., in the evolutionary planes from below upwards.

[4] The Gnostic, perhaps Valentinus, takes as literal fact the hint given in Mk. 9: 13, which seems inconsistent with Elijah's appearance along with Moses on the Mount of Transfiguration, not in the person of John.

[5] I think she cannot be equated with that in Mani's faith; she is rather the 'Mother of the Living', Barbēlō, in the Eighth Heaven of Epiphanius. GIG tells us that she presides over the Baptism of Fire.

Receivers;[1] they brought it to the Sphere of the Rulers [2] and it was inserted into Elisabeth's womb. So the Power of the little IAŌ of the Midst and the soul of the Prophet Elijah —it is they that were bound in the body of John the Baptist (PS 12).

4. After this, at the First Mystery's command I again looked down on the world of mankind and found Mary, who is called my Mother according to the body of matter. I spoke with her also in Gabriel's form,[3] and when she turned herself up to me [4] I inserted [5] in her the First Power that I had received from Barbēlō, that is, the body I had worn on high; and in place of the soul I inserted in her the Power I had received from the Great Sabaōth [6] the Good, who is in the region of the Right [7] (PS 13-14). So as for thee, Mary, thou hast as to matter a form that is in

---

[1] *i.e.*, those who arrange bodies for incarnating souls.

[2] *i.e.*, of Fate, that is, our world.

[3] See page 133, foot-note 1.

[4] *i.e.*, submitted to, with the word 'Fiat,' let it be done.

[5] *lit*: threw.

[6] Sabaōth is named by Epiphanius as Lord of the Seventh Heaven; the word *sab'a* means 'seven'.

[7] *i.e.*, of the good and upward-trending; *cf.* GG 38:1.

Barbēlō, and as for light thou hast received a likeness that is in the Maiden of the Light[1] (PS 116).

5. Now it is the Twelve Powers of the Twelve Saviours ... whom I had taken from the Twelve Ministers in the Midst,[2] I inserted them into the Sphere of the Rulers. And the Rulers' decans[3] and their servants were thinking that they were souls of the Rulers, so the servants brought them and bound them in the body of your mothers. Then when your time was full you were born in the world, no soul of the Rulers being in you, but you got your portion from the Power which the

---

[1] The Gospel of Bartholomew says: " I give the peace to all who believe in my name and in Mary my Mother, the true Virgin, the Pearl-Treasure, the Source of salvation for all the children of Adam "—a doctrine now implicit in modern Mariology. In the Peter-Gospel quoted by Haase, pp. 36-37, Christ revealed himself to Mary in Gabriel's form and was inserted into her womb. So too Ep. Ap. 14 says: "On that day whereon I took the form of the angel Gabriel I appeared to Mary." It is clear that Gabriel was by some equated with the Holy Spirit.

The Apocalypse of Nicotheos says: " The Son of God, capable of all things and becoming all things as much as he wills, appears as he will to each for the sake of devout souls, so that he may draw them out of the sphere of Destiny to the Bodiless."

[2] Copt: *pmṅtsnous ṅdiakonos et-hn-tmesos*.

[3] Copt: *diakonos*; there are three ' decans ' in each zodiacal Sign of 30 degrees, so each contains 10 degrees; they are subordinate to the Sign-Rulers.

Last Helper breathed into the Mixing,[1]. . . . and it happened in all those who are in the Mixing (PS 14).

Reminding them of how it was while he sat alone in contemplation, recalling that his mission on earth was ended yet God had not yet glorified him (cf. Jn. 17 : 5), he tells them that in that very dawn the time came for his last act—to raise the chosen few to the highest initiation of which they were capable.

First, then, he tells why they were chosen; it was no personal favouritism but that they were of a different origin from the common run of men, belonging to the Race Above. Their souls were not subject to the stars of destiny, but Powers from the Treasury of Light, and so could resist the whirling forces of the lower chaos, this world, and save others for the Light. So too John the Baptist was no ordinary man, but came from between the Firmament and Heaven, and was actually the soul of Elijah; in the body of Mary, Joseph's spouse, in the very form of Gabriel Christ placed a 'soul' from the yet higher realm of Heaven itself. The Light shone in the darkness of the Rulers' ignorance and was not recognised; the saints appear as men, yet are beyond mere human frailty.

46. The Glorious Light-Robe

1. Add joy to your joy, for the times are complete for me to put on me my Robe which was prepared for me from the first and

---

[1] Copt: *tai ṅtafnife ṁmos eḥoun epkerasmos ṅci phāe ṁparastātēs*. The 'Mixing' is this lower world wherein Light is mingled with the darkness of Matter; GG 41: 2 speaks of the Five Helpers.

THE GLORIOUS ASCENSION 137

(which) I had left in the Last Mystery. . . . See now, I have donned my Robe and have been given all authority by the First Mystery.[1] Yet a little while, and I shall tell you the mystery of the universe, . . . and from this hour I shall hide nothing from you (PS 16); I shall perfect you in all mysteries of the Kingdom of the Light (PS 104).[2]

2. When the sun rose in the east, a great Light-Power containing my Robe came down, . . . and on my Robe I found a mystery written in the script of those of the Height: "ZĀMA ZĀMA ŌZZA RAḤAMA ŌZAÏ,"[3] whose meaning is this: "O Mystery that is outside the world, on whose account the universe has come into being, . . . come down to us, for we are Thy fellow-members, and also we are all with Thee—we are one and

---

[1] *Cf.* Mt. 28 : 18; this total authority comes only with the Robe of Glory.

[2] Probably the 'Mystery of the Ineffable', cosmic consciousness, spoken of in GG 85, is here referred to.

[3] These mysterious sentences in an unknown language, whereof we can occasionally pick out a word of Egyptian or Hebrew (*e.g.*, *raḥama*: mercy), were dearly loved by the later Gnostics; the Bruce Codex is full of them. Interpretations are usually given, which are vastly longer than and bear no apparent relation to them. It may be noted, however, that the line marking abbreviation is over the whole mantram, and these five words may be only the first of a long prayer.

the very same![1] Thou art the First Mystery who has from the first been within the Ineffable before ever He came forth; and we all are the Name of That! So now we all together meet Thee at the Last Boundary,[2] which is the last mystery from within; it is itself a part of us.[3] Now then we have sent thee thy Robe which was thine from the beginning and which thou hast left in the Last Boundary . . . until its time was completed, according to the command of the First Mystery. See, its time is come; put it on thyself! (PS 16-17)

3. "Come to us,[4] for we all draw near to thee to put on thee the First Mystery with all His glory at His very own command, the First Mystery having given it to us—. . . there being two Robes to clothe thee in besides this that we have sent for thee, because thou art worthy of them since it is thou who wast

[1] A touching appeal to the essential oneness of the Soul with God, for whom she alone exists.

[2] This is the 'Boundary' of GG 14 : 2, and in GPM the Rescuer came to the 'Boundary' to save the Soul from the Darkness.

[3] This 'Boundary' is indeed "a part of us," for it is our finite human nature which keeps us apart from God; when this is transcended we fly into Him.

[4] H. P. Blavatsky says much of this phrase in 'The Secret Doctrine'; it is the 'Call' of Mani's faith, which rouses the Soul and draws it home to God.

before us. ... In the first there is all the glory of all the names of all the mysteries and all the emanations of the planes of the spaces of the Ineffable, while in the second Robe [1] is the whole glory of the name of all the mysteries and all the emanations which are in the planes of the two spaces of this First Mystery (PS 17-18).

4. "Now in this Robe which we have sent now to thee there is the glory of the name of the Revealer [2] who is the First Decree,[3] and the mystery of the Five Impressions,[4] and the mystery of the Ineffable's Great Envoy who is this great Light,[5] together with the mystery of the Five ... Helpers.[6] Also in that Robe there is the glory of the name of the mystery of all the planes of the emanations of the Treasure of the Light, as well as their Saviours,

---

[1] The First Robe is universal awareness; the inferior Robe the awareness of God as manifest.

[2] Copt: *pmēneutēs*.

[3] *i.e.*, the words "Let it be!" which began creation and the incarnation of the Christ; thus they are the Incarnate Word.

[4] Copt: *ptiou ṅkharagmē*; *cf.* the seal-impressions of GG 5 : 5, which result in the appearance of this universe and its creatures.

[5] This may well be the 'Messenger of the Light' whereof Mani has so much to say, and his Divine Prototype.

[6] *Cf.* Note 6 to GG 41 : 2.

and also the planes of the Orders,¹ which are the Seven Amens and are also the Seven Vowels,² together with the Five Trees and also the Three Amens and the Twin-Saviour —who are the Child of the Child—and also the mystery of the Nine Guards of the three Gates³ of the Treasure of the Light (PS 18).

5. "Furthermore, there is in it the whole glory of the name (of those) who are in the Right,⁴ together with all those who are in the midst; also there is in it the whole glory of the name of the Great Unseen, who is the Great Forefather; also the mystery of the three 'Triple-Powers'⁵ and . . . all their region, besides the mystery of all their Invisibles, together with all those who are in the Thirteenth of the Aeons,⁶ . . . and also all those

---

¹ How to translate this? *mn ṅtaxis ṅṅtaxis*; it equates at once with the Seven Vowels, God's mystic Name, whose number is 9879, says GIG 113.

² *lit*: voices.

³ There are three Guards to each Gate of the Treasure, as also several diagrams in the Bruce Codex clearly show.

⁴ *i.e.*, the righteous, of the upward-trending path.

⁵ *i.e.*, the human soul.

⁶ Mead explains that in a mass of spheres twelve touch each one and so a dodecahedron is formed; the thirteenth is thus the central sphere. The number 13 seems to have had a fascination for the Gnostics, perhaps because Jesus is the Thirteenth, with his twelve disciples.

who are in the Twelve Aeons, and the whole mystery of the name of all those who are in the (Realm of) Destiny and all the heavens, also ... in the Sphere, together with their firmaments and all who are in them, and also all their regions [1] (PS 18-19).

6. "See then, we have sent thee that Robe which no one has known from the First Mystery down, because the glory of its light was hidden in it.... So hasten and put this Robe upon thee. Come to us, for at the First Mystery's command we draw near to thee to put on thee thy two Robes [2] until the time set by the Ineffable is complete. Now see, the time has come; come then swiftly to us and we shall put them on thee; ... for there is still a little time, a very little, thou comest to us and shalt leave the world. Come swiftly, then, to receive all thy glory which is the glory of the First Mystery" (PS 19-20).

Jesus then speaks of the glorious Robe of Light he is putting on, veiled for the moment from their eyes; in it are all the wonders of the universe, every living

---

[1] In fact, the Light-Robe contains all mysteries of the whole manifested universe, above and below. "She gave him twelve powers serving him, and she gave him a Robe to enclose everything in it," says GL 256.

[2] *i.e.*, those named in paragraph 3.

creature being reflected therein. Arjuna saw this in Sri Krishna; the cosmic vision knows that all are in the One. This is the secret of the Gnosis, realised at the 'boundary' of the individual self, where it dissolves in the infinity of the Divine. This is the glory of the Gnosis, where the individual becomes the All—as Clifford Bax has it in 'The Marriage of the Soul' "O, I have reached the boundaries of the self; I am becoming one with all things!" The higher stage: "O, I am nothing, nothing; Thou art all!" comes later on the inward way. The Light-Powers embrace the Christed one into their number, explaining how all beings of the universe are at-oned in them; all the mysteries and mighty Forces of the Heavens are included in these shining vestures he must now put on—omitting only the evil powers of the 'Left' or of Darkness—before he leaves the lower world for ever and can no more manifest God's glory to mankind.

47. Jesus Puts on the Robe[1]

So it was, when I saw the mystery of all these things in the Robe which He had sent me, I put it on me in that moment, and I shone most exceedingly and soared on high. Then I came before the gate of the Firmament,[2] ... and the gates of the Firmament shook against each other and all opened at once.[3] Then all

---

[1] "If you follow righteousness, you will attain and put it on like a Robe of glory," said Ecclus. 27: 8, in the 2nd c. B.C.

[2] *i.e.* the Boundary between our human sky and the heavenly spheres.

[3] *Cf.* the story of the 'harrying of Hell' in the old Gospel of Nicodemus and in the Gnostic Revelation of Bartholomew, recently found in Coptic.

the Rulers . . . therein trembled together because of the great light that was in me; and they gazed at the Light-Robe on me, . . . they saw the mystery on which were their names, and were extremely afraid. Then all their ties were loosed . . . and everyone left his rank[1] and they all prostrated in my presence and worshipped, saying: "How has the Lord of the Universe passed us without our knowing?"[2] and all together they hymned the Inmost of the Inmost.[3] Now me they were not seeing, but they saw only the light, and they were in great fear (PS 20-21).

Realising that this 'Robe' is itself omnidentity, the cosmic consciousness, Jesus loses no time in taking it to himself. Then in unspeakable glory he rose into the 'firmament,' the visible sky, where all the Rulers trembled at the knowledge that their names, *i.e.*, powers, had been assumed by him; they burst into adoration of the Supreme manifested in him.

[1] Copt: *auō apwe pwa lo hn teftaxis*: *lit*: each one ceased (to be) in his order.

[2] The same idea of Jesus passing unknown through the Powers of the Air; *cf.* CJ 12: "Remember also that I was with you without your having recognised me." Also Asc. Isa. 10: 23-24: "When he descended into the third heaven, he made himself like the form of the angels in the third heaven; and those who kept the gate of the heaven demanded the password, and the Lord gave it them in order that he should not be recognised"; and (*idem* 11: 24): "How did our Lord descend in our midst, and we perceived not the glory which we see has been on him from the sixth heaven?"

[3] *Cf.* Note 5 to GG 43:1.

48. He Enters Plane after Plane

1. I left that place[1] behind me and went up to the First Sphere, shining ... forty nine times more brightly than I had shone in the Firmament.[2] ... And I left behind me that place[1] and came to the gate of the Second Sphere, which is the (Sphere of) Destiny. ... Then I left that place [1] behind me and went up to the great Aeons of the Rulers. I came before their veils and also their gates, ... and all their Aeons were shaken at once [3] ... because of the great light that was in me— ... For the world cannot bear the Light as it is in its truth,[4] or the world would at once dissolve with all that are thereon— ... because of the great fear that had come on them as they did not know the mystery that had come to pass (PS 21-25).

[1] Copt: *pma etmmau*, a vague term, differing from the technical word '*topos*'.

[2] "The glory of my appearance was undergoing transformation as I ascended to each heaven in turn" (Asc. Isa. 7: 25).

[3] There is no resistance in the first two Spheres; it is only the Rulers of the Second Sphere, who dwell above it, who have to be overcome.

[4] This is one of the countless Johannine touches which suggest that this book may be from Valentinus or a disciple of his. His 'Gospel of Truth,' now found, opens and continues in a somewhat Johannine way. As by St. John, the Light is contrasted with the 'world'.

THE GLORIOUS ASCENSION 145

2. Then Adamas the great Tyrant,[1] with all the tyrants who are in all the Aeons, began to fight in vain against the Light (PS 25), desiring to hold it back among them so that they might continue [2] further in their Rulership [3] (PS 38); but they did not know with whom they fought,[4] because they saw nothing but the overwhelming Light. So it happened when they fought the Light they all became feeble together and fell down into the Aeons—they became like dead men of earth with no breath in them. Then I took a third part [5] of the power of them all lest they be active in their evil ways, and so that if the men in the world invoked them in ... their sorceries, ... which the Angels who had transgressed had brought down,[6] ... they might be unable to carry them out (PS 25).

---

[1] Adamas is, in this book, (*cf.* GG 62 and 67), the demon power of fallen or evil humanity—nearly Satan.

[2] *lit.* delay

[3] The same idea as we have in GPM 2: 3 etc.

[4] Even in the 7th c. B. C. Zarathushtra stresses the ignorance of the evil spirit (*cf.* GZ 45 : 2).

[5] *Cf.* Rev. 8 : 10.

[6] An allusion to the old legend of the 'Watchers' found in the Books of Enoch, in the Manichean Book of Giants, and in the late Book of Adam and Eve.

Passing on, Jesus with fast-increasing glory penetrated the inner planes—the first, the second of the great lords of Destiny, ruled by the planetary lords who administer the 'laws of karma', and on into the third where are the eternal worlds of the Rulers—probably the 'Hebdomad' of GG 24:4. Here too all was thrown into confusion, Adamas—St. Paul's 'old man'—fiercely resisting the inrush of new light into his realms, in his ignorance that it is invincible. The Redeemer weakens the Powers of this region so that they, the 'evil angels' of Enoch's story (GY 103 note), might no longer aid men in all their wickedness.

49. And Hastens the Day of Liberation

1. Then did I at the command of the First Mystery change the paths and courses of their Aeons [1] . . . and confused them greatly, . . . and thereafter they could no longer turn to the refuse of their matter to devour it.[2] Then I made the path of their course hasten, so that they might be quickly purified and raised on high.[3] . . . Further, their times and their periods have been shortened, so that the perfect number of the souls who are to receive

---

[1] *i.e.*, changed the planetary orbits, and so upset the whole of their influences over human life.

[2] They had no longer power over even the material body.

[3] The idea is that of Mani in GPM 25 etc., matter being refined and the Soul raised to heaven with such matter as has become pure enough, the subtle body.

mysteries and to be in the Treasure of the Light may be quickly completed, ... that is, the Elect. Now if I had not shortened their periods, no material soul would have been saved,[1] but they would have been destroyed in the fire that is in the flesh of the Rulers [2] (PS 38-40).

2. Now it happened when Jesus finished saying these things to his disciples they all prostrated at once and worshipped him; and they said to him: " It is we who are blessed above every man in that thou hast revealed these great exploits " (PS 40)![3]

> He violently alters the laws of movement of their planets and deprives them of the power to rob mankind of spirituality; he shortens the periods of their revolution, lessening the duration of the ages, and so of individual human lives (GPM 85:1), so that the consummation might be expedited and souls be sooner rescued from the dangers of physical incarnation which might drown them in fleshly desires. This news delights the disciples, so they adore the Saviour.

---

[1] An allusion to Mt. 24 : 22, *et al.*

[2] Mani also has this thought; the desire of the flesh is indeed a destructive fire, able to destroy all but the truly spiritual souls (*cf.* GPM 57 : 2).

[3] An almost Buddhistic ending to the first part of the book " Pistis Sophia " (*cf.* GPM 95 : 3).

CHAPTER NINE

THE SOUL REDEEMED

JESUS proceeds with the detailed story of how he rescues the faithful but fallen human Soul from the dark chaos of material life, and leads her stage by stage back into the glorious Light-realm where she belongs.

As in GG 14, we learn that she fell by an over-impulsive urge to something beyond her—a kind of pride, as was the fall of Lucifer in later Jewish legend —and misled by the counterfeit Angel of Light which is her own ego (Authades, Arrogant, or Self-Willed). Her sin was pardonable because it arose from her very love for God the Light, deceived and lured into the Darkness by the element of spirituality which alone makes the ego possible. She has broken the bounds of the twelve " Zodiacal Signs " by this self-willed urge to immediate merging with God, and has to suffer and repent for and through each of these in turn—the original text being here long-winded to the point of boredom.

Towards the end of her long repentances Jesus comes to her and gives her a little spiritual strength on his own authority, raising her to a higher level of wisdom among men, but the enemy renews his violent assaults. Egoism stands firmly to block her upward progress and to drag her again to the depths, until the sacramental life surrounds her and crowns her with light and spiritual power. Again egoistic Pride assails her, joined by the downward tendencies of the ' old man', until Jesus again pours grace into her and lifts her on high and tramples her spiritual foes under her feet. While she rejoices at this escape, Jesus tells her how it will be made eternal when every soul of the Race of the Light is liberated. Then at the end of time the evil inherent in lower creation, Adamas, once more lifts up its head; the Redeemer finally draws the Soul into her everlasting home, the realm of supreme Light where she belongs, and she then joins her fellows in the thanksgiving Hymn.

It will be of great interest to compare this late 'Valentinian' version of the Myth with the Gospel parable of the Prodigal Son (Lk. 15: 11-32), the earlier version from the same 'school' of Gnostics in GG 14-19, the Bardesanian poem in GG 70-77, the late Manichean version in GPM 1-10, etc., and the so-called 'Prayer of Cyriacus' in App. III.

50. Jesus Finds the Faithful Wisdom

1. (Jesus said): After these things I ascended as far as the veils of the Thirteenth of the Aeons;[1] then when I came upon their veils they withdrew of themselves and opened to me. I went in to the Thirteenth of the Aeons, and at the bottom[2] found the faithful Wisdom[3] ... all alone, none of them being with

[1] *i.e.*, the chief of the eternal worlds, as the teacher is head of his twelve disciples.

[2] At the bottom of the highest 'Aeon', she is still above the twelve Rulers, and thus awakens their jealousy.

[3] Copt: usually *tpistis sophia*, lit. 'the faith-wisdom'. The point of the whole story is that even in her fall the human Soul clings to the Light she has once seen, even though in the 'veil'. Sometimes the name 'Wisdom' alone is used, and to avoid the constant

her.[1] Now she was sitting there, grieving and lamenting that she was not admitted to the Thirteenth Aeon, her region on high, and ... because of the pains which Arrogant,[2] who is one of the 'Three-Powered' ones, had made for her (PS 42), the one who had disobeyed in not emitting all the refinement of his power in him ... at the time when the Rulers had given their refinement (of Matter), desiring to lord it over the whole Thirteenth Aeon and those below it (PS 44-45).

2. When the faithful Wisdom saw me shining most exceedingly, ... she fell into great agitation. Then she gazed out into the light of my Robe, and she saw in my Robe the mystery of her name,[3] as well as the whole glory of its mystery. For she was formerly in the higher region of the Thirteenth Aeon, and was wont

repetition of the whole appellation, clumsy in English, I prefer to call her 'Wisdom' always, as in GG 14-16 and in 92—occasionally prefixing the adjective 'faithful'. In GG 11 : 2 'Faith' is defined as that "whereby the mysteries of the Ineffable have been believed", even before personal direct experience.

[1] She is in the solitary void, as in GG 16 : 1.

[2] Copt: *authadēs*, one who does what he likes. This undoubtedly describes the ego, which is one of those who refuse to give God all the glory and try to keep back something for themselves, in order to rule over the worlds around them.

[3] As one of the Powers, her name too is in the Robe, for she is a part of the universal consciousness (GG 46 : 5).

THE SOUL REDEEMED

to hymn the Higher Light which she had seen in the Veil[1] of the Treasure of the Light (PS 43).

3. Then looked all the Rulers who are with the two great 'Three-Powered' ones,[2] together with her unseen who is paired with her,[3] and the twenty-two other invisible emanations—since the faithful Wisdom and her twin . . . make up twenty-four emanations[4] whom the Great Unseen Forefather had emanated (PS 43).

Empowered by his Robe of universal knowledge, Jesus passed beyond the twelve 'aeons' of manifestation to the lower border of the mysterious 'Thirteenth', where he found the human Soul deserted by her celestial brethren and afflicted by all the miseries brought her by the false light of Egoism, which ever tries to hold for itself what is meant to be shared by all. At the first sight of his brightness, the Soul was afraid ('modest' in GG 17 : 1) until she found herself reflected in his Robe of Power; then all the forces of the manifested worlds also gazed at him.

---

[1] Even the prototype of the human Soul can see Him but "as in a glass, dimly", for His glory is veiled for our sake, else we could not dare look on it.

[2] *i.e.*, those associated with humanity.

[3] *viz.*, "Willed" (*Thelētos*), destined to be the Twin-Guide or Spouse of the human Soul, as God's Will is all its joy; *cf.* GG 14:1.

[4] *i.e.*, twelve pairs', each one for one of the 'Aeons'.

51. How She Made Enemies

1. It came to pass while Wisdom was in the Thirteenth of the Aeons,[1] in the region of all her brethren, these Invisibles, . . . so it happened by the First Mystery's command, Wisdom looked up and saw the light of the Veil [2] of the Treasure of the Light, and she longed to go there but could not go to that region. Yet she ceased performing the mystery of the Thirteenth Aeon,[3] and was hymning the Light on high that she had seen in . . . the Veil (PS 44).

2. All the Rulers . . . who were below hated her because she had ceased from their mysteries and because she wished to go up and be above them all.[4] For this reason, then, they were enraged at her . . . and hated her. . . . Then Arrogant . . . joined himself

---

[1] This looks back in time, to tell how Wisdom came to fall into the chaos of dark Matter.

[2] The Veil is man's own spiritual nature; to raise it he must transcend individuality, break death, and enter the Light to behold God (*cf.* TGH 1 : 62).

[3] Seeing God, she forgot her own normal duties of life.

[4] It is jealousy of the Soul's power to enjoy God that stirs the lower self to hate all things good; it soon finds allies in the 'rulers' of the natural forces of the world.

to the Rulers of the Twelve Aeons, and he too raged against the faithful Wisdom (PS 44-45).

Now she had fallen into this strait through longing to enter the higher life that was still beyond her reach, and through ceasing to live the normal life of the human status, while lost in adoration of the Most High. This stirred up the lower powers against her, and they enlisted on their side the mighty force of egoism or self-will. So she deserted her real partner, God's Will, (GG 13 : 1) and her natural companions and, aiming over high, fell from her own estate, much as through pride Lucifer fell and dragged Adam and Eve after him by their ambition.

52. The Lion-Faced Power

1. He evolved from himself a great power with lion's face,[1] and from his matter in him emanated a host of other very mighty[2] material emanations.[3] Then he sent them into the lower regions, to the parts of the Chaos,[4] so

[1] In GPM 57 : 1 the "roaring lion" is Greed, one of the two great demons that afflict the Soul; this 'lion-faced Power' may well be the desire to overthrow the higher faculties of the Soul and take its powers for itself. Abraxas, p. 53, quotes Paris Papyrus 21: 12 "A statue girt about with lion's face, holding in the right hand a wand whereon a Dragon stands, and a certain asp twisted all round the left hand, and fire is breathed out of the lion's mouth." Ginzā 278 : 19 speaks of "his head (as) that of a lion", while MP 57 : 18 refers to "this lion-faced dragon".

[2] Mead takes this as 'violent'; Copt: *eunaṣt emate*.

[3] These are the evil thoughts which assail the Soul at the call of ambition and its lord egoism.

[4] It is clear from other places that the 'Chaos' and the 'Darkness' are simply names for this our plane of gross matter.

as to trap Wisdom there and carry her power away from her, because . . . she kept mourning and seeking after the Light that she had seen (PS 45).

2. So it was . . . at the First Mystery's command [1] this great 'three-powered' Arrogant . . . persecuted Wisdom in the Thirteenth Aeon, so that she should look down [2] and see his Light-Power there which was lion-faced, and long for it,[3] and go to that region, and have her light taken from her (PS 45-46).

3. It happened, then, after this, she looked down and saw his Light-Power in the depths, but she did not know that it belonged to this 'three-powered' Arrogant but thought it was of the Light that she had seen from the first on high,[4] which came from the veil of the Treasure of the Light. Then she thought in herself: "I will go to that region without my Twin,[5] and

---

[1] God wills this suffering, because He can see its final result is the Soul's glorification.

[2] *lit.* to the lower parts.

[3] It is the divine element in ambition which draws the Soul down into Matter, where she is doomed to lose her spiritual powers.

[4] It is easy to mistake ambition as spiritual; we dream of doing great things for God—which is egoism.

[5] *i.e.*, without consulting God's will, on her own.

THE SOUL REDEEMED

take the Light, and fashion it for myself into light-aeons,[1] so that I may be able to go to the Light of these lights which is in the Height of heights" (PS 46)!

4. Thinking this, then, she went out of her region, the Thirteenth Aeon, and she came down to the Twelfth Aeon.[2] ... Again she left the Twelfth Aeon and came to the regions of the Chaos, and she made her way to this lion-faced Light-power to devour it.[3] But all the material emanations of Arrogant surrounded her, and this great lion-faced Light-Power swallowed the light-powers in Wisdom; it both refined her light and devoured it, while her matter was thrown out to the Chaos.[4] In the Chaos it became a lion-faced Ruler whose half was fire and the other half

---

[1] Yes, she planned to build God eternal worlds of light; Satan also trapped Adam and Eve with such sublime ambitions to be like God!

[2] Evidently passing through all the other 'Aeons' on her way down from the Thirteenth to the lowest world of dark Chaos.

[3] Her idea was to use ambition for her own high ends; but countless evil thoughts overwhelmed her and she was enslaved to the very ambition she hoped to control.

[4] So her body became grosser and became physical; she was incarnated here—which is the real 'fall of Man'. H. P. Blavatsky has much to say on the gradual densification of the first cloudy human bodies.

was darkness—that is, Ialdabaoth.[1] . . . So when these things happened, Wisdom became greatly enfeebled while that lion-faced Power was busy in taking away all the light-powers in Wisdom, and all Arrogant's material powers surrounded Wisdom at once and pressed upon her (PS 46-48).

Through self-inflation Egoism awakens greed in the heart, the desire to acquire more and more of what is not one's own; and this fierce, lion-like force arouses countless more desires which ensnare the Soul and rob her of spirituality. But, strange as it is, all this is at God's mysterious Will; He lets the Soul experience the folly of the unreal so that in time she may turn with greater love and steadiness to embrace the Real. Seeing the Divine reflected in the individual self or ego, the Soul thinks in pursuing that end she is nearing the Divine Light she really seeks, and that out of this little light she can create eternities to His glory and so become like Him.

So she steps down from her own spiritual life of grace, and comes into the darkness of physical matter and illusion, hoping to absorb, satisfy, this ambition; but she at once becomes prey to all the countless shapes egoism assumes, becomes a prisoner in matter, and is stripped of all her spritual power, while her subtle body is degraded into gross physical matter. Ambition, forgetful of its origin, half passionate desire and half ignorant delusion, now predominates on earth, and the human Soul loses all its glory to its foes.

---

[1] Here the Soul became a blend of passion and ignorance, the ' Ialdabaoth ' said by Epiphanius to rule the Sixth Plane, probably our ' lower astral '.

53. Wisdom's First Appeals

1. She cried out extremely loud, ... she cried to the Light of these lights whom she had seen and trusted from the first, and she uttered this Repentance,[1] saying thus: "... O Light of Truth, Thou knowest that I have done these things in my innocence,[2] thinking that the lion-faced Power belonged to Thee, ... and because of the delusion of Thy Light I have become alien[3] to my brethren, the Invisibles. ... Save me from this darkness of the Chaos,[4] ... lest I be swallowed up in it; ... let it not shroud[5] all my power! ... Amid the darknesses have I waited for my Twin to come and fight for me, but he did not come"[6] (PS 48-51)!

---

[1] Copt: *metanoia*, which here bears a special technical meaning as a cry for help, admitting that God alone can give that help which is so greatly needed.

[2] Copt: *ñtaier nai hn tamntbalhēt*. There was no sin of malice, but only of ignorance and of presumptuous desire for God, as in GG 14:1, 3.

[3] This word runs through all the mystery-religions of the day. We belong to heaven, but our exile down here has made us foreigners to it.

[4] Copt: *hm pikake ñte nekhaos*; the word 'chaos' is in the plural, for which English has no equivalent.

[5] *i.e.*, cover over like the dead.

[6] She sought God's will, but having no reply acted on her own without it; had He given His aid, there would have been no fall. Mary explains this First Repentance with reference to Ps. 68.

2. The faithful Wisdom went on again, she sang a Second Repentance, speaking in this way: "Rescue me, O Light, from this lion-faced Power and from the emanations of divine Arrogance;[1] for it is Thou, O Light, in whose light I have believed, and I have trusted to Thy Light from the first; ... it is Thou who shalt save me. ... Now then, O Light, leave me not in the Chaos; ... do not abandon me, O Light, for ... they have desired to carry off all my light in me; they have kept watch on my power, saying to one another all at once: 'The Light has forsaken her; seize her, and let us take away all the light in her'"[2] (PS 56-59)!

Oppressed by the misery of her fall, the Soul cries out to the God once faintly seen afar and still remembered, protesting that the calamity was due to her very eagerness for Him, and appealing for His direct help, as she could not surrender to His Will thus shown. She begged Him to save her from egoism which is stripping off her spiritual strength, and to free her from the dark world of gross physical matter (cf. GPM 70-71).

---

[1] Copt: m̀pauthadēs ǹǹnoute; lit. of the Gods. The ego in man is really of divine origin and needs only to be in subjection to the Supreme.

[2] This Second Repentance Peter explains with reference to Ps. 70.

54. Four More Cries for Help

1. She continued again and spoke the Third Repentance,[1] saying: "Let those who would take my power be turned to the Chaos and put to shame, let them be swiftly turned to the Darkness; ... let everyone who seeks after the Light rejoice and be glad! ... Thou, then, O Light, Thou art my Saviour; ... hasten and save me out of this Chaos" (PS 60-61)!

2. She went on ... in the Fourth Repentance,[2] saying, before she was oppressed the second time, so that the lion-faced Power and all the material emanations ... might not take away the rest of her light in her: ... "Because of the voice of the fear and the power of this Arrogant[3] my power has vanished in me; I have become like a strange demon dwelling in matter[4] with no light in him. ... O Light, all this has befallen me

---

[1] Martha explains this Third Repentance by referring to Ps. 69.

[2] This Fourth Repentance is explained by John as related to Ps. 101.

[3] The very sight of egoism deprives the Soul of spiritual power until it flees for help to God.

[4] Copt: aiṣōpe enthe ṅouhidios ṅdaimōn efwēh hn ouhulē. The word hidios really means something peculiar to the self, and is thus suited to the growing ego.

through Thy decree; . . . **it** has brought me down, and I have descended like a power of the Chaos, and my power is numb within me.[1] . . . My time has come that Thou shouldst seek after . . . my soul, and this is the time Thou hast decreed to seek me out" (PS 62-64)!

3. The emanations of Arrogant again oppressed the faithful Wisdom in the Chaos, . . . and not yet was her decree fulfilled to bring her out, . . . nor had the command yet come to me from the First Mystery [2] to rescue her from the Chaos. So it was when they oppressed her . . . she cried out, speaking the Fifth Repentance:[3] " . . . O Light, . . . let Thy light come down on me, for my light in me has been taken and I am in misery; . . . for my power is filled with darkness, and my light has gone down to the Chaos, . . . to the Darkness below. . . . And I have spread out my hands up to Thee and cried out . . . with all the light in me. . . . I hymn Thee in the region on high, and again in the Chaos" (PS 67-68)!

---

[1] Copt: *auō atacom ōcr hrai ṅhēt.*

[2] *i.e.*, God Manifest, the Father who sends the Saviour.

[3] This Fifth Repentance, a prayer for grace, was explained by Philip as referring to Ps. 87.

THE SOUL REDEEMED

4. The faithful Wisdom cried out to the Light: He forgave her sin that she had left her region and come down to the Darkness. She uttered the Sixth Repentance,[1] speaking thus: . . . "Let every power in me trust in the Light while I am in the Darkness below, and again let them trust in Him if they come to the higher region; for it is He who shall pity and save us, and there is in Him a great saving mystery [2] (PS 73-74)."

She asks for the defeat of her human desires and for the victory and happiness of those who seek for God. It is this very self-will which has isolated her from heaven, exiled her from the Light; but even this must be a part of His supreme Will, as too must be the salvation that she craves.

Thoughts of self-esteem again attack her, perhaps aroused by this very claim on God's assistance; in her agony she appeals desperately for aid. With all her heart she seeks God's grace, for all that was in her is lost and she is poor and in deepest misery. Yet she will cling to Him in sorrow even as she did in joy and glory.

Then God forgives her sin, though she must still suffer its results. She urges herself to perfect trust in Him even while in the depths, as she had ever done while on the heights of joy. Her acceptance of His will is now growing more perfect, and the hour of liberation, yet unseen, draws near.

---

[1] Andrew refers the Sixth Repentance to Ps. 129. It is a noble appeal.

[2] Copt: *auō un ounoc m̅musterion n̅nouhm n̅hētf.*

55. Three More Appeals

1. She again turned herself up to see whether her sins had been forgiven her, and to see whether she would be brought up out of the Chaos. But by the First Mystery's command she had not yet been listened to, that her sin should be forgiven [1] . . . She saw all the Rulers of the Twelve Aeons laughing at her and rejoicing over her because her repentance was not accepted from her (PS 77).

2. She was greatly grieved, she lifted up her voice on high, saying in the Seventh Repentance:[2] . . . " The Light is good and just;[3] this is why He will grant me my way to be rescued in my trangression. . . . For all the Gnoses of the Light are saving means,[4] and there are mysteries for every one who seeks after the regions of his inheritance.[5] . . . To every one who trusts in the Light He will

---

[1] In GG 54 : 4 we are told that her sin was forgiven, yet here it has not yet been (fully) absolved, because the Mystery, the Crown of Light, has not yet come.

[2] Thomas explains this Seventh Repentance by Ps. 24.

[3] Copt: *wagathos auō efsōutōn pe (pwoein).*

[4] Copt: *je ṅsown tērou ṁpwoin hennouhm ne.*

[5] *i.e.,* at every stage there are spiritual means to raise each aspiring Soul.

give the mystery suited to him, and his soul shall be in the regions of the Light. . . . Well, I have always believed in the Light, for it is He who will rescue my feet out of the chains of the Darkness (PS 77-79)!"

3. Not even yet had the order come to me through the First Mystery to save her and bring her up from the Chaos. But on my own authority alone, compassionately and unbidden,[1] I led her to a somewhat wider region in the Chaos. Then they ceased . . . a little pressing on her, thinking that she would be brought up from the Chaos altogether.[2] . . . Wisdom was not aware that it was I who helped her, nor did she at all know me, but she persisted in hymning the Treasure of the Light whom she had formerly seen and in whom she had believed, and she thought it was even He who had helped her (PS 82-84).

4. So it was when Arrogant's emanations knew that **she** had not been brought up from the Chaos, they turned round again all together, violently oppressing her. For this

---

[1] Copt: *alla anok ebol-hitoot m̄min m̄moi hn oumntnaēt ajn keleusis.*

[2] Now she is regarded as a spiritual person, somewhat freed from temptation, but really in constant danger of fresh falls.

reason, then, she spoke the Eighth Repentance,[1] saying: ". . . . I have set my hope on Thee, O Light; . . . be to me a Saviour . . . and lead me to the foot of Thy Light! . . . Thou hast brought me to a region that is not constrained, . . . and Thou shalt also release my power from the Chaos (PS 84)!"

5. It happened, then, when this lion-faced Power knew that the faithful Wisdom was not led altogether up from the Chaos, it came again with all Arrogant's other material emanations, and they again oppressed **her**. . . . She cried out in this same Repentance, saying: . . . " My power has begun to wane while I am in these afflictions, . . . and all the powers in me are shaken. . . . All the Rulers of the Height have counted me as Matter wherein no Light is;[2] . . . do not cause me to get contempt, for it is Thou to whom I have sung, O Light (PS 84-86)!"

6. After this when Arrogant's emanations pressed upon **her** in the Chaos, she uttered the Ninth Repentance,[3] saying: "O Light,

---

[1] Matthew refers this Eighth Repentance to Ps. 30; it falls into two halves.

[2] Copt: ñarkhōn tērou m̄pjise auopt etootou n̄nouhulē emn woein n̄hēts.

[3] The Ninth Repentance refers to Ps. 34, says James. The Soul now becomes more desperate and vengeful in her plea.

smite down those who have taken my power from me, ... for it is I who am Thy power and Thy light; come and save me! Let a great darkness cover my oppressors, ... let their power become like dust, and let Thy Messenger IEOU [1] smite them ... and throw them to the lower Darkness. For ... they have risen against me, lying about me and saying that I know the mystery of the Light on high, wherein I have believed, ... this which I do not know.[2] ... How long then, O Light, dost Thou let them oppress me, ... for I am the only one among the Invisibles who is in this region? ... Hasten, O Light, vindicate me and avenge me, ... for I desire the Thirteenth Aeon, the region of righteousness [3] (PS 89-92)!"

---

[1] As always, the name IEOU is marked with the sign that it is an abbreviation of *some* word not to be spoken, the four-lettered Tetragrammaton YHWH. PS 86 says: " IEOU, he is the Overseer of the Light," and GIG 122 speaks of " the Great Man who is the King of this whole Light-Treasure and whose name is IEOU, . . . the Father of the Light-Treasure."

[2] Her ambition and egoism have led her to think she already *knows* God, is in fact a Gnostic; this is not yet true, for she has not yet been crowned with the Light from on high, which comes on her as an act of Grace when she is ready.

[3] Here the Thirteenth Aeon is almost the 'Kingdom of Light' referred to in all the scriptures of the Mystery-Religions.

7. Again this lion-faced Power pressed upon her, wishing to take away every power in her; again she cried out to the Light, saying: "O Light, in whom from the first I have believed, for whose sake I have endured these great pains, help me (PS 98-99)!"

But not yet was her love wholly purified by the fire of suffering and loneliness; indeed, her faith is made to seem ridiculous and vain. Yet in her sorrow she clings to a blind faith in God's saving goodness, which will be extended to everyone who cries to Him, in the measure he can avail of it.

This leads Jesus himself, out of his own kindness, to draw her a little out of the worst sufferings of material life into a 'region' slightly freer from the cruelties of greed, ambition and self-esteem. She does not know it is he who helps, but rightly gives the thanks to God; when her foes again assail her, just because of this partial relief—"I am God's devotee, so He has to save me!"—she again begs Him to make it full freedom, admitting the total loss of spirituality in her through these assaults, and imploring rescue if only for the sake of God's own honour.

She is now led to pray for the utter humiliation and overthrow of self-esteem, for she has now the true inner humility on which alone spiritual life can be built, admitting that of herself she can do nothing. The memory of her lost glory again awakes the lower desire to be above the powers of manifestation, and now—as it were, afraid to say many words lest they rouse fresh pride and new desires—she merely cries for help to the One she trusts and loves.

56. Jesus Comes to Help Her

1. Now in that very hour her repentance was accepted from her; the First Mystery listened to her, and at His command I was sent and came to help her.[1] I led her up from the Chaos because she had repented and ... believed in the Light, and had endured these great troubles and ... dangers. She had been deluded by this divine Arrogant and not ... by anything other than a Light-Power, because of its likeness to the Light wherein she had believed. So for this reason was I sent ... to help her secretly.[2] But I did not at all go yet to the region of the Aeons, but went out among them all without any Power knowing—either those of the very Inmost or those of the very Outmost—save only this First Mystery (PS 99).

2. So it was, when I came to the Chaos to help her, she saw that I was understanding [3]

---

[1] It is her simple prayer, not the wordy hymns she has sent up hitherto, which at last wins God's help.

[2] Note the usual reference to the secrecy of Christ's help; every mystic will understand why this is stressed—who can *speak* of spiritual realities?

[3] Copt: *noeros*; *i.e.*, intelligent, intuitional, able to understand her need.

and shining brightly and was compassionate to her, for I was not arrogant like this lion-faced Power. . . . Then the faithful Wisdom saw that I was a myriad times brighter than it was, . . . and she knew that I was from the Height of heights, in whose Light she had believed from the first[1] (PS 99-100).

God accepts the soul surrendered to His will, humble and suppliant at His feet. He sends the Saviour to lift her up from materiality by a certain secret mystical aid, unknown even to the very Powers which close her in on every side. She at once recognises that the Saviour comes truly from the Light which "shines in the Darkness", because he is meek and gentle in his approach; she welcomes him as a messenger from the lost, yet still-loved, God on high.

57. The Four Last Appeals

1. So Wisdom took courage, and she spoke the Tenth Repentance,[2] saying: . . . "I have cried unto Thee, O Light, in my affliction, and Thou hast listened unto me (PS 100)!"

2. When this lion-faced Power saw how I had drawn near to the faithful Wisdom shining

---

[1] Seeing Christ's kindness and glory, the Soul at once knows he is from God, and now recognises the ambitious dreams of egoism for what they are—of the Pit.

[2] Peter refers this Tenth Repentance to Ps. 119.

most brilliantly, it grew still more furious, and poured out from itself other hosts of extremely mighty emanations. When this happened, then, she uttered the Eleventh Repentance,[1] ... saying: "Why has this mighty Power raised itself in evil ... like a sharp sword? ... So for this reason will the Light take away all their light; ... then these twenty-four emanations shall see what has befallen thee, O lion-faced-Power, and they will fear and not be disobedient (PS 101-102)."

3. After this I drew near to the Chaos ... to take away the light of that lion-faced Power. As I was a bright light, it was afraid and cried out to its god Arrogant[2] to help it. Then at that very time the divine Arrogant looked out of the Thirteenth Aeon,[3] he looked down into the Chaos, extremely wrathful and eager to help his lion-faced Power. And immediately this lion-faced Power surrounded Wisdom with all its emanations, wishing to take away all the light that was in **her** (PS 104-105).

[1] Salome refers this Eleventh Repentance to Ps. 51. The Soul is now bold enough to threaten the lower desires with extinction.

[2] Copt: *asōṣ ehrai epesnoute ṅauthadēs*. Or: "to its self-willed god".

[3] Arrogant seems quite at home in the "Thirteenth Aeon", sphere of the righteous Soul. The righteous are often egoists.

4. She cried out to the Height, calling on me to help her. Then it was ... she saw Arrogant very furious, and she was afraid. She spoke the Twelfth Repentance [1] ... in this way: " O Light, forget not my hymn, for ... they have hated me (only) because I sang praise to Thee ... and ... I have loved Thee! Let the darkness come down upon Arrogant, ... and let all his powers of his light in him be extinguished! ... Let the Receiver, the refiner of the lights,[2] refine all the lights that are in Arrogant and let him take them away! ... Because they have not spared me, but ... have wished to take away all my light in me, they loved to go down to the Chaos; they shall be in it, and not be brought up from now on! ... But Thou, O Light, have mercy upon me because of the mystery of Thy Name, and save me in the kindness of Thy grace (PS 105-107)."

5. Afterwards she cried out to me, ... saying: "O Light of the lights, I have transgressed in the Twelve Aeons and come down

---

[1] Andrew relates this Twelfth Repentance to Ps. 108.

[2] This is done by the Sun and Moon in GPM 25. The Soul, with the subtler 'body', is drawn out of Matter, purified and raised to heaven. *Cf.* GG 79 : 3.

from them; this is why I have uttered the Twelve Repentances, one for each Aeon. Now then, O Light of light, forgive my transgression that I have forsaken the regions of the Height and come down, and dwelt in the regions of the Chaos—for it is very great [1] (PS 110)."

6. Again she went on in the Thirteenth Repentance [2] saying: "Hear me hymning Thee, O Light of the lights, . . . so that the Thirteenth Repentance of the Thirteenth Aeon may be fulfilled—those I transgressed when I came down out of them. . . . . O Light, save me through Thy great Mystery and forgive my transgression; . . . give me the Baptism and put away my sins, and purify me from my transgression, . . . this lion-faced Power [3] (PS 110-111)!"

But her very welcome rouses in her new flames of personal ambition, a 'spiritual ambition' now, and

[1] To the Gnostics, this is the greatest sin for a very Child of God to turn from Him and plunge into this filthy life of materiality, seeking things of no value and forgetting Him.

[2] Martha explains this Thirteenth Repentance from Psalm 50; it begs for restoration to the lost Kingdom through the mystical baptism of grace, followed by the even greater mystery of absolution; cf. GG 81 : 3.

[3] The lion-faced Power, i.e., greed or ambition, is the transgression for which she suffers down here; it was the desire to make 'light-worlds' of her own—Aeons like those of the Father in GG 13 : 1—which drew her after the false light created by her own egoism.

she cries out in amazement at this unexpected result of the longed-for help, demanding the full enfeeblement of ambition, so that all other bad thoughts be led to submit.

Jesus proceeds to overthrow this selfishness, but in its self-defence it calls up the very sense of individuality, the ego representing God as the Monad within (GG 10). Thus reinforced, ambition plays havoc once again with the spiritual powers, and she now cries for the total destruction of the ego-sense itself, so that only the Divine Spark, round which it has grown as an excrescence, may remain. Once the One true Light pours His grace on her, it is sure that foolish thoughts glorifying anything else will perish.

She has suffered for each of the sins committed in being thus lured out of her proper sphere; each Zodiacal Sign has taught her its spiritual lesson; so now she can hope for full deliverance from the bondage of exterior manifestation in flesh. To qualify her for re-entry on that lost Kingdom of the Soul beyond form, she prays for full forgiveness and the mystical baptism with the Gnosis.

58. Arrogant Tries to Prevent her Escape

1. The time was come for her to be brought up from the Chaos, and on my own authority, without the First Mystery,[1] I brought a Light-Power out of myself and sent it down to . . . this upper region of the Chaos, until the command should come from this First Mystery that she be led altogether up from the Chaos.

---

[1] It is Christ who lifts the Soul from the depths into a somewhat more spiritual life as, say, a disciple of one of the exoteric schools.

THE SOUL REDEEMED

Then my Light-Power brought up the faithful Wisdom to the regions that are above the Chaos [1] (PS 112).

2. Then it was when Arrogant's emanations knew that **she** had been brought up, ... they pursued her even upwards, wishing to take her again to the lower regions of the Chaos.[2] ... She sang again and cried out to me,[3] saying: " Leave me not in the Chaos! ... Thou hast sent me Thy Light from Thyself and saved me and led me to the upper regions of the Chaos; ... let them not come to the upper regions to see me! But let a great darkness come down upon them, ... and let them not see me in the light of Thy Power. ... Because they have planned without Thy permission,[4] O Light, ... they could not carry away my light; because I have believed in the Light, I shall not fear, and the Light is my Rescuer (PS 112-114)! "

Jesus sends the Soul the Light that shines in the baptismal water, the light of grace (*cf.* Gospel of the

---

[1] *Cf.* the deathbed scene in GPM 75.

[2] Spiritual egoism, more dangerous than all else, now awakes in the Soul to drag her down from the slight progress already made.

[3] Salome refers this prayer to the Odes of Solomon, 5.

[4] *lit*: decree.

Hebrews), to raise her from the chaotic darkness of materiality. The old devil of self-esteem is again awake in her through this favour, and tries to drag her back with thoughts of her superiority to those who have not received such graces. In her misery at this discovery, she cries for protection from such temptations—which she is sure God cannot have willed to lie in the very sacramental life itself—and declares her confidence that this aid will come.

59. She is Crowned with Light

1. When Wisdom ceased saying this, . . . I made this Light-Power . . . a Crown of Light on her head,[1] so that Arrogant's emanations might henceforward be powerless against her. . . . Then all the evil matters in her were shaken, and they were all purified in her, they withered and fell into the Chaos, while the emanations of Arrogant watched them and rejoiced over them. Then the refined pure Light in Wisdom gave power to

---

[1] The Crown of Divine Light shakes out all the impure matter in her which could vibrate to lower desires; even the sight of this lower matter that was in her delights her latent egoism. The Odes of Solomon speak of this: "I was crowned by God, He is my living Crown (17: 1); the Lord is on my head like a Crown, and I shall not fall away from Him (1: 1)." "This is the Crown which the Universal Father has given the Individual, wherein there are 365 kinds and they shine filling the universe with incorruptible and inextinguishable light. This is the Crown which gives strength to every Power, and this is the Crown for which all the Immortals pray," adds GL 240.

the Light of my Power [1] which had become a crown for her head (PS 115).

2. It also happened, then, as it surrounded the pure light that was in Wisdom, and her pure light did not go out of the Crown of the Power [2] of this Light-Flame, lest Arrogant's emanations should snatch it away—then ... the pure light in Wisdom began to hymn ... my Light-Power that was a Crown on her head; it ... said: ... " Though all the matters shake, yet I shall not move, ... for the Light is with me, and I myself am with the Light [3] (PS 115-116)!"

Jesus then crowns the Soul with his Grace, so that egoistic pride may no longer prevail against her. This at once expels all that is impure in her, and it drops away into the evil realms where it belongs; her own innate goodness gives added strength to the grace she has received, and expresses itself in a song of joyful confidence in the God with whom she is now united.

---

[1] *i.e.*, she co-operates with grace. In GIG the spiritual Anointing, or Christing, comes after baptisms of Water, Fire and the Holy Spirit, and of the Absolution. These are elaborately described in that mysterious book.

[2] She keeps her thought on the real source of the grace received, lest egoism arise again in her and deprive her of its help.

[3] Mary, Mother of Jesus, refers this little hymn to the Odes 1. The Soul now realises its essential oneness with the Saviour, the Light so long worshipped from afar. *Cf.* The Gospel of Truth, 42: " The Father is in them, and they are in the Father "—a close parallel with Jn. 14: 11.

60. The Light-Stream Flows Down

1. Now in that hour was fulfilled the decree of all the trials assigned to Wisdom for the sake of completing (the command) of the First Mystery,[1] ... and the time came for her to be rescued from the Chaos and ... all the darknesses. For her Repentances had been accepted by the First Mystery. And He, that Mystery, sent me a great Light-Power from on high,[2] that I should help the faithful Wisdom and bring her up from (?) the Chaos. Then I looked above the Aeons and saw the Light-Power ... coming from the Aeons and hastening towards me—now I myself was above the Chaos—and another Light-Power came out of me that it too might help Wisdom;[3] and ... they met each other and

---

[1] The Soul has suffered enough to learn that God alone can save and that it is He alone on whom we must rely in every need.

[2] This is the 'sanctifying grace' of the Christians.

[3] To co-operate with the new Power, Truth rises from Jesus to blend with the Grace come down from God—as we are told is the meaning of Ps. 84:10-11. In the text, here follows an interesting story from some lost Gnostic apocryphal Gospel, about how Mary saw a phantasm from heaven uniting with Jesus as a Child; this is almost certainly the 'Twin' spoken of also by Mani; *cf.* GPM p. xxv.

THE SOUL REDEEMED

became a great Light-Stream, ... exceedingly bright [1] (PS 117-118).

2. I called Gabriel down from the Aeons together with Michael,[2] at the command of my Father, this first introverted Mystery;[3] I gave them the Light-Stream and had them go down to the Chaos to help Wisdom and to take the light-powers away ... from them and give them to **her** (PS 128-129).

3. And as soon as the Light-Stream was taken down to the Chaos, it shone extremely bright [4] ... and spread out in all their regions; and Arrogant's emanations ... were afraid all together. Then that Stream drew out of them every light-power that had been taken from the faithful Wisdom,[5] and **they** dared not lay hold on that Light-Stream in the dark Chaos, ... with (all) the skill of Arrogant who controls the emanations (PS 129).

---

[1] Jesus the Christ blends with God's Spirit at the 'Baptism', and becomes a mighty Stream of Grace, the Gnosis.

[2] Gabriel (*cf.* GG 45 : 2, 4) and Michael are the two greatest Archangels invoked even by the latest Gnostics of the 6th century.

[3] *i.e.*, He who ever contemplates Himself, because there is none other whom He can contemplate outside Himself.

[4] The brighter because of the surrounding darkness of physical matter.

[5] The power of God's grace restores to the Soul all her lost spiritual forces, so long at the disposal of mere egoism.

4. Then Gabriel and Michael led the Stream of Light over Wisdom's material body, and all her lights which had been taken from her were poured into her; and her material body received all (the) light,[1] and also all her powers in her received light. . . . Then the other light-powers . . . which Arrogant's emanations had not taken away rejoiced again and were filled with light; . . . they became again as they had been at first, and also increased in sensitivity to light.[2] Then all Wisdom's light-powers knew one another and were saved by my Light-Stream. . . . Then the Stream of Light . . . returned and went up from the Chaos (PS 129-131).

So comes the hour of her liberation, and God sends down a second 'Light-Power', the 'Holy Spirit' of GG 15 : 1, which joins the Power of the Christ to become a very River of Light. The two mighty Angels of the Throne bear this down to the Soul in the lower world, and its glory shines so brightly it robs all egoistic thoughts of their power. Then they pour this mighty Grace on the Soul's spiritual body; all her original spirituality returns, she is filled with 'light' again, and saved from the darkness of materiality.

[1] God's power now covers even the very body of the Blessed with a radiant spirituality, the *tejas* of the Hindus.

[2] *i.e.*, there is now the power to recognise Spirit in all its activities; we have in GIG 41: "O Light that is in the light which has lighted all our hearts."

61. Arrogant Attacks Again

1. Then after these things, when Arrogant's emanations knew that, ... and also saw the faithful Wisdom was bright as she had been from the first, they were enraged at **her**, and again cried out to their Arrogant to come and help them and take away once more the powers in Wisdom [1] (PS 135).

2. Then Arrogant sent from on high in the Thirteenth Aeon another great Light-Power; it came down to the Chaos like a flying arrow, ... and ... the emanations ... took great courage, and they again pursued Wisdom ... and oppressed her. ... One of them changed into the form of a great snake,[2] another again took the form of a seven-headed basilisk,[3] yet another took a

---

[1] When the Soul realises it has now a spiritual outlook, egoism naturally stirs once more.

[2] I cannot identify the sinful thoughts specified by these 'emanations'. In PS 254-258, pitilessness, wrath, cursing and thieving are associated with a punishing demon with dragon face, and slander and adultery go with a lion-faced one, while murder is punished by a demon with crocodile's face. But as in the same context Ialdabaoth is linked with robbery, strife, ignorance and sloth (*i.e.*, fiery passion and dark ignorance, as in GG 52 : 4), I think we cannot press this too far. See also the Cyriacus Prayer in the Appendix.

[3] Is this monster in any way connected with the seven-headed Hydra? There are also seven capital sins, and it may refer to these.

dragon-form. Further, the other first Power of Arrogant which was lion-faced, together with all his other very many emanations, they too came together and oppressed the faithful Wisdom; they brought her again to the lower regions of the Chaos and again terrified her greatly (PS 135-136).

Once more the help she has received awakes in her, swift as an arrow on the wing, a sense of superiority; again the old enemy afflicts her, taking various fearful forms, variants of the Ancient Snake of Eden (*cf.* GG 29 : 1). Once more ambition for the separate self awakes in her, and by all these thoughts she is again dragged down to the former depths of misery.

62. Adamas Joins In

1. She ran from them, and came to the upper regions of the Chaos, and the emanations of Arrogant ran after her and alarmed her exceedingly.... Afterwards Adamas the Tyrant, who was also enraged with **her** because she longed to go to the Light of these lights, who is above them all, looked out from the Twelve Aeons.... He saw Arrogant's emanations pressing on the faithful Wisdom until they took all lights in her [1] (PS 136-137).

[1] Frightened by these new egoistic thoughts, the Soul flees as far upwards as she can go; and there she has also to deal with the wickedness innate in all human nature.

2. Now it happened when the Power of Adamas came down to the Chaos,[1] ... he threw Wisdom down, and ... all the other very many emanations of Arrogant surrounded **her** all at one time, wishing to carry off her powers once more.... She cried out again to the Light, ... saying: " O Light, it is Thou who hast helped me; let Thy Light come down on me ... and it is Thou who shalt rescue me (PS 137) !"

Vainly using her own strength, she tries to escape from these evil thoughts. But the badness still inherent in her, the ' old man '—can we call him ' Original Sin '?—overthrows her while robbed of her spiritual strength. In her fear of this constantly reawakening egoism, she cries almost in despair so that the God who has helped her once might now save her altogether from herself.

63. The Light Prevails

1. Then again, at my Father's command, ... I sent Gabriel and Michael with this great Light-Stream, that they might help the faithful Wisdom; and I bade Gabriel and Michael

---

[1] Note that Adamas, whom we have already met in GG 48 : 2, does not himself come down; there is no need for personal devils to intervene in every fight—there is in every soul a ' fifth column ' ready for treachery at all times.

take **her** upon their hands,[1] that her feet might not touch the darkness below, and ... guide her in the regions of the Chaos. ... Then again all Arrogant's emanations and the emanation of Adamas saw the Light-Stream was exceedingly bright, ... and they were afraid and left Wisdom.[2] Then the great Light-Stream surrounded **her** on every side ... and became a Light-Crown upon her head [3] (PS 137-138).

2. She took very great courage and ... feared them no more, ... nor did she even tremble at the demon-Power of Adamas which had come out of the Aeons. ... Then the faithful Wisdom remained in the midst of the Light, and all the emanations of Arrogant ... could not bear the great light of the Stream which was a Crown on her head; ... rather, they all fell on one another ... and could do nothing evil to **her** because she was trusting in the Light [4] (PS 138-139).

[1] This time she is herself lifted up, as in Ps. 91 : 11-12.

[2] Egoism and latent sinfulness cannot fight against God's active grace.

[3] For the second time; this will be the Second Initiation spoken of by the modern Theosophists.

[4] Nothing can now separate her from grace, nor can egoism arise in her mind.

THE SOUL REDEEMED

3. Next, at my Father's command, . . . I myself went down to the Chaos, shining exceedingly. I made my way to this lion-faced Power which was shining brightly, and I took all its light that was in it, and I held fast all the emanations of Arrogant to prevent them from going to their region, that is, the Thirteenth Aeon, any more.[1] Then I took away the power in all of **them**, and they all fell into the Chaos, being powerless (PS 139-140).

4. Then I led out the faithful Wisdom on the right of Gabriel and Michael, and this great Light-Stream entered into them again, and she beheld with her eyes her enemies, . . . how I had taken away the light-power from them.[2] So I brought **her** out of the Chaos, while she trampled on Arrogant's snake-faced emanation[3] and also . . . **on that** with seven-headed basilisk face;[4] . . . and trod upon

---

[1] Christ himself now takes away human ambition and subdues the ego sense to its proper field. It then "falls down".

[2] This final triumph of the Soul over dark powers corresponds with the Third Initiation, the Transfiguration, whereat the Conqueror has an 'Angel' on each side, as in the canonical Gospels Jesus has Moses and Elijah.

[3] The 'snake-faced' may be a symbol of sex-desire or lust, which stands between the Soul and all true Gnosis (*cf.* GG 84 : 1-2).

[4] *Cf.* : "He who has by my hands overthrown the seven-headed dragon, and set me at its roots that I might destroy his seed"

this lion-faced Power and this dragon-face. I made **her** remain standing on the emanation ... which was basilisk-faced, ... for it exceeded them all in its evils. Then I, the First Mystery, stood beside her,[1] and took away all the powers that were in it, and I destroyed its whole matter so that henceforth no seed might arise in it [2] (PS 140).

The two Angels again bring the sacramental River of Grace, at the very sight of which glory the Soul's enemies flee away, and she is crowned therewith again. This gives her full faith as she " abides in the Light " of God Himself, where none can touch her. Jesus himself then goes down like the Hero in GPM 21: 8 to the lower planes and deprives ambition of all its strength, putting the sense of a separate self under control, so that such thoughts may no longer defile the region proper to the Soul; he makes her trample on her enemies, while he takes away their power and destroys them, for the Soul must herself fight for her own freedom.

64. Wisdom's Thanksgiving

1. She cried out again, saying: " I have been rescued in the Chaos and loosed from

---

(Odes of Sol. 22 : 5). Herakles found the seven-headed Hydra most hard to fight, for its lopped heads were continually renewed. Copt: *ńtos de nesjoor eroou tērou hn nespethoou.*

[1] *or*: over it, *i.e.*, the basilisk-faced Power.

[2] Hereafter sin has no more power over the Soul.

the bonds of the Darkness; I have come to Thee, O Light, for Thou hast become Light on every side of me,[1] ... and the emanations of Arrogant which opposed me Thou hast hindered with Thy Light.[2] ... Now hast Thou covered me with the Light of Thy Stream and hast purified in me all my evil matters. ... I have become encouraged by Thy light, ... and have shone in Thy great power, for it is Thou who savest always (PS 148-149)!"

2. And she continued hymning me..., saying: "I hymn Thee at whose decree Thou hast led me out of the high Aeon ... and brought me down to the lower regions;[3] ... and Thou hast scattered far from me Arrogant's emanations which pressed on me and were enemies to me;[4] and to all my Limbs which

---

[1] The singer of the Odes of Solomon, 21 : 2, says: " I have laid aside the Darkness and clothed myself with Light." From the dark chaos of physical matter the Soul has been restored to the radiance of the Spirit.

[2] The very sight of God's glory overcomes the charms of egoism.

[3] As often in Coptic, there is here some confusion in the pronouns; at God's decree the Saviour has imperilled the Soul; as taught also in GG 54 : 2, all our woes, even the fall into Matter, are God's will. In the glad recognition of this lies our peace.

[4] God's will now ordains the overthrow of evil forces and the restoration of the Soul to her own plane.

had no light in them Thou hast given a refined light out of the Light on high. Thou hast placed in me the light of Thy Stream, and I have become light refined. . . . O Light, Thou hast rescued me and brought my light up from the Chaos, Thou hast saved me from those who went down to the Darkness (PS 153-160)."

3. These things also she spoke, . . . she went on . . . in this hymn; she said: " The Light has become Saviour for me and has changed for me my darkness into light; He has rent the Chaos that surrounded me and girded me with light![1] . . . My power, sing to the Light, and forget not all the powers of the Light! . . . All powers that are in me, sing to the Name of His holy Mystery . . . which has filled thee with refined light, and thy beginning shall be renewed as an Invisible of the Height!"[2] These words was the faithful Wisdom singing because she was rescued

[1] In this sentence there is a certain literary beauty; Copt: *afkte pakake nai euoein, auō afpeh pekhaos etkōte eroi, afmort ñouwoein.* Martha relates this passage to Ps. 29 : 10-11, as Mary related the previous sentence to Ps. 29 : 1-3. Of this section paragraphs 1 and 2 were related by Thomas and Matthew respectively to the Odes of Solomon 25 and 22.

[2] *i.e.*, the glory which was the Soul's before the world began becomes her own again; she is the ' Son ' of Jn. 17 : 5.

and remembered all the things I had done for her [1] (PS 162).

The Soul bursts into a paean of victory, knowing she is in God's very Being, enfolded in the Light she has always loved from afar, and freed from all the forms of darkness. It is He who brought her down, that she might find Him even in the depths; it is He again who has led her up, so that now she is herself all Light within and without. She calls on everything in her to adore the saving God who is even now restoring her to the lost inheritance above.

65. She Rejoices in Her Ascent

1. I took the faithful Wisdom and led her up to a region below the Thirteenth Aeon, and I gave her a new mystery of the Light, one not belonging to her Aeon, the region of the Invisibles. Then I gave her also a hymn of the Light,[2] so that the Aeon-Rulers might not henceforth be able to act against her, and I placed her in that region until I should come after her and take her to her (own) region that is above (PS 164).

2. She spoke again in this hymn,[3] saying it in this way: " I have faithfully believed in

---

[1] Mary compares this song of joy with Ps. 102 : 1-5.

[2] This is the ' new song ' given the Blessed to sing in heaven for evermore, spoken of in Rev. 14 : 3.

[3] Andrew equates this song with Ps. 39 : 1-2.

the Light, and He has remembered me and hearkened to my hymn. . . . Now then, O Light, all the Rulers will see what Thou hast done with me, and fear, and believe in the Light!" This hymn she kept repeating, . . . rejoicing that she had been brought out of the Chaos and led to the regions below the Thirteenth Aeon [1] (PS 164-165).

The Soul is now led to the lower boundary of her own realm and taught how to repel any attack from the lords of destiny just below her, till in the last days Jesus returns to restore her to her home. She replies in joyful confidence that, seeing what he has done for her, no one hereafter will dare oppose God's will or try to drag her down again.

66. Her Doubts are Solved

1. So it was when I brought her to the region below the Thirteenth of the Aeons, I was about to go to the Light and depart from her.[2] She said to me: . . . " Adamas the Tyrant [3] will be knowing that . . . he who is

---

[1] She must wait on the 'Boundary' until the consummation of the ages when *every* Soul of the Light has been restored, as in GG 19 : 2.

[2] Copt: *aiei nabōk epwoein ṅtalo haros*. Now the hour of the last triumph over the darkness, won through such suffering and destitution, draws near.

[3] Egoism, and all its derivative thoughts, have been subdued, and now the danger comes only from her own inner human weakness.

to save me is not (here); . . . and they will all come and press upon me at once, and take away all my light from me. . . . So now, . . . my Light, take the power of their light from them, so that they may be unable to oppress me from now on (PS 166)."

2. I answered her, saying: "My Father has not yet bidden me . . . take their light from them,[1] but I shall seal the regions of Arrogant . . . and . . . Adamas, with their Rulers, so that not one of them shall be able to fight with thee until the time is come . . . when three times [2] are completed (PS 166-167)."

3. The faithful Wisdom replied; she said to me: "O Light, how shall I know when it is the three times, so that I may be glad in myself and rejoice (PS 167)?"

4. And I answered, I said to her: "When thou seest the Gate to the left of the Treasure of the Great Light opened to the Thirteenth

---

[1] In effect she asks to be divinised, but Jesus says the time for that will come only after the 'dark night' has passed over her, during which she will be under his protection.

[2] The 'three times' are the past—when Light and Dark were separate; the present—when they are mixed; and the future—when they will be separated again; Mani and Zarathushtra both taught this. When all these three are at an end, when Time is no more, the Soul is finally merged in the Light of God.

Aeon, . . . those who are in all the Aeons will know because of the great light there will be in all their regions.[1] . . . They will not venture anything evil against thee until the three times are completed; but thou wilt there have the right to go down to their Twelve Aeons when it pleases thee, and to return again and go to thy region . . . wherein thou art now. But thou wilt not have the right to enter the Gate of the Height which is in the Thirteenth Aeon, so as to enter thine (own) region whence thou hast come. Rather . . . will Arrogant and all his Rulers again oppress thee to let them take the light from thee. . . . Now then, . . . hymn to the Light, and I . . . will come speedily to thee [2] . . . and go down to their regions and take away their light from them, and come to this region where I have left thee . . . until I take thee to thy region whence thou didst come (PS 167-169)."

---

[1] *i.e.*, when spiritual light pours forth everywhere unchecked, and the " glory of God covers the earth as the waters the sea ", then will humanity become divine.

[2] Jesus warns the Soul of the last trial, the 'Crucifixion' of Theosophical books, which precedes the glory of Nirvāṇa; in that trial Christ will come speedily (Rev 22 : 20) to answer her cry for aid. The ego must die that the Self may shine.

5. So it was ... she rejoiced with great joy, while I for my part placed her in the region below the Thirteenth Aeon; I went to the Light and left her (there) (PS 169).

Seeing her Saviour about to leave her, the Soul doubts lest the old human frailty stir once more in his absence and give her further trouble; she begs him to free her from this and make her all divine. Jesus assures her that she has nothing to fear until when past, present and future have all gone and Time is no more. This will be when Heaven's doors are flung wide and Light ineffable pours out on every plane. Meanwhile the Soul will be free to go up or down among all the planes below where she is now installed; she may even enter into incarnation once again if she will, fearing nothing from her old enemies till the end. When the attack is then renewed, she has but to call on him, and he will at once deprive her foes of all their strength and take her safely home. With this she is satisfied. It is the promise with which the Christian Revelation ends—"Even so come, Lord Jesus!"

67. Evil Makes its Last Attack

1. While I was in the world of mankind, ... the time was completed.[1] ... Adamas looked out from the Twelve Aeons, he looked down to the regions of the Chaos; he saw his demon-Power which had no light in it at all;

---

[1] The speaker assumes the end of time to have been while Jesus was on the earth, the common assumption of the first two generations of Christians. Time ceases when the Self manifests.

... and he saw it was dark and could not go to his region, the Twelve Aeons.[1] Adamas again remembered the faithful Wisdom and was most extremely furious with her, thinking that it was she who had held his Power fast in the Chaos and ... taken its light from it [2] (PS 169-170).

2. Then was he greatly embittered; ... he evolved from himself a dark emanation, and another mighty one, chaotic and evil, so that by them he might terrify Wisdom. He also created a region of darkness within his region, so that he might constrain Wisdom therein.[3] He also took hosts of Rulers,[4] who ran after Wisdom to bring her to this dark Chaos which he had created, and to oppress her in that region. Then these two dark emanations terrified her ... until they should take all her light from her, and take it to the

---

[1] Humanity is a poor thing, powerless and unable even to rule its own fate.

[2] The aspiring Soul is naturally blamed for this exposure to human weakness when apart from God. The worldly look on religious folk as insulting human dignity when they pay devout homage to the unseen Divinity.

[3] The darkness and chaos, ignorance and confusion, of mere human nature now try to strip the Soul once more of her spiritual glory and to imprison her once again in the dark physical body.

[4] *i.e.*, the lords of 'karma', or the planetary forces which control man's horoscope and destiny.

great dark lower Chaos, and insert it in his dark chaotic Power so that it might perhaps be able to come to his region [1] (PS 170-171).

So at the end of time [2] Jesus was born in the world, and the evil innate therein remembered that it was the human Soul, empowered by God's Light, which had bound it fast and robbed it of all its strength. Two terrible thoughts are put out to capture the Soul—Cruelty and Ignorant Confusion?—and a prison is made for her in the depths. So frightened is Wisdom that she might well have lost her strength and courage to this evil force and let it grow in power.

68. Wisdom Again Cries for Help

1. So it came to pass when they chased the faithful Wisdom, she again cried out: ... "O Light of the lights, I have trusted in Thee; save me from all these Rulers who ran after me! ... Adamas has raged against me, saying these things: 'It is thou who hast held my Power fast in the Chaos!' Now then, ... if it is I who have done this, all these Rulers who ran after me shall take away my light

---

[1] This plan was frustrated, for the Soul crowned with Light can no more be enslaved in Matter. An Arhat may be born, but only as a liberator of others.

[2] Based on Mt. 24 : 34 and Jn. 21 : 22, the strange idea that the world was about to end even in the first Christian generation, appearing here, proves a very early source to have been used by the author of "Pistis Sophia".

from me ... and put my power in the Chaos [1] (PS 171-172)!"

2. She turned back to see whether Adamas had retreated with his Rulers, to go back to their Aeon, and she saw them pursuing her. She turned to them and said to them: [2] ... "Very well, the Light is a Vindicator, and He is a mighty one; [3] ... and this is the time of which He told me. So then if you ... cease not to run after me, the Light shall ... take your light that is in you, and you will become dark [4] (PS 173)!"

3. She looked at the region of Adamas, and saw the dark chaotic region he had created, and she also saw the two dark and very mighty emanations; ... she was afraid and cried out to the light (PS 173-174).

In her new distress the Soul cries out as she has been bidden, denying that it was she who had prevailed over her foes; by this humble admission of the truth

---

[1] She knows it is God's power, not her own, which has vanquished all evil thoughts. If it had been she, she would be willing to surrender to them once for all. James refers this passage to Ps. 7 : 1-7.

[2] Finding that her appeal has not checked the assailants, she turns to threats.

[3] Copt: *tenou ce ourefti ēp pe pwoein, auō oujōōre pe.*

[4] As light is life, so is dark death; what cannot be seen because of the darkness is considered as having no real existence.

she thus renounced the egoism of the self which had so long troubled her. When her ambition still tried to drag her down, she denounced it with full faith; it thought to ruin her but would itself be wholly destroyed by her Redeemer. This she said when she realised the miserable state to which her human weakness, unaided, would have brought her.

69. She Returns Home

1. After all these things I took the faithful Wisdom and led her into the Thirteenth Aeon,[1] ... I entered into the region of the Twenty-four Invisibles. ... Then they trembled with a great trembling; they looked, and they saw Wisdom was with me, and they knew her. But me they did not recognise, who I was, but their thought of me was like an emanation of the Land of the Light[2] (PS 176).

2. So it came to pass when Wisdom saw her fellows, the Invisibles, she rejoiced in great joy, ... she wanted to proclaim the wonders I had wrought with her below in the land of mankind until I rescued her. She

---

[1] Christ no longer leaves her to Angels; he himself brings her homewards.

[2] The Mind alone can know God and the deified Christ (*cf.* GG 13:2); even the highest Powers in heaven can recognise only the liberated human Soul.

came up into the midst of the Invisibles and hymned me among them, saying:[1] . . . " O Light, I shall reveal to Thee how Thou hast saved me, and how Thy wonders have taken place in the human race![2] . . . Thou hast smashed the high Gates of the Darkness together with the mighty bolts of the Chaos,[3] . . . and I have come up through the Gates of the Chaos [4] (PS 176-177)! "

And then the faithful Soul, who in all her woes had clung only to the God she had always loved, came to the happy end of all her troubles. Jesus led her by the hand home to her own realm of the Unseen Ones (GPM 79), and when she saw them she rejoiced exceedingly and began to tell of all the wonders the Lord had worked in the world—overcoming its darkness and confusion, liberating her from the prison of flesh, and bringing her once more home into the eternal Land of infinite Light and Joy.

---

[1] This hymn of rejoicing is parallel to that in GH 7, 47; Philip compares it with Ps. 106 : 1-14.

[2] " He raised me up by His love and lifted me up by the greatness of His beauty," says the Odes of Solomon, 29 : 3.

[3] Elements derived from the old story of the ' harrying of hell ' found in the Revelation of Bartholomew, the Gospel of Nicodemus, and in other Gnostic books.

[4] The last scene of the story, which should tell of the Soul's Marriage with Christ her Spouse (cf. GG 19 : 2), is here omitted— possibly because in this particular school such teachings were not put in writing for general readers.

CHAPTER TEN

THE SONG OF THE PEARL[1]

Here we have in a lovely Syriac poem, in all likelihood written by Bardaisan himself, the same enthralling story of the Soul's descent into the world and, roused by the Call from on high, its glorious Rising again into the Kingdom of the Father. The Pearl he is to seek in Egypt, the body, is certainly the Gnosis, and the terrible Serpent is the passion of egoism—within which lies the truth (*cf.* GG 87). In this version, as in that of Wisdom, it is God who ordains the Soul's going forth, and also her eventual return home.

The story may also be compared with that of the Pearl in Griffith's Demotic Magical Papyrus, London and Leyden,[2] and with the countless fairy stories built upon the same eternal Quest. "This (Wisdom) is the essence of Souls", says Hip. Ref. 6 : 29, and 1 Enoch (42 : 2) tells us: "Wisdom went forth to make her dwelling among the children of men and found no resting-place; Wisdom returned to her place and took her seat among the Angels." Wisdom is here God's Son.

[1] In the footnotes to this Chapter I have made much use of Mead's intuitional comments in his "The Hymn of the Robe of Glory".

[2] See also John Bunyan's famous allegory, "The Pilgrim's Progress".

70. The Soul is Sent Forth

1. When I was a little child [1]
    and lived [2] in my Kingdom,[3] my Father's House,[4]
And in the riches and glories [5]
    of my parents took my delight,
From the East, our Homeland,[6]
    my parents provided me [7] and sent me forth,
And from the wealth of our Treasury
    they had tied up a bundle for me.[8]
It was large [9] but light [10]
    that I might carry it without help:

---

[1] *i.e.*, a tiny Spark of the One Light, as Haase shows. That this poem is not primarily Christian is held by this scholar: " Als Verfasser kann man deshalb mit mehr Recht einen unbekannten, nicht-christliche Dichter ansehen " (p. 66).

[2] *lit*: caused to rest.

[3] The Thirteenth Aeon, the Kingdom of the Light where the Soul belongs.

[4] *i.e.*, the home of the Higher Self, the Wisdom Above.

[5] In the fullness and beauty of Divine Life.

[6] The Land of Light, where the Sun rises.

[7] *lit*: they took abundantly.

[8] The Soul brought with him the fruits of past experience—both his own and that of the Race Above—treasures of the spiritual Mind held in the heart or memory.

[9] *or*: precious (Syr: *sgyaa*).

[10] Because non-material.

Gold of the highlands [1] was there,
and silver of Jazzak the Great,[2]
With Indian rubies [3]
and agates from the House of Qashan [4]
(HRG 1-7).
2. Then they girded me with adamant [5]
which was stronger than iron,
And stripped me of the brightness [6]
which in their love they had made for me,
And my radiant [7] mantle
that was measured and woven to my stature.[8]
Then they made with me a contract
and wrote it in my heart that it be not forgotten:

---

[1] Either 'Gīlā', Media (*Jilyā*); or, with the Gk. "land of the higher ones" (*ᵃaliyā*). The Gk. here reads: "Gold of the great treasures uncoined".

[2] *i.e.*, Takht-i-Suleiman in Azerbaijan, where was a famous Parsi temple.

[3] India was anciently famed for her rubies found near the modern Golconda.

[4] Bevan says this may be the Koshān of Tabari, a hilly region north of Ispahan in Persia.

[5] *Cf.* App. I: 5 : 4, the 'plasm' of man, his body.

[6] Syr: *zhyta*; it refers to the Gnostic Robe of Light; the Gk. has: "Robe of gold tissue incrusted with jewels".

[7] or: purple, iridescent—referring to the rich colours of the human aura, says Mead. The Syriac word for mantle is the Latin '*toga*'.

[8] *i.e.*, exactly fitting his own spiritual quality; *cf.* GG. 76 : 1.

Saying: " If thou goest down to Egypt [1]
and bringest the one Pearl [2]
Kept there in the midst of the Sea
that contains the roaring Serpent,[3]
Thou shalt resume thy brightness
and thy mantle laid over it,[4]
And with thy Brother, our Viceroy,[5]
thou shalt be heir in our Kingdom "
(HRG 8-15).

From Heaven we come forth, as Wordsworth reminds us in his lovely Ode, and God equips us with all we need for the long pilgrimage in the lower planes; we have to leave our spiritual glory behind us in His home, till we have earned the right to it once

---

[1] Egypt is the body of flesh, to which at God's will the Soul descends.

[2] *i.e.*, the living Gnosis, self-realisation, which is the finding of God. Mead adds that the spiritual man steals from within the shell of flesh the gem produced by the disease of self-will, or egoism.

[3] Gk. reads: " the Serpent, the Swallower "; this is Typhon, the violent passions of the form-plane. Lipsius thinks the text corrupt here, and wants to read *serpens venēnum spirans*; it is the hissing Serpent or Wind of GG 5 : 9.

[4] Wright here adds *anta*, to read: " with which thou art contented "; this to me seems needless. In the Ginzā (211 : 5-10) we read: " When thy measure is full for thee, thou wilt come clothing thyself in thy stola of splendour and covering thyself with thy great turban of light, and they will put around thee thy fadeless Crown; thou wilt sit on thy throne of rest." In the Kauṣītaki-Upaniṣad 1, the ascending Soul is given garlands and robes and adorned as God, we are told.

[5] *i.e.*, the Christ.

more (GG 46 : 1). From the dark Sea of Matter, the *samsāra-sāgaram* of Sanskrit poetry, we have to take the Pearl of true God-knowledge, of *jñānam*, which is guarded by the monster of self-will and individuality. Bringing this prize home with her, the Soul will inherit eternal life in God's realm.

71. He Descends to the World

1. I threw off the East and went down,
   two Messengers[1] being with me,
Because the way was risky and hard
   and I very young to tread it.
I passed by the borders of Maishan,[2]
   the mart of Eastern merchants,
And came to the land of Bābel [3]
   and entered within Sarbug's walls;[4]
I went down to Egypt's borders
   and my companions parted from me.

---

[1] We have here the Persian word *perwānak*, letter-carriers; Mead says they are Rays from the Divine Mind; they may be the twin guardian angels.

[2] Under the Parthians Maishan, near the mouths of Tigris and Euphrates, was a separate kingdom. To the Mental Plane souls bring the merchandise of each life's trading—an idea prominent in Mani and the Mandean books, also.

[3] The confusion of the emotions on the lower astral plane, Babylon.

[4] Perhaps the etheric level, formed before physical birth in the world. The name 'Sarbug' is not sure; it may be Hierapolis in North Syria, on the highway from Babylon to Egypt.

I hastened straight to the Serpent;
near him I took up my dwelling,[1]
Till he should slumber and sleep
and from him I could snatch my Pearl[2]
(HRG 16-22).

2. Now I was single, I was alone,
I was a stranger[3] to the sons of my kin.
A son of my Race, a son of freedom,
from the Easterners I saw there,
A youth fair and gracious,
a son of anointing[4] . . . . .
. . . .
then he came to me and was a companion;
I made him my intimate,
a comrade with whom I shared my Merchandise;[5]

---

[1] Persian: *aspanzh*, inn; Gk. has 'den' or 'hole', indicating contempt for the prison-body.

[2] The Soul vainly hopes passion will of itself subside and let the Pearl of true wisdom be taken away.

[3] In all the mystery-religions the Soul incarnate is called an 'alien' to the Race Above, its true kindred.

[4] Syr: *br-msha*; Wright thinks: 'Son of oilmen', but that gives no sense here; the word is clearly that known to us as Messiah, 'anointed' of the Lord, *i.e.*, he is one 'consecrated' to the spiritual life. Mead thinks this is the Conscience; perhaps. The break in metre shows there is here a break in text.

[5] *i.e.*, spiritual knowledge.

He warned me [1] against the Egyptians
  and against their ways of uncleanness[2]
    (HG 23-28).
3. Then I dressed in raiment like theirs,
  lest they insult me[3] that I came from afar,
That I might take away the Pearl
  and arouse the Serpent against me.
But somehow or other
  they noticed I was not their countryman;
So they dealt with me with their cunning
  and fed me also their food.
I forgot that I was a son of Kings[4]
  and served the King of their land;
Then I forgot the Pearl
  for which my parents had sent me,

---

[1] The text, apparently by some error, reads: "I warned him", which does not cohere well with the story. I have ventured to correct this.

[2] Egypt is the body, as we learn in App. I: 5 : 5, and the Egyptians are those spiritually ignorant, the 'fleshly men'. Speaking of the Peratae, Hip. Ref. 5 : 11 has: "All who are ignorant are Egyptians; and this is the departure from Egypt, the body." The 'unclean ways' include sexuality.

[3] In the 2nd c. Acts of Phocas we have: "Keep my spirit ... lest the Dragon breathe on me, lest his feet trample me, for he could not by gold or silver persuade me to lose the precious Pearl." Noldeke reads *nkrwhy*, "lest they should recognise me" here.

[4] This is the 'oblivion' referred to in GG 79 : 1 and in most parallel works; it is the spiritual *ajñānam* which it is the function of Gnosis to disperse; of it the Gospel of Truth has much to say of interest.

And under the load of their foods[1]
I lay in a heavy sleep[2] (HRG 29-35).

The Soul is escorted by two guards: Conscience and Revelation, or in another version Michael and Gabriel, and passes by the busy Mental Plane (Maishan) and the confused planes of the Astral (Bābel); passing through the etheric densification of matter (Sarbug's walls), he comes to the physical, and is there born into a body of flesh (Egypt), whither the spiritual companions cannot follow him. He at once hastens to the 'arrogant' Serpent of egoism or separativeness, in whose vicinity he takes up his abode.

In his loneliness, a spirit imprisoned in matter, he rejoices to find there a single spiritual man, who seems to play the part of a Guru, having been initiated in the Gnosis, and for a time trusts to this friend's guidance, but then becomes too clever to take the advice of another. He pretends to be a man of the world like those around him, hoping thus to deceive the watchful Serpent of the ego and win the Gnosis. But the worldly folk soon find out he is none of theirs and, like the folk of Vanity Fair in Bunyan's wonderful version of this same story, do all they can to overcome his resolution. As these martyred Faithful, so the men of 'Egypt' poison the Prince with their worldliness and plunge him in a drunken sleep, wherein he forgets his real nature and his mission (*cf.* GPM 49 : 1-3).

---

[1] *Cf.* PS 282: "And the babe eats of the delights of the world of the Rulers"; nourished on fleshly delights, the Soul is weighed down with heavy matter (*cf.* GG 81 : 2). The book of Wisdom (9 : 15) says: "The corruptible body presses down the Soul" —a commonplace in Hermes, Mani, and the Platonists.

Here the Gk. word is used: *trophai-hōn*; the Soul thus becomes carnal and gross. *Cf.* PS 281: "the very heavy weight of their forgetfulness".

[2] The "drunken sleep" of all parallel scriptures, *e.g.*, GH 8 : 2.

72. The Father Sends a Reminder

1. But all these things that befell me
    my parents saw[1] and grieved for me;
Then was announced in our Kingdom
    that all the people to our Gate should hasten—
Kings and Chiefs of Parthia [2]
and all the magnates of the East.[3]
Then they wove on my behalf a plan
    that I be not in Egypt forsaken;
And they wrote to me a Letter [4]
    and every great one wrote his name on it
    (HRG 36-40).

2. "From thy Father the King of Kings,
    and thy Mother the Queen of the East,[5]

---

[1] Providence, watching all, prepares for the Soul's liberation at the due time.

[2] The naming of this State, which perished in A.D. 226, proves that our poem is certainly older than this; there is no reason at all to put it later than the time of Bardaisan (155-223), and it dates probably in the earlier part of his life.

[3] I cannot accept Mead's idea that the Princes are "facets of the King", *i.e.*, prior lives expressing man's spiritual mind. To me, they are simply the heavenly Powers, the 'Invisibles' of GG 69 : 2, etc.

[4] This 'Letter' is the Gospel of GG 26, the Call of GPM, the Preaching of GH 8 : 1-2.

[5] GG 93 and 97 stress the feminine side of Deity; no Mediterranean religion even in our own day, can ignore the early trinity of Father, Mother, Child.

And from thy Brother, our Viceroy,[1]
    to thee, our Son in Egypt, peace!
Up and arise [2] from thy sleep
    and hear the words of our Letter! [3]
Remember thou art the Son of Kings;
    see the slavery and whom thou servest!
Recollect the Pearl
    for which thou didst hasten to Egypt!
Think of thy brightness,
    and recall thy glorious mantle,
Which thou shalt wear as adornment
    that thy name be read in the list of Heroes; [4]
Then with thy Brother, our Viceroy,
    thou shalt be with him in our Kingdom!"
    (HRG 41-48).

    The Divine is watching all that happens to the Prince and calls on all Heaven's resources to unite, that he may be reawakened to his task—much as the Aeons in GG 15:2 unite to bring forth Jesus, the Perfect Fruit. The Gospel is sent down as a great Call (GPM 4:8) to rouse the Slumberer to memory of his royal spirituality and of why he has been sent down to the world,

---

[1] *lit.* ' Second ', *i.e.*, next in rank, *i.e.*, the Christ.

[2] The word literally means ' shrink ' *i.e.*, withdraw (from ignorance).

[3] The Letter reminds the Soul of his real spiritual origin and purpose; his coming to the world is not to luxuriate in ' Egyptian food ', the delights of materiality, but in the Gnosis of God.

[4] *Cf.* Rev. 3 : 5.

promising him also a share in God's glory on his victorious return.

73. He Fulfils His Mission

1. As for my Letter, it was a letter
   the King had sealed with his right hand
(Safe) from the evil sons of Bābel
   and the fierce demons of Sarbug.[1]
It flew in an eagle's likeness,[2]
   the king of all the birds;
It flew and (then) rested beside me,
   and all of it became speech.[3]
At its voice and the sound of its whisper [4]
   I started and rose from my sleep;
I took it up and kissed it,[5]
   then loosened its seal, and I read;

---

[1] God Himself has ensured the safety of the Gospel on its way to Man, lest the powers of the air corrupt or destroy its message; Jesus passes unknown among them on his way.

[2] In Mandaism, God's Messenger, Mandā d' Haiye, is a white eagle; Mead notes that the Eagle is the highest grade in the Mithraic rites. It often symbolises also the mystical Rapture of contemplatives.

[3] *i.e.*, the voice of conscience within, rousing the Soul from heavy sleep.

[4] *or*: rustling. Its message was only for the Soul to hear, not for the 'men of Egypt'; fleshly men can make nothing of the teachings of the Gnosis.

[5] As an act of respect to the Sender, welcoming the Gospel to the heart.

And according to what was in my heart [1]
  the words that in my Letter were written
  (HRG 49-55).
2. I remembered I was a Son of Kings,
  and my free Soul longed for its nature; [2]
I remembered the Pearl
  for which I had been sent to Egypt.
Then I began to bewitch him,
  the Serpent roaring and terrible;
I hushed him and put him to sleep,
  for my Father's Name I uttered over him, [3]
And the Name of our Viceroy
  and of my Mother, the Queen of the East.
Then I snatched up the Pearl
  and turned to go back to my Father's House;
Their raiment filthy and unclean [4]
  I stripped off and left in their land,
And I took up my road to come
  to the Light of our Homeland, the East
  (HRG 56-63).

---

[1] The Soul knew at once the truth of what he read, because it stirred the old memories of past experience Above.

[2] *i.e.*, desired to be free from all unspiritual excrescences. Wright reads: "My noble birth asserted its nature."

[3] Himself awake, he now puts the fleshly passions to sleep by the use of the Divine Names, supreme *mantram*.

[4] *i.e.*, the physical body; "the wearing of flesh, which is the garment of the visible world" (Datastan-i-denik 37 : 33, q. Widengren). The Soul escapes into the free life of disembodiment.

Now this 'Gospel' of the Truth came down unknown to the Rulers of the astral and etheric worlds (*cf.* GG 26 : 1), for their emotions would have perverted the pure spirituality of its message (*cf.* GG 56 : 1). It came like an eagle straight to the Prince, and its message roused him from his sleep of ignorance (*cf.* CJ). He welcomed it reverently, opened it and read it to himself, finding it said only what he in his heart already knew to be the truth. So he recalled to his memory how he came to be in the world and at once overcame with the Name of God, *i.e.*, the power of His Son (*cf.* CJ), the fearful serpent of the separate self which opposes God's will. Gnosis is then easily attained, and with it he hastens homewards, like the Prodigal Son when he remembers his Father's house, leaving in the world where it belongs his filthy body of physical matter.

74. The Homeward Way

Now my Letter, my Awakener,
   before me on the Road I found,[1]
And as with its voice it had roused me,
   so too with its light (was it) my Guide,
Which shone with splendour (?)
   before me on the road to be travelled (?),
While with its voice and its guiding
   it encouraged me also to hasten,
And with its love it drew me
   (along the dangerous way?).[2]

---

[1] However fast we may travel homewards, the **Ideal** is always ahead of us and leads us on.

[2] This line is a speculative restoration by me.

I went forth, I passed by Sarbug,
  left Bābel aside to my left,
And came to Maishan the Mighty,
  the harbour of the merchants
That sits on the shore of the sea;[1]
  (I came to the boundary of the East?)[2]
  (HRG 64-71).

Not only does the Gospel arouse the sleeping Prince, but it is also his guide along the Path, encouraging him in all its difficulties and shining like a lamp before him through the dark night. So he retraces his steps through the lower planes to the Boundary of his Homeland, the Kingdom of the Light.

75. The Coming of the Light-Robe

1. Then my brightness which I had discarded, and my mantle[3] wherein it was wrapped,
From the (far) heights of Hyrcania[4]
  my parents sent thither

---

[1] The return journey follows inversely that taken when travelling outwards or downwards into matter.

[2] There must have been some such line as this in the place now broken away; it is at the Boundary that the Robe of Glory meets the Soul (*cf.* GG 46 : 2).

[3] The Latin word ' *toga* ' is again used in Syriac here.

[4] *i.e.*, the ' highlands ' of GG 70 : 1, Heaven. Syr: *Warqan*, the mountain land where Parthian and Sassanian Kings spent the hot season, we learn.

THE SONG OF THE PEARL

By the hands of their treasurers,[1]
  who for their faithfulness were trusted with it.
Now because I had not remembered its appearance,[2]
  as in my childhood I had left it (in) my Father's House,
Suddenly when I went to meet it
  the Garment seemed to me my mirror[3] (HRG 72-76).
2. All of it I saw in the whole of me,
  and also in it I went to meet my all;
For we were two in separation,
  but only one in a single likeness.[4]
And also those treasurers
  who brought it me I saw likewise

---

[1] Widengren well describes the role of the 'treasurers' in contemporary religion; they take the place of the Angels carrying the Robe, Garland, etc., to the escaping Soul in GPM 75: 2.

[2] The Soul had forgotten his heavenly glory, as in Wordsworth's Ode.

[3] Bevan thinks this may be: "I seemed to myself like the mirror of the garment," but other Gnostic texts speak of the Robe as mirroring the universe, *cf.* GG 46. Even the liberated Soul can see only a reflection of his own glory; *cf.* 2 Cor. 3 : 18. The Robe exactly fits his own development, and on seeing it he dimly realises what he himself *really* is.

[4] The Gk. of this difficult passage reads: *exaiphnēs de idontos mou tēn esthēta hōs en esoptrōi homoiōtheisan (emoi), kai holon emauton ep' autēn etheasamēn, kai egnōn kai eidon di' autēs emauton, hoti kata meros diēirēmetha ek tou autou ontes, kai palin hen esmen dia morphēs mias.* The Soul realises his absolute oneness with the Robe of Light which he has won.

That they (were) two, their likeness one,
   for one Sign of the King stamped on them—[1]
Whose hands restored to me
   my treasure and my riches in their hands:
My many-coloured radiance
   which was raying glorious hues;
With gold and with beryls,
   and rubies and agates,
And sardonyx of various colours
   it too was prepared in its highland;
While with stones of adamant
   all its seams were fastened,
And the Image of the King of Kings
   was fully depicted in it all;
And like the sapphire stones
   so too were its manifold hues [2] (HRG 77-87).

   Here he finds his Robe of Light awaiting him in the care of the King's trusted messengers, just as it was when he left it behind him on setting out. Because it is the exact return or reward for all he is and has done, it seems to him like his mirror-image or reflection, indeed, his own 'higher self' (GZ 43 : 3). So too were the angels who met him there exactly like each other,

---

[1] He perceives the Angels are also one, both being reflections of God Himself because doing His will.

[2] The beauties of the Light-Robe are again detailed, in words whose deeper significance still escapes me. It is to be noted that the whole is God's Image (Gen. 1:27).

for each is in the image of his King. The splendour of that radiant Garment surpasses words; it scintillates rays of every hue, is indestructible and celestial, reflecting the Divine likeness in every part of it. Such is the glory of the "risen Soul" that has "put on Christ".

76. He Puts It On

1. Moreover I saw that in it all
   the motions of Consciousness stirred,
And as though to speak
   I saw it also preparing;[1]
The sounds of its tones I heard
   which it spoke to its bearers,
Saying: "I am active in the works (?)[2]
   for which they reared me in my Father's presence,
And I had also noticed in myself
   that my stature grew with his labours[3] (HRG 88-92).
2. Then in its royal movements
   it was all flowing out towards me,

---

[1] Being in no way other than the Soul himself, the Robe is full of life.

[2] A very hard passage, perhaps corrupt; it seems to read in Syr: *d'hw ana zrya 'bda*.

[3] As the Soul worked for God, so his Robe became greater and more lovely; the same idea is found in all Iranian religions.

And on the hands of its givers
it hastened as though I should take it; [1]
Also me too my love impelled
that I should run to meet and welcome it.
So I stretched out and grasped it,
with the beauty of its hues adorned,[2]
And my mantle of glorious colours
I threw it all entirely on.[3]
I clothed myself therein and soared on high
to the Gate of Peace and Adoration [4]
(HRG 93-98).

The Prince finds his Robe to be full of life and hears the words it speaks to the bearers, telling how it exactly matches its wearer, for it has grown as he grew in spirit. The Robe then eagerly rushes to the returning Soul and is embraced and put on with equal love and joy, after which he can rise swiftly to the Gateway of the King, his Father on high.

[1] The Robe itself seeks the victor-Soul, who has need only to accept it, though its beauty also makes it infinitely attractive.

[2] So too does Jesus in GG 47.

[3] "Throw round you a double robe of the righteousness that comes from God, and set a diadem of the glory of the Everlasting on your head" (1 Bar. 5:2); "They shall have been clothed with garments of glory, ... robes of life from the Lord of Spirits (which) shall not grow old" (1 Eno. 62: 16); "Take Enoch out of his earthly garments and anoint him with My sweet ointment, and put him in the robes of My glory" (2 Eno. 22:8); "(Adam) was girded about with a tunic of pearls and rays of light shot out from his face, as they do from the sun when he is about to rise" (Gospel of Bartholomew). Similar passages might be selected from all the scriptures, even back to the Pyramid Texts.

[4] In Arabic this would read: "ilā bāb isSalām wa'sSajd"; Peace because the struggle is over, and Adoration because the Soul is entering God's Kingdom.

77. The Father's Welcome

I bowed my head and adored Him,
    my Father's Majesty [1] who sent it me,
For I had carried out what He had bidden me [2]
    and He too had done what He promised me.
Then at the Gate of his Princes
    I mingled with His noble magnates; [3]
For He rejoiced in me and welcomed me,
    and I was with Him in His Kingdom;
And with the voice of spirit [4]
    all His servants (were) glorifying Him.
So He assured me that also to the Gate
    of the King of Kings I should speed with Him, [5]

---

[1] It seems clear that the 'Father's Majesty' is distinct from the 'King of Kings', the 'Second God' from the First Unmanifest, hidden Father of all, the First Space and Fountain of GG 6. Mandeism uses this word *zīwā* for the Angels.

[2] The Soul's mission is ordered by the manifested God, who in the Coptic works sends the Light-Spark into Matter.

[3] We can hardly distinguish the 'princes', 'magnates' and 'great ones'; they must be different Orders of Spiritual Powers. The word used is from Persian *waspur*, son of a house, *i.e.*, a member of one of the seven great families; they may possibly be the Seven Rulers of the Gnostic planets.

[4] So reads Lipsius, but Bevan prefers "of praise" (reading *de-doksā* for *de-rūḥā*), an easy change. This is the Hymn of Praise also found in GG 69:2 and 93:3, and in all parallel scriptures.

[5] Gnosis can carry the Soul even into the nameless Glory of the Hidden One.

And with my Gift and my Pearl [1]
appear with Him to our King (HRG 99-105).

The mission has been accomplished, and God too has now fulfilled His promise; welcomed by the Powers of Heaven, the Soul enters into His glorious Presence amid the rejoicings of all His servants, and is assured that the Pearl he brings will carry him to the very Inmost of all, God Unmanifest, who abides eternally alone in silence and in bliss ineffable.

---

[1] Probably aposiopesis: " with my gift of the Pearl ".

CHAPTER ELEVEN

BITTER WATERS

We now turn in somewhat greater detail to the life the Soul lives in the world. Naturally we ask ourselves first how she comes to be in the world at all, and how and when she may escape therefrom. It is sin, that is, the turning away from Spirit to things material, which entangles the soul in flesh and puts her in the slavery of the lords of fate. According to his desires, so is a man's life in the world; if there be no lower desires in him he cannot be held in matter but will flash back to the Source of Spiritual Light. Sin arises from ignorance of the true nature of the Soul, which is akin to God; knowledge destroys sin, and lets the Soul return to God. While ignorance endures, the Soul falls again and again into the chaotic darkness of this life, forgetting the joy and loveliness of the life in Spirit she has already known. When liberation draws near, the Soul is made restless in her slavery; she yearns for freedom, until the Messenger from on high comes down to her, awakens her to her true nature, and leads her home.

78. Sin and the Mysteries

1. There is nothing in this world that is of the quality of Heaven [1] (PS 84). If I take you

---

[1] This is the lowest of the supramundane planes, yet even this is immeasurably better than the physical.

to the region of the Rulers of Destiny, you will see the glory they are in, and because of this great excelling glory you will consider this world before you as darkness of darkness, and you will look upon the whole world of mankind as being a speck of dust [1] (PS 184).

2. For the emanations of the Light do not need the mysteries, for they are refined;[2] but it is the human race who need them, because they are all material refuse.[3] . . . Woe to them, the children of men, for they are like blind men groping in the dark and see not (the way) out![4] . . . There is no flesh shall be saved, . . . whether righteous or sinning [5] (PS 100, 372, 351).

---

[1] Copt: *efnaertoot nounapne nsois*. Who, having once seen those enduring splendours, could value any more the trashy tinsel of earthly life? " I do not mean the flesh wherein (you) dwell, but the flesh of . . . the ignorance which is in the unknowing that leads many away from my Father's (Word) ", says GIG 43.

[2] *Cf.* GG 69 : 1. The Angels need no special Gnosis, for they " always behold the face of my Father ", says Jesus, and they are wholly Spirit.

[3] A very strong phrase! Man is made from the lowest material elements—the " dust of the earth ", as Genesis put it long ago.

[4] *Cf.* the groping in GG 88 : 1. Life is a labyrinth for the blind souls of men.

[5] An emphatic denial of the absurd doctrine that material flesh can " rise again from the dead "; it was not known even to Paul, perhaps our earliest Christian writer; *cf.* 1 Cor. 15:40, 50, etc., the latter verse being very close to our Gnostic text: " Flesh and blood cannot inherit the Kingdom of God; neither does corruption

3. Watch over yourselves; do not sin,[1] lest ever you heap evil on evil and go out of the body without repenting, and (so) you become alien to the Kingdom of the Light for ever.[2] ... If **a man** sins (even) once or twice or thrice, he too shall be thrown into the world, according to the type of the sins he has committed [3] (PS 311, 263).

4. Because of the sinners have I troubled myself and come to the world, that I might save them;[4] ... before I came to the world no soul entered the Light, but now when I came I opened the gates of the Light and opened the ways that lead into the Light [5]

---

inherit incorruption." From where on earth does the later, purely pagan, idea of the 'resurrection of the flesh' arise? Ignatius (Eph. 8) writes: "Those who are of the flesh cannot do the works of the Spirit, nor they of the Spirit the works of the flesh." And what would the organs of the abdomen do in heaven?

[1] "Be at all times mindful of the Lord, and you shall not sin," tells Hermas (2 Herm. 4).

[2] Even now in the body we are estranged, alien, from our inheritance and Race Above; if we die in sin, that unhappy state becomes permanent.

[3] Even one unrepented sin is enough to bring about the hell of rebirth in the flesh, in such circumstances as may bring the results of that sin.

[4] Christ comes for sinners (*cf.* Lk. 5:32). "Because of those who corrupt my words have I come down from heaven" (Ep. Ap. 39).

[5] From some such source must come the present orthodox belief that even the righteous in earlier days could not enter heaven; it is elaborated on in the Gospel of Nicodemus.

(PS 354-355). I forgive, and I will forgive; so for this reason has the First Mystery sent me, to forgive the sins of everyone [1] (PS 252); (yet) I tell you that one shall be found in a thousand, two in ten thousand, to fulfil the mystery of the First Mystery,[2] . . . for they are all under sin, and they all need the gift of the mysteries.[3] . . . Because even for the righteous who have never done any kind of evil, nor have sinned at all, it is necessary for them to come upon the mysteries [4] (PS 354-355); in a word, there is no power to take a Soul to the Light without the mysteries of the Kingdom of the Light (PS 263).

5. Every man who is to receive the mysteries, if they knew the time wherein they would come out of the body, they would watch

---

[1] A noble universalism, limited only by man's power to accept the freely offered grace.

[2] Most scriptures have verses parallel to this; it were tedious to mention all, but we may note GH 49 : 2 and Gita 7 : 3.

[3] " I stood in the midst of the world and was seen of them in the flesh, and I found all drunken and found not one of them athirst, and my soul was pained for the sons of men that they were blind in their heart and saw not, deaf and have not known their destitution " (Agraphon 49).

[4] Even those wholly sinless cannot reach God until initiated into Gnosis; so says the Valentinian Epistle of James: " Thus alone is it possible for you to gain the Kingdom of the Heavens; if you do not at all obtain it by Gnosis, you will not be able to find it " (CJ 8).

themselves and not sin, so that they might for ever inherit the Kingdom of the Light.[1] . . . Now then, let him who shall do what is worthy of the mysteries receive the mysteries [2] and go to the Light. . . . He who is to receive the mysteries . . . becomes a great fire, very mighty and wise, and it burns up sins, and **the flames** secretly enter the Soul and consume all the sins which the Imitative Spirit [3] has fastened on it; [4] . . . and that Soul surrenders their destiny, saying to the **Rulers of Destiny**: " Take to yourselves your destiny; henceforth I come no more to your region; I have for ever become alien to you, being about to go to the region of my inheritance[5]" (PS 310, 355, 300, 290).

The beauties of this material world are as dust and ashes before those of spirit, but humanity blindly

---

[1] Who would sin, knowing it the last moment on earth and that sin would for ever deprive him of such unmeasured bliss?

[2] Initiation absolutely demands a state of worthiness, of righteous dealing and of freedom from the evil deeds listed in GG 81:3.

[3] This phrase will be explained in GG 79:1.

[4] So the Vaishnavas declare that even *one* perfect utterance of God's Name, with full faith and devotion, destroys all the sins of crores of lives; where is then the childish bogey of past 'karma' needing ages to burn away?

[5] Hereafter the soul is free from the laws of 'karma', free from the bondage of the planets and of destiny, free from the need of rebirth on earth. Copt: *ṅtinēu an enetntopos jin mpeinau; aier-allotrios erōtn ṣa-eneh, einabōk eptopos ṅtaklēronomia.*

clings to this worthless flesh which can never put on incorruption. It is most vital while in the body to gaze up, or in, to the Spirit, so that you may escape the futility of rebirth and avoid continued exile from the real Homeland of the Soul. This is why the Saviour came for us, that at least a few might turn from sin and seek the Light, and so be guided stage by stage into its highest levels; nothing else can save the Soul from falling back into the darkness of material life down here. Wise then are they who seek the Light while still in the body, and earn the right to be initiated into it; thus they burn up all the sins and worldly desires which might bring about rebirth in the world, and are freed for evermore from slavery to destiny or the laws of ' karma '.

79. Rebirth in this World

1. Everything allotted to each one by destiny, both every good and every sin . . . comes in them,[1] . . . (for) it is the Rulers of Destiny who compel the man until he sins. . . . When an old soul [2] is about to come down through them, the Rulers of the Great

---

[1] *i.e.*, through the Rulers of Destiny. All things in life, pleasant and wretched, come to us through forces indicated by the position and aspects of the planets in the hour of birth. Like the Hermetist, the Gnostics admitted the force of evidence to the scientific truth of Astrology. It is not that the physical planets govern us, but they show what is already in store for us, by God's will or our own deserts.

[2] *i.e.*, one that has already been incarnate before. This implies that some souls are newly created at birth, coming here for the first time; it may be so.

BITTER WATERS

Destiny ... give the old soul a cup of forgetfulness [1] out of the seed of the evil,[2] filled with every different desire [3] ... and with the water of forgetfulness. ... Then as soon as that soul drinks of the cup it forgets [4] all the regions it has visited and all the chastisements [5] wherein it has wandered; and that cup of the water of forgetfulness becomes a body outside the soul [6]

---

[1] Called by the old Greeks the 'river of Lēthē', forgetfulness; few of us remember our past lives on earth, or where we were on the inner planes before we were born. This is no evidence against reincarnation, of course.

[2] *i.e.*, as the result of the evil we have done in previous lives. Copt: ṣauti ṅtepsukhē ṅarkhaion ṅwapot ṅebṣe ebol hm psperma ṅtkakia efmeh ebol hn epithumia nim etṣobe.

[3] " The irrational part, and that which is of a corporeal nature, being then moistened and made fleshly, awakens the memory of the body, and from this memory come a yearning and a desire which drag down the soul into generation " (Vision of Aridaeus in TGH 1 : 454-455). " The Soul descends into this world in order that it may make trial of things and learn to know them; but when it is here, it neglects its business of seeking and learning Truth; it is drawn away to the pursuit of worldly goods and pleasures, and forgets the purpose for which it came down to earth " (Hermes de Cas. Ani. 2 : 6, q. Scott). *Cf.* also many passages in GZ, GH, GPM, etc.

[4] " Intoxication is there first experienced by souls in their descent by the influx of matter into them; from which cause also forgetfulness, the companion of intoxication, then begins secretly to creep into souls " (Cicero Rep. 6, q. in TGH 1 : 415).

[5] Copt: *kolasis*, probably referring only to the results, nice or nasty, of its past deeds.

[6] Copt: ṣafṣōpe ṅsōma pbol ṅtepsukhē; the body itself is (the cause of this) forgetfulness; how can a new brain carry memories gathered by a mind through a brain that perished long ago?

and comes to resemble the soul in every respect,[1] ... that is, it is called the 'Imitative Spirit' (PS 350, 336, 380, 336-337).

2. Now the 'Imitative Spirit' leads the soul astray and compels it and makes it do all its lawlessnesses,[2] together with all its passions and all its sins continually; and it stays attached to the soul and is its enemy,[3] making it do all these evils and sins. ... Moreover, even when it would rest by night (or) by day, it comes and moves it in dreams [4] or in worldly desires, and makes it long for everything of the world (PS 283).

3. Afterwards [5] comes a Receiver of the Little Sabaoth the Good,[6] him of the Midst, and he in his turn brings a cup filled with

---

[1] *lit* : figure (Copt: *smot*); the body is modelled on the soul and closely resembles it.

[2] It is the desires of the body that lead the soul away from God.

[3] Christians have always been inclined to give the body too much importance, as though it were in some way a vital part of the self, instead of an external and rather troublesome tool which often gets out of order.

[4] Bodily desires, and those of the subconscious mind, get a hold on us by way of our dreams, both while asleep and when 'awake'.

[5] *i.e.*, at last, after all our lives come near their end.

[6] He is the subordinate of the 'Great Sabaoth', whence Jesus drew the soul for his own manifestation on earth (GG 45 : 4).

thoughts and wisdom¹ containing sobriety. Then he gives it to the soul, and she is thrown down into a body² which will be unable to sleep or to forget,³ because of this cup of sobriety that has been given her. But it will be continually lashing her heart, asking after the mysteries of the Light, until at the command of the Maiden of the Light⁴ she finds them and inherits the everlasting Light.⁵ ... Now the Inner Power moves the soul to seek after the region of the Light as well as the whole Godhead (PS 388, 283).

[1] An Orphic Tablet reads: "I am a child of Earth and Starry Heaven, but my Race is of Heaven; this you yourselves know. Lo, now I am parched with thirst and perish; give me swiftly of the cold water flowing forth from Memory's Lake."

[2] Even the spiritual soul has to enter the flesh for the last time in order to receive the Mysteries. But in her the memory of her real nature is always awake, and she leaves the body no rest in her ceaseless search for God and for the Gnosis which will unite her with Him.

[3] Harpocrates said of Jesus that "his soul, having been made strong and pure, remembered the things seen by it in the circuit with the Uncreated God" (PG 16 : 3338).

[4] It is the 'Maiden of the Light' who mediates this supreme grace; Catholics may see here a faint foreshadowing of their own doctrine of Mariology.

[5] Harpocrates taught: "The souls are transferred from body to body until all the defects are set right, but as soon as nothing remains then they are freed to depart to that God above the world-making Angels, and thus all the souls are saved. But certain, ... paying off all the debts at one time, will be freed from ever again being born in a body" (PG 16 : 3339).

Inherent in the flesh itself is the tendency to sin which leads to enslavement to fate. When about to come down into incarnation, the Soul is made to drink the Cup of Lethe or Oblivion, and at once forgets her real home and nature and all the joys and beauties of the spirit-planes, so that she eagerly plunges into the bottomless abyss of matter. Her desires take shape around her as a ' body of desire ', in all ways like herself; and this constantly urges her further and further away from Heaven, making her dive ever deeper into the sea of passion and desire, and so playing continually the tempter's part. Even her dreams are haunted by desires, which leave her neither time nor inclination to remember or long for her true home; she is ' asleep ' with folly and drunkenness.

But the soul who draws near to liberation is made to drink at birth of the Cup of Memory, and though her past desires still draw her into a body she constantly remembers and longs for the glorious lost life of spirit, to which she really belongs. So that soul is ever seeking for the Truth, searching out a Teacher of the Mysteries who can initiate her into the Gnosis and lead her to the Kingdom of the Light and to the feet of God.

CHAPTER TWELVE

THE GNOSTIC IN THE WORLD

The Soul whom we have just seen seeking for the Light comes upon His Messenger, who gives her the law of love and righteousness, teaches her how to be worthy of the mysteries and able to turn from all materiality to the infinity of the Spirit, being thus cleansed from all her sins and defects. We stress then the urgency of this 'repentance', lest the Soul postpone it to some other life, and the importance of moral and ethical conduct. Nor are the mysteries to be progagated like the exoteric religion; they are only for the few who are worthy, and those who teach such souls are assured great glory in the Light. The sense of sex and the sense of separateness are to be transcended, and then the Soul will be led up to the heights of Cosmic life and crowned with divinity, even while outwardly still a mere human being. To know the One who abides ever as the inmost Self behind the apparent separate self—this is true Gnosis, this is the fulfilment of all life, the purpose of creation.

80. The Messenger of Light

1. Then did Setheus[1] send a Creative Word;[2] . . . now when he saw the grace

---

[1] *Cf.* note 1 to GG 11: 1.
[2] Copt: *logos ndēmiourgos.*

which the hidden Father had given him, ...
he wished to turn the universe back to the
hidden Father—for it is His desire to have the
universe return to Him.[1] ... Then lights [2]
were given him, and he was given the authority over all the secrets, so that he might distribute to those who had striven.[3] Now they
fled before the matter of the Aeon, putting it
behind them, and they ran up to the Aeon of
the Self-Father and took the Promise to themselves [4] (GL 247, 254-255).

2. He gave them the Glory and Joy and
Jubilation, Happiness and Peace and Hope,
and Faith and Love and Truth which changes
not;[5] ... and they have become blessed and

---

[1] The outward wave having ended, the water must now return to the infinite Sea from whence it came; God's love, which once sent the Pilgrim forth into Egypt, now calls him home again.

[2] *i.e.*, means of knowledge—the same use as among modern Catholics.

[3] Only those who have tried to become worthy can be initiated in the mysteries.

[4] *i.e.*, surrendered to God, abandoning the delights of the world and claiming the promise in Mk. 10: 29-30.

[5] A list of the ennead of Gnostic graces; Copt: *souṣou, raṣe, telēl, ounof, irēnē, helpis, pistis, agapē, alēthia*—the first four are Egyptian, and the last five Greek names. *Cf.* CJ 31: " He has given them the Thought, the Wisdom, the Pity, the Health, the Strength-spirit (issued) from the infinity and the sweetness of the Father." These last are rather the ' Five Trees '.

perfect, and have come to know the God of Truth,[1] . . . and have become Gods and Perfected Ones.[2] . . . And he gave them the Law:[3] to love one another, and to honour God[4] and bless Him and seek Him—who He is and what He is—and that they should wonder at the place whence they have come,[5] how narrow and difficult it is, and not return to it again but run after[6] the one who has given them the Law (GL 256-257).

3. Then he brought them out of the darkness of Matter that is a mother to them,[7] and he told them what is of Light, for they had

---

[1] Though we cannot distinguish their meanings, the Coptic always carefully marks off *pnoute ntalēthia*, the 'God of Truth', from the 'true God'.

[2] Copt: *auō nse-er-noute auō nse-er-telios*; this is one of the rare assertions in our texts that the end of Gnosis is deification.

[3] It would be hard to surpass this statement of the Law.

[4] Pope Xystus (Ring, 44) writes: "The greatest honour thou canst render to God is to know and imitate Him." There was slight difference between the Gnostics and the Catholics in the first two centuries.

[5] *i.e.*, the womb of a mother.

[6] *i.e.*, follow closely.

[7] Human beings are born from a material womb. The Mithra-Ritual says: "It is beyond my reach that, born under the sway of death, I should soar on high, together with the golden sparklings of the Brightness that knows no death; . . . translate me, now held by my lower nature, unto the Generation that is free from death, in order that, beyond the insistent need that presses on me, I may have vision of the Deathless Source, . . . in order that I may be reborn in Mind, so that I may become initiate and the Holy Breath may breathe in me" (4, 2).

230   THE GOSPEL OF THE GNOSTICS

not yet known the Light, whether it exists or not. Thereupon he gave them the precept never to do harm to one another,[1] and he went away from them up to the region of the Mother of the universe [2] (GL 257-258).

The Messenger comes down to turn the universe back to God, and to give of the Light freely to those who earnestly seek it, those who flee from the world to God and claim His promise of salvation. He gives those who listen to him all the graces, and he leads them towards perfection along the road of love for God and one another, preferring this to the hard ways of the world and constant birth therein. So he leads them out of darkness into Light, teaching perfect gentleness, and afterwards he returns to whence he came.

Though perhaps Jesus was specially in the Gnostic's mind while writing this, it is clear that all God's messengers act alike, and these words may be taken as a standard by which to recognise them.

81. Who Can Be a Gnostic

1. Be calm in yourselves,[3] and let each one of you bring the power of the feeling[4]

---

[1] The singling out of this as the Teacher's chief precept is very striking; could it reflect an Indian influence somewhere? Basilides was in touch with Indian thought, as Kennedy in part shows us.

[2] The Universal Mother, who prays for her children in GG 97, is invoked in GG 93, and referred to in GG 95: 8.

[2] Copt: *ernēphe m̂mōtn*—the first need for spiritual life, which is almost impossible amid the whirling storms of egoism and outer conflict.

[4] *or*: sensitivity to (Copt: *aisthēsis*). The gross and carnal are insensitive to subtle forces, while the refined are ever aware of them.

of the Light before himself, and you will certainly feel it¹... and receive the mysteries of the Light and ascend to the Kingdom of the Light² (PS 216, 259).

2. The calm, ... humane³, ... gentle, ... peaceful, ... kind, ... charitable,⁴ ... serving the poor and sick and troubled, ... devotional,⁵ ... righteous, ... good, ... (and) all-renouncing⁶ ... : these are all the boundaries of the ways of those who are worthy of the mysteries of the Light. ... So for this reason, ... renounce the whole world and all the matter in it;⁷ nay, he who takes and gives⁸

---

¹ The Odes of Solomon (26 : 13) have: "It is enough to know and to rest."

² Valentinian Letter to Reginus says: "He has risen, having whelmed the visible in the invisible, and he has furnished us the way of our immortality. ... If we have manifested in the world having put on the Christ, we are Christ's rays, and we are upheld by him until our setting, *i.e.*, our death in this life: we are drawn by him to Heaven like rays by the sun, nothing being an obstacle for us. This is the spiritual Resurrection, which surpasses the psychic as well as the fleshly" (CJ 45-46).

³ Copt: *mairōme; lit*: loving man.

⁴ Copt: *naē ... mntna*.

⁵ Copt: *mainoute; lit*: loving God.

⁶ Copt: *apotasse mptērf*. Or: renouncing the universe.

⁷ "Separate your souls from everything that is of the senses, from everything that appears and does not really exist" (Acts of Peter, 37); "flee the shadow of this world, receive the joyfulness of your glory" (2 Esd. 2: 36); "you who are, make yourselves like those who are not, in order to be with them" (CJ 12-13).

⁸ *or*: buys and sells; *i.e.*, has any business with the world. "Accept nothing from any man, nor possess anything in this world" (Agr. 171); *cf.* Mt. 6: 19.

in the world, and eats and drinks of its matter,[1] and lives in all its cares and contacts,[2] gathers in to himself other[3] matters to his other matters; because this whole world .... and all its contacts are material refuse,[4] and each one of them shall be asked about their purity.[5] ... To these, therefore, who have in this way totally renounced give the mysteries of the Light, and do not at all hide them from them[6] (PS 259, 250, 260).

3. Now he who would receive any of these mysteries must (first) receive the Mystery of Absolution;[7] ... any man who believes in

[1] Not literally that taking food and drink for the body enslaves the Soul to Matter, but looking on material things as 'food and drink', essentials.

[2] *or* : affairs (Copt: *homilia*).

[3] *or* : fresh.

[4] Copt: *hensorm ṅhulikon*, a phrase already used of the human body in GG 78: 2.

[5] Before admitting a soul to the Light it must be shown free from coarse defilements; the phrasing here reminds one of the Qur'ān. Hermes (de Cas. Ani. 2: 8, q. Scott): " If you desire true pleasures and unceasing joys, you must put off your unclean garment, cast off the burden of your body (*cf.* GG 73: 2), and guard against things repugnant to your being; and having done so, turn to the world of true pleasures and unceasing joys, clothe yourself in garments congruous with your true being "—*i.e.*, the Robe of Light.

[6] They can be given only to renouncers, and to them they must be given, not withheld.

[7] The first step is to wash away the stains of sin; *cf.* GG 2: 1. The Bruce Codex goes into very great detail on several of these mysteries in turn, describing the actual rites and detailing the mystic names and mantrams to be used in each of them (see GIG

the Kingdom of the Light may perform the Mystery of Absolution only once;[1] ... (then) all the sins they have committed, knowingly or unknowingly: ... their calumnies and their curses, their perjuries and thefts and lies, their false charges, their lusts and immoralities, their coveting and robberies,[2] together with (all) that they have done from their childhood up to this very day, ... they must all be destroyed ... and made pure light; then the Soul steadily leaps from region to region until it comes to the Treasure of the Light and enters in[3] ... and is taken to the Light of these lights, ... because *it* has received mysteries before coming out of the body[4] (GIG 117, 104, 117, 110, 104, 99, 104, 100).

[1] St Cyprian also held this idea, which was later condemned as a heresy; it led naturally to deathbed baptisms, lest later sins lose the purity thus gained.

[2] This Gnostic list of sins is of some interest; PS adds sorcery as among the foulest and most unforgivable of them.

[3] Nothing but sin can hold back the Soul from her upward rush into the Light, where by right she belongs (*cf.* GG 22: 1); "you shall shine as the lights of heaven, you shall shine and be seen, and the portals of heaven shall be opened to you," says 1 Eno. 104: 2.

[4] There is great stress on initiation while *in* the body; the mysteries have less effect on those receiving them while on the inner planes—if indeed that be at all possible, for the Gnostics never speak of it. The 'spirits' lay the same stress on spiritual progress being easier down here in these hard conditions of life.

The first qualification is 'Calmness'—"Be still, and know that I am God" (Ps. 46: 10)—and the last is a total renunciation of all worldly things, which alone can make the soul pure and able to receive the Mysteries. But before that stillness of heart can be attained, it must be purged of actual sins against God and the fellow-man, after which its progress into the Light is very swift. It is an old taunt of the ignorant against the Gnostics that they cared little for conventional morality: in fact this was so obvious a prerequisite that the Gnostics did not always feel the need to state it in cold language.

82. Seriousness of Purpose

1. Preach to the whole world: Fight yourselves [1] and receive the mysteries of the Light in this afflicted time,[2] and go into the Kingdom of the Light. Do not add day to day or cycle to cycle, hoping to come to receive the mysteries when we come to the world in another cycle.[3] Now such people do not know when the number of the Perfect Souls will be

---

[1] A striking phrase, full of the reality of spiritual life; Copt: miṣe erōtn ṅtetnji ṅmmustērion ṁpwoin hm peiwoeiṣ ethēj. Apok. 74b, reads: "to fight with and disregard the flesh, yielding to it no lack of control for the sake of pleasure, but to enlarge the Soul through Faith and Gnosis".

[2] i.e., of limitation or restraint; the Soul is cramped in the body; this is the same word so often used for oppression in GG 52-67.

[3] There is plenty of time, so why worry, the foolish soul thinks. But time is not infinite and will one day come to an end—then what awaits the dilatory?

complete, ... (and) I shall shut the Gates of the Light, and from that time no one shall go in, nor does anyone come out afterwards, because ... the mystery of the First Mystery[1] has been accomplished, for whose sake the universe has come into being (PS 317).

2. Now you have come into great troubles and great afflictions during the rebirths in various bodies of the world; and after all these pains you have of yourselves alone striven and fought, having renounced the whole world and all the matter in it, nor have you ceased from seeking until you found all the mysteries of the Kingdom of the Light which have refined you and made you pure (and) very refined light (PS 248-249). And there is no one who shall hinder you from what you desire; you shall produce for yourselves Aeons and worlds and heavens,[2] so that the intuitional[3] Spirits come and dwell in you. Then shall you become Gods and know that you are of God, and you shall see Him (as) God

---

[1] *i.e.*, God's mysterious purpose.

[2] Those who become "Gods and Perfect Ones" naturally create their own worlds, as we are told spirits do on their own plane— the dream of Wisdom in GG 52:3.

[3] Copt: *noeros*, that significant word hard to translate adequately.

in you, and He shall dwell in your Aeon[1] (GL 261-262).

Nor is it true that the Gnostics hugged their knowledge to themselves, indifferent to the outer world; like those of Hermes, they knew few could receive the Gnosis, but its existence and the terms whereon it can be found must have been widely spread even by open preaching.

The danger of a belief in rebirths is just this: that the soul puts off to an easier future what can actually be done today; such a soul may in fact never attain at all, for there will be a time when the doors will be closed because those who are to be perfected in this universe have already entered in. Having endured so much in countless earthly lives, happy indeed are those who now at least give all their hearts to seek for the purifying Light, for they have infinite powers even to create their own environment and in it to welcome the spirits of understanding and heavenly wisdom to their hearts, uniting them with God and making them divine.

83. Receive, and Give

1. Seek, all of you, after the Light,[2] so that the power of your Soul that is in you may live.

---

[1] The final end of the Gnosis is union with God dwelling in the Soul and its environment; Copt: *auō tetner-noute ṅtetneime je ṅtetn henebol hm pnoute, auō tetnenau erof efo ṅnoute ṅhēttēutn, auō fnawōh hm petnaiōn.* Hermes says (de Cas. Ani. 3: 13), "If it returns to its Source and Root, then it is still and at rest, and it reposes from the misery and debasement of its wandering in a foreign land."

[2] This reminds us of Dr. Besant's saying that the teaching of Ancient Egypt was, "Seek out the Light". Though unacquainted with the language or texts of old Egypt, she had a correct intuition of their spirit (*cf.* our GP). Copt: *ṣine tērtn ṅsa pwoin, taresonh ṅci*

... Do not desist from seeking by day and by night, until you find the purifying mysteries ... of the Light which refine the body of matter and make it pure light very refined[1] (PS 52, 250).

2. Now then, to all men who come to you[2] and believe in you and listen to your words and do what is worthy of the mysteries of the Light, give the mysteries of the Light and do not hide them from them[3] (PS 280). But before everything command him to whom you are to give these mysteries not to swear falsely,[4] nor even to swear at all ... but let their Yes be Yes and their No, No,[5] ... nor to be immoral or commit adultery, nor to steal or

tcom ñtetnpsukhē ethn-tēutn. Ignatius (Rom. 6) says: "Let me enter into pure Light, where being come I shall indeed be the man of God"—which shows how close the earliest Fathers were to the Gnosis.

[1] Contrary to the doctrine of GG 78: 2, this does suggest that even the physical body can be changed into pure Light, as it is said happened to that of Sri Ramalingaswamy, the famous Tamil Saint of the 19th century at Vadalur.

[2] The initiative must rest with the candidate, though the Gnostic must let everyone know of the possibility of Gnosis.

[3] The disciples say: "Not only are we pitiful to our own selves, but we are pitiful to the whole race of humanity" (PS 88).

[4] The ethical law binds even the initiate; there is no hint of the slander of their opponents that as the Gnostic cannot be stained by sin he might freely defile himself; on the contrary, see the warning in GG 81: 3.

[5] It is easy here to see the quotation from Mt. 5: 37.

covet anything, nor to love silver or gold, nor for any purpose to name the name of the Rulers or . . . their Angels,[1] nor to rob or curse, nor to slander falsely or accuse; . . . in one word, to fulfil the good commandments (GIG 102).

3. These mysteries that I shall give you, guard them;[2] do not give them to any man unless worthy of them; do not give them to father or mother, to brother or

---

[1] Prohibiting both sorcery and false worship.

[2] The law of secrecy was common. Pope Xystus writes: " Impart not to everyone the word concerning God; . . . before a crowd try not to speak of God. . . . Let him who utters a word about God to those who may not lawfully hear it be regarded as a betrayer of God." Philo: "We give a higher teaching of the divine mysteries to initiates who are worthy of the holiest rites. . . . Receive these things into your souls . . . as truly sacred mysteries, and see that you speak not of them to any who may be without initiation, but storing them away in your hearts, guard well your treasury " (de Cher. 12, 14). Odes of Solomon: " Guard my secret, you who are kept by it! " (8 : 11). Gospel of Bartholomew: "As many as are faithful and can keep them to themselves, to them thou mayest entrust these things; for there are some who are worthy of them, but there are also some others to whom it is not proper to entrust them." The Justinite vowed: " I swear by the Good over all to guard these mysteries and to divulge them to no one, and not to fall back from the Good One to the creature " (PG 16: 3203). Elkhasai: " Do not recite this account to all men, and guard carefully these precepts, for all men are not faithful, nor are all women straightforward " (Hip. Ref. 9 : 12). Abraxas: " Transmit the mysteries, but only to a child worthy of immortality to be initiated in this Power of ours " (p. 163). See also the note on GH p. 235, and Gita 18: 67. It is false, ignorant, to deny the existence of esoteric Christianity in early days; even the Gospel Agraphon 84 reads: " Guard the mysteries for me and the sons of my house."

sister or relative.[1] ... Guard them; do not give them to anyone at all for the sake of the goods of this whole world. ... Do not speak to them of these mysteries of the Treasure of the Light, save to those who shall be worthy of them, having left the whole world and all its affairs, ... being in no faith other than the Faith of the Light [2] in the way of the Children of the Light, listening to one another and treating one another as Sons of the Light [3] (GIG 100-101).

4. He who shall give Life to a single soul and save it, besides the light that is his (own) in the Kingdom of the Light, he shall receive other glory in return for the soul he has saved, so that he who shall save a host of souls, besides the glory he has in the Glory he will receive another host of glories for the souls whom he has saved [4] (PS 265).

The Teacher urges perseverance on the seeker, and at the same time a generous sharing with the

---

[1] It is human to wish to enrich one's relatives first, even with spiritual wealth.
[2] This seems to be the Gnostic's own special name for his religion, as it later was of Mani's; Copt: *tpistis mpwoein*.
[3] Doing as they would be done by, in perfect brotherliness.
[4] *Cf.* Dan. 12: 3.

deserving of the fruits of that search—the definition of worthiness being substantially in accord with the demands of morality—sorcery being specially condemned, as latter by Mani (GPM 54: 2). Nothing is to be given for the sake of nepotism, but only to those who have truly turned from Matter to the Spirit and are faithful to the Religion of the Light. Those who thus lead others to the Light greatly increase their own glory therein.

84. Gospel Fragments

1. To Salome,[1] asking how long men will die, the Lord said: "So long as you women give birth, for I have come to abolish the works of the female."—Now 'of the female' (means) 'of desire', and 'works' (are) genesis and decay.[2] When she was saying: "Then I have done well in not bringing forth?" the Lord replied: "Eat every plant, but do not eat that which has bitterness"[3] (Gosp. Eg.).

2. When Salome asked when those things of which she enquired would be known, the

---

[1] Salome, one of the favorite disciples among the Gnostics, elicits the teaching of encratism.

[2] The Gnostic commentator explains the 'works of the female' as sex desires which lead to birth and death. Xystus says (317): "Seek not for good in the flesh," and "So long as the flesh is filled with longing the Soul knows not God" (136).

[3] Man has a right to every experience, but it is wise to abstain from that which, like sex, leads only to his misery. Gk: *pasan phuge botanēn, tēn de pikrian ekhousan mē phagēs.*

THE GNOSTIC IN THE WORLD

Lord said: "When you shall tread on the vesture of shame,[1] and when the two shall be one, and the male with the female neither male nor female,[2] ... (and) when you shall strip and not be ashamed"[3] (Gosp. Eg.).

3. "I am a Voice of awakening[4] in the age[5] of the Night; henceforth I begin to make naked the Power from the Chaos[6] (PG 16: 3159 ff). And I have not sown children to the Ruler,[7] but have torn up his root; I have

---

[1] *i.e.*, the fear of bodily nakedness, which arises from sex-desire, conscious or hidden in the heart; the pure find no evil in nudity. Gk. *hotan to tēs aiskhunēs enduma patēsēte*.

[2] *i.e.*, no difference is felt between the sexes; "He will take your souls to the Light of these lights, ... to the region wherein there is no woman or male, nor form in that region, but it is light that remains ineffable" (PS 143).

[3] "When wilt thou manifest to us, and when shall we see thee? ... When you have put off your raiment and are not ashamed" (Oxyrh. Frag. 655). "(God) is present with only one class of men—with those who, having stripped themselves of all things in genesis, even to the innermost veil and garment of opinion, come to God with unclad and naked minds", says Philo in his de Gigan. 12. Such are the true Gymnosophers.

[4] *i.e.*, from the 'drunken slumber' of ignorance of the Soul's true nature and mission.

[5] *or:* world. The 'Night' is of course the darkness of Matter and Ignorance. Gk. *egō phōnē exupnismou en tōi aiōni tēs nuktos*.

[6] *i.e.*, I strip away the power of Matter and make it harmless to my soul; I deprive the evil 'powers' of their 'light', as the "Pistis Sophia" puts it.

[7] *i.e.*, I have taken no part in producing children; I am a Virgin and have shared in no sexual acts.

gathered together the limbs scattered abroad,[1] and I know thee who thou art, for I am of those Above [2] (Gosp. Phil.). I am thou, and thou art I,[3] and wherever thou art, there am I; and I am sown in all, and from wherever thou wilt thou gatherest me, and gathering me thou gatherest thyself" [4] (Gosp. Eve).

These fragments from lost Gnostic Gospels stress the impossibility of sex-life in one who would be devoted to the search for spiritual Light. The former, with all its ceaseless and clamorous demands on thought and action, leaves neither time nor energy to the aspirant; it is only those who have firmly turned away from its dark lures, so that the very sense of sex-difference has faded away, who can begin to realise their absolute Oneness with the One manifested in every form. Such are indeed of the Heavenly Race, like Angels neither marrying nor seeking in marriage, and they find their own total fulfilment in spiritual atonement with Him who is in all.

---

[1] I have withdrawn my whole life-force from worldly things and concentrated them on the Soul. *Cf.* the scattering of the Limbs of Osiris in GP; Dionysus too was torn by the Titans limb from limb, and after his burial the pieces came together again to reconstitute the God.

[2] I belong to the Race from Above, the Gnostics, spiritual and enlightened, no longer subject to the Powers of the middle and lower regions.

[3] This formula appears in Hermes-hymns in TGH 1: 87 and 89; also in the Kosmopoiia (Abraxas, p. 196): "For thou art I and I thou; what I say must come into being; for I have thy name as a guardian in my heart." It is of Egyptian origin.

[4] The Soul declares its absolute oneness with all that exists.

85. The Way to the Higher Mysteries

1. Each of them in its (own) time, all the souls of the Light come,[1] ... and those of the Midst will baptize them ... and seal them in their seals of their mysteries; and (then) they enter into them all and go to the region of the inheritances of the Light.[2] ... Everyone receiving a mystery of the Light will remain in the region whose mystery each one has received, and has no authority to go up to the planes that are above it.[3] ... But he who has received the real Mystery ... of the Ineffable ... has the right to wander in all the planes of the spaces of this three ' triple-spiritual ',[4] ... from out inwards and from in outwards; and ... in a word he has the right to move about in all the regions of the inheritances of

---

[1] Not that all souls of every kind attain the Light, but only that those who are spiritual, of the Race Above, will achieve in due course the glory destined for them.

[2] Having duly passed through the lower, they enter on the higher planes of the Light.

[3] Each soul is in its own plane; it may go lower but cannot rise above its own natural level; the ' spirits ' teach the same. "Everyone shall learn his own measure and shall take his reward according to his measure" (2 Eno. 44: 5).

[4] Only the soul knowing it is one with the All can enter every plane which is the field of humanity.

the Light, and ... to remain in the region pleasing to him in ... the Kingdom of the Light (PS 195-196, 203, 205-206).

2. Do not grieve, then, my disciples, about the Mystery of the Ineffable, thinking that you will not understand it. Truly I tell you that that Mystery is yours and everyone's who shall listen to you and renounce all this world ... and every evil thought ... and ... all the cares of this Aeon, ... while he surrenders to the Godhead.[1] ... That Mystery is far easier than all the (other) mysteries of the Kingdom of the Light.[2] ... Now it is that Mystery which knows why all the regions in the space of the Ineffable have evolved,[3] with all that are in them, and ... why it has troubled itself[4] to come out of the Ineffable (PS 217-219, 225).

---

[1] Copt: *auō nfhupotasse ṅtmntnoute*.

[2] For all its sublimity this 'mystery' is in fact very accessible: it may come in a flash, even to one quite unprepared, if he be only turned away from material pleasure to the inner joy of the Spirit, surrendering his whole being to God. I remember J. Krishnamurti saying much the same in 1927.

[3] *or*: spread out; *i.e.*, the one with true cosmic consciousness knows the purpose of everything that exists in this whole universe, being one with all.

[4] Copt: *afskulli ṁmof*—the same phrase as in GG 78 : 4.

3. Now the soul which receives the Mystery of the Ineffable will soar on high, being a great Stream of Light, ... nor is there any power at all able to restrain it¹ ... until it reaches the region of inheritances of the Mystery ... and becomes united with its limbs.² ... He is a man while in the world, but he has excelled all the Angels,³ and ... he will reign with me in my Kingdom,⁴ ... (for) he is a King in the Light. And truly I tell you that man is I, and I am that man, ... for that man is truly the First⁵ and is like to Him (PS 228-230, 254).

As their day of maturity comes, each soul of this Divine Race is led into the mysteries through the gate

---

¹ Nothing can hold back the Advaitin who has known for himself that all is one.

² *i.e.*, until all its thoughts and deeds are folded up in itself and it is still. Xystus (167) tells us that "Wisdom guides the soul on the way to God".

³ Though apparently a mere human being, the true Gnostic (Skt: *jñānī*) is a King of Light, in no way really different from the King of Kings, and identical with the Christ, who is God manifested in the world. Marcus Aurelius (Conf. 7: 67) says: "Never forget that it is possible to be at once a divine man, yet a man unknown to all the world."

⁴ "Souls ... when separated from the irrational part of their nature and made clean from all matter, have communion with the Gods and join them in the governing of the whole world" (Sallustius: On the Gods and the World, 21).

⁵ *i.e.*, the First Father of GG 6.

of a spiritual (and formal?) baptism, and then is free to move to and fro in all the planes up to that wherein she is initiated. A soul that has realised the One in all, the Cosmic truth of Omnidentity, being one with all is free of every human plane—perhaps beyond this there are other inconceivable Gnoses?—and to abide in any state she will. This supreme Mystery is not beyond our reach, for one who has renounced the lower life can easily attain it; and it gives direct experiential knowledge of all the secrets in the manifested universe. Once possessed thereof, a soul soars into the highest and is made one with all glories; in the world of man her glories may not be recognised, but her spiritual royalty is obvious in the inner worlds, for she is one with God Himself.

86. The Greatness of the Initiate

1. Blessed is he who has found the mysteries (of the first space) [1] outside, and a God is he [2] who has found these words of the mysteries of the second space of the midst; but a Saviour and an Unattainable [3] is he who has found the worlds of the third space which is within; I tell you in God's truth ... they are

[1] These few words have evidently been dropped in error from our text; the handwriting shows the copy was made by an old man, and there are many careless repetitions and omissions.

[2] Xystus says: "A man worthy of God is a God among men" (376a); GIG 104 has: "Ever since they were on the earth they have already earned God's Kingdom and have a share in the Light-Treasure, and are immortal Gods."

[3] Copt: *akhōrētos*, the word often used for the Supreme Uncontainable One. The soul that has reached the Inmost has become the One, and saves his fellows.

the Limbs of the Ineffable [1] (PS 253-254), a host of Powers with Him wearing crowns upon them and their crowns shedding forth rays [2] (GL 247).

2. Now the brightness of their bodies is living in the region to which they have come,[3] and the word coming out of their mouth is everlasting life, and the light that comes from their eyes is repose for them; the movement of their hand is their flight to the region whence they have come,[4] and their gazing into their faces is the gnosis into themselves;[5] their walking towards them is their return home again, and the spreading out of their

---

[1] *i.e.*, they function as the universe itself, *or*: they become God's perfect instruments. The 'Ineffable' is both the totality of Cosmic life, and the Unnamed God behind and within it all. Copt: *ntow ne mmelos mpiatsaje erof*.

[2] Copt: *ere neuklom nej-aktin ebol*, as in the case of the Manifest God Himself in GG 7 : 3.

[3] Their radiance shows to which level of spirit-life they have reached.

[4] *i.e.*, they return to God as easily as they wave a hand.

[5] When they look at themselves in calm water or a mirror, they see the Real Self there; also when others look at them, they see them as they really are; *cf.* GG 30 : 4. "The wise man's understanding is a mirror of God", says Pope Xystus (450); the Codex Jung, p. 13, has: "Do not raise yourself above this Light that illumines, but be face to face with yourselves (*cf.* GG 87), as I myself am face to face with you."

hands is their firm establishing;[1] the hearing of their ears is the feeling that is in their heart,[2] and the joining of their limbs is the ingathering of Israel's dispersed;[3] the holding of them is their strengthening in the Word, and the number in their fingers is ... the total that has come forth [4] (GL 247-248).

Happy are those who have even the lower mysteries, but those initiated in this last and supreme Mystery are like Gods, vehicles of the Ineffable and radiant with every glory. Every part of them manifests the wonder they have attained; they have become the Saviour, the Mystic Cross that upholds creation and draws the scattered units of God's Life into one whole.

87. The Final Secret of the Self

Cease to seek God in creation and things like these,[5] and seek Him from thyself;[6] and

---

[1] 'Establishing' is a function of the Cross, which is the spreading out of the hands of the Heavenly Man; *cf.* GG 34: 2. Of course, balance is thus secured.

[2] *i.e.*, they hear in their own hearts the 'Voice of the Silence'.

[3] As their limbs are joined together, so are the 'limbs' which were scattered abroad in the creation drawn together through them; *cf.* GG 84: 3.

[4] *i.e.*, the perfect number, ten.

[5] Gk. *katalipōn zētein Theon kai ktisin kai ta toutois paraplēsia*. Most interpreters have understood here a word like 'outside'; but it seems to me that the second *kai* (and) has confused the orthodox refutator, who could not have sympathised with, or understood, the doctrine, and he has put *kai* here also instead of *eis* (into). I have ventured to correct the text.

[6] 'Light on the Path' teaches a dual search: "Seek the way by retreating within; seek the way by advancing boldly without."

learn who it is that absolutely appropriates everything in thee and says: " My God, my mind, my understanding, my soul, my body."[1] Then learn whence is sorrow, and rejoicing, and love, and hate, and being unwillingly awake, (and sleeping when one would not),[2] and getting angry against one's will, and falling in love when one would not. Now if thou enquire exactly into these things,[3] thou shalt find Him in thyself[4]—one and many

---

There is no real opposition here, for what is within is also without; but Monoimus advises us rather to find God in the self, the one which always says 'I'. Agraphon 56: "The Kingdom of the Heavens is within you, and whoever shall know the self shall find this." Hermes in de Cas. Ani. 12: 5 writes: "All things that you ought to get knowledge of are in your possession and within you. Beware then of being led into error by seeking (elsewhere) the things that are in your own possession," and in 14:7: "Withdraw yourself in imagination, O Soul, from the physical world, and then see whether you can find anything besides your own essence and its existence " (both q. Scott).

[1] Gk. *mathē tis estin ho panta hapaxaplōs en soi exidiopoioumenos kai legōn.* "He appears not to these bodily eyes, but is found by the eyes of the mind" (Acts Thom. 65). Pope Xystus says: "Know thou who is God; learn what that is which thinks within thee..... Seeing God, thou wilt see thyself" (394, 446).

[2] Some such clause is surely needed to keep the balance so carefully maintained elsewhere. Read: *kai to hupnousthai mē thelonta.*

[3] Gk. *kai an tauta epizētēseis akribōs.* "Who hast not withheld thine own compassion from me when lost, but hast shown me how to seek myself and to know what I was, and what and how I am now, so that I may become again what I was; whom indeed I know not, but thou whom I knew not hast sought me out and taken me to thyself" (Acts Thom.). This is Ātma-vichāra.

[4] " Perceiving then, O man, all this in yourself, that you are immaterial holy light akin to Him who is unborn, that you are

like the atom [1]—(thus) finding that way (out) from thyself [2] (PG 16: 3358 ff).

This striking passage is from a letter of Monoimus the Arabian, and might well have come from any Hindu Advaitin. We can hear in it the voice of Sri Ramana Maharshi, bidding the seeker of the Real ask " Who am I? " and therein finding the Self beyond all separation, immortal. The old Gnostic, following the ancient dictum *Gnōthi seauton* (Know thyself), tells us to turn away from seeking God outside in the universe, and to seek Him out from within the self. Who is it that constantly says " I, my and me "? Knowing this, the seeker will understand the changing moods and fancies of individual life and enter the stillness of the eternal Self, infinitesimal yet infinitely reflected in countless images; thus will he find escape from the miseries of ego and of separate life, and merge into the universal and deathless One beyond all Being.

---

intuitional, heavenly, translucent, pure, above the flesh, above the world, above Rulers, . . . understand yourself in your (true) state and receive full (Gnosis), and realise wherein you excel; and beholding your face in your essence break all bonds asunder " (Acts of Andrew, 352).

[1] Gk. *hen kai polla kata tēn keraian.*

[2] This is parallel to the thought in GG 88 : 1.

CHAPTER THIRTEEN

GNOSTIC HYMNS AND PRAYERS

I have included here a small selection of typical Gnostic poetry and petition, some of them more on the Pagan, others more on the Christian, side. They come from various sources: from orthodox refutators, from isolated Coptic papyri, from catholicized Gnostic Acts of the Apostles, and from the uncorrupted Gnostic codices which have come to light in the Egypt of our own day, after who knows what vicissitudes of time!

Some of these touch the heights of majestic thought and speech, some are full of devotion, some sound the depths of magic incantation; all bear in them the mark of true Gnosis, such as that we are now studying, and a few bear signs of real personal mystical experience. Many link closely with the thought and diction of other sections in this ' Gospel '.

88. The Naassene Psalm

1. A Law productive of the universe was the First Mind,[1]

---

[1] *i.e.*, the First Mind, God, produced all things according to Law.

and the Second was the outpoured
Chaos of the Firstborn,[1]
while Thirdly Soul received a Law to
be laboured at.[2]
Therefore, swathed in a deer's form,[3]
overpowered by death, (she) works
at practice (of it).[4]
At times, having a kingdom, she looks
at the light;
at times thrown into misery, she
weeps,
and at times (she) mourns (and)
rejoices;
And at times she wails (as) she is judged,[5]
and sometimes she is judged (and) dies;

---

[1] When Mind became creative (Gk. *gonimos*), secondly came the whirling 'chaos' of creation.

[2] *i.e.*, carried out, obeyed. The Soul, with its moral law, was the 'third outbreathing'; Gk. *tritatē psukhē d' elaben ergazomenēn nomon*. As usual in poetry, the language is rather terse and elliptical.

[3] In the Bacchic rites a fawn-skin was worn and a thyrsus carried (*cf.* Plutarch de Iside 35 : 2); this *nebris* was symbolic of death and rebirth.

[4] *or*: labours at her task beneath death's rule. Though constantly dying, and being reborn, she keeps trying to learn and practise the moral law.

[5] This word (*krinetai*) probably has some technical sense whereof I am not aware. It certainly does not refer to any 'day of judgment' in a Christian sense.

GNOSTIC HYMNS AND PRAYERS

    While at times the unhappy one finds
        no way out from evil,
      being led astray, she has entered a
        labyrinth [1] (PG 16: 3159).
2. Said IAŌ-ZEĒSAR:[2] " Father,
      a seeking of evils on earth [3]
      wanders about (far) from Thy Breath,[4]
      and seeks to flee the bitter Chaos [5]
      but knows not how it will escape.[6]
    On this account send me, Father;
      having seals, I shall descend,
      shall make way through all Aeons,
      shall explain all mysteries

---

[1] *or*: in misery she enters in her wandering the labyrinth of ills. It takes all the magic power of true Gnosis to free the soul from the ' ocean ' of life and death.

[2] The actual Codex reads: *eipen diēsous esor*, which early editors took as *eipen de Iēsous* (*christos*), certainly playing rather loose with the last word; even the reading *Iēsous* (Jesus) is almost certainly an error of the refutator. It is Mead who says it is probably a broken down *Iaō Zeēsar*, words common in this ' sect ', and I have accepted this suggestion. It combines the name of the Lord of the highest Heaven with that of the Mediator between the Above and Below, *i.e.*, the Mystic Cross of GG 39: 2, whose name in App. I : 6 : 1 is that of the " Jordan flowing upwards ". Thus it is the secret name of the God upon the Cross, by whom all Souls rise to their heavenly Home.

[3] *i.e.*, one who seeks worthless pain-giving things.

[4] The ceaseless search for worldly things takes the Soul ever further away from God's Spirit, which is true Life.

[5] As in the ' Sethian ' system of GG 5 : 8.

[6] *i.e.*, the painful life in physical matter.

and show (the) forms of Gods;
and the hidden things of the Holy Path,
having called (them) Gnosis, I shall impart" [1] (PG 16 : 3160).

Hippolytus appends this striking poem to his long account of the Naassenes which we have used in our Appendix I, to which it is in no way directly related, save that it was used by the same group of Gnostics. It is probably pre-Christian, if we can judge from the use of the mystic name for the Saviour, instead of the 'Jesus' usual in later days. The Soul's varied experiences in the body—joy and sorrow interchanging or even co-existing—are touched upon, and as she finds no way out from the miseries of earth-life Zeësar (*cf*. App. I : 6 : 1), link between earth and heaven, offers to guide her from the labyrinth into freedom, promising to initiate her also in the saving mysteries of the Gnosis.

89. Valentinian Poems

1. That sublime Light had come to be in every place,[2]
and in every place where he was he taught of the Father;

---

[1] Gk. *kai ta kekrummena tēs hagias hodou | gnōsin kalesas paradōsō*. Mead suggests that the original read 'Naas' for Gnosis; I doubt this. In English we must invert the order of the last two lines. The work of the Christ is to bring the Gnosis to those who wander in the darkness.

[2] *'lya nwhra hw | bkla tr hwa* (Syr.). This clearly refers to the work of any Messenger of the Light, as in GG 80, penetrating everywhere; *cf*. GPM 32.

(he threw one committing iniquity down into the Void),
but was kind to the contending Aeons and merciful to the Lady who came from the rejected.[1]
The sublime Firmament [2] limited strife among the quarrelling worlds;
what was going out he expelled,
he healed the branches with first fruits,
but (cut away) the rotten ones which began to wither ... (JAOS, February 1918).

This fragment was recognised by Newbold in 1918 as a Syriac poem in garbled Greek lettering, copied unintelligently by Hippolytus as though it were a magic formula in gibberish. It evidently refers to the work of the Demiurgic Power and is more or less parallel to GG 10-11, the establishing of order in the universe shaken by the first Outpouring of life.

2. I see all things depending on Spirit; I gaze upon all things depending on Spirit: Flesh depends on Soul, Soul is upheld by Air, Air hangs from Ether—Fruits brought into

---

[1] *i.e.*, the Soul, or Wisdom, rising out of the dark Void outside the Fullness.

[2] Another name for him who establishes all things and separates the good from the evil—like the 'Boundary' or the 'Cross' spoken of elsewhere in this 'Gospel'.

being from the Deep, Babe born of the womb (Hip. Ref. 6: 32).

G. R. S. Mead gives us this little poem on the consonance of all things, each dependent on another, each derived from another.

3. Greeting from unweary Mind to minds that nothing can fatigue![1] Now shall I wake again in you the memory of Mysteries above the very heavens—the Mysteries whereto no name can anyhow be given, whereof no tongue can tell [2]—the Mysteries no Rulership and no Authority, no subject or mingled nature can understand, but that yet have been made plain to the understanding of the Mind that stands above all change [3] (Epiph. 1: 31: 5).

From Mead's FFF I have also drawn this allusion to the ineffability of the supreme Mystery, which can yet be understood by the eternal Mind, attainable by minds that earnestly desire it; I have not seen the Gk. original of this little poem.

---

[1] Divine Mind illumines the little human mind, which like itself is actually beyond human frailties.

[2] *i.e.*, the Mystery of the Ineffable of GG 85.

[3] One gifted with this Mystery is beyond all change, all death, all failure in spirituality. It is the Mystery of the Light-Robe in GG 27-28.

90. From a Turin Papyrus [1]

1. O great Aloneborn, hear me this day when I cry to thee, O One-Father, almighty Spirit hidden in the Father,[2] the firstborn of every living being and every Aeon! ... Help me, O holy Angels! May all my enemies and slanderers (?) swiftly flee away from me, ... so that you may come to me, remain with me, and chase all impure spirits from before my eyes, ... be they celestial, or of the earth or air! ...[3]

2. I adjure thee, Gabriel,[4] by the Four Angels who rest on the Four Pillars, whose feet are firmly fixed on the foundations of the holy Abyss![5] ... Purify this place for me to a distance of sixty myriad cubits,[6] ... that they

---

[1] Published by Rossi in Cinque manuscritti copti della Biblioteca Nazionale di Torino, II, XVIII.

[2] *i.e.*, the 'Second Space' of GG 7, ever hidden in the eternal Unknown Father, yet manifesting Him in all creation.

[3] To drive away evil spirits is to open the way for the higher spirits (Gk. *noeros*), as in the Closing Prayer of this 'Gospel'.

[4] The Angel of Purity, and so of vast Strength, who announces the Christ to his Virgin Mother, and brings the stream of grace that saves and adorns the repentant human soul.

[5] The Spirits of the four Cardinal Points, and the Four Gospels of the Christian Canon, as Irenaeus is absurdly at such pains to convince us.

[6] *i.e.*, about 170 miles.

come not near to me! ... I invoke thee, Gabriel, by the Father's great Name and His holy Glory and by those who dwell in thy presence; ... by the glory of the Father's throne whose eyes (?) are flames of fire; ... by the Father's light whereby the Cherubim and Seraphim are illumined,[1] together with the dwellers of all the heavens and those of the whole earth; ... by the great glorious Virgin in whose Bosom the Father was concealed from the beginning[2] ...! May my body be purified from every impure spirit, ... so that He may come to me![3]

This typical late Gnostic prayer, half petition and half conjuration, contains much else of little interest save to the specialist. It is in the main an appeal for protecting spirits under the overlordship of Gabriel (the Strong One of God), always a mighty name to be invoked, and it harks back to several Egyptian ideas of extreme age—such as the Four Pillars, the Abyss, and the Virgin from whom arose the First of Fathers. Hebrew influences, common in the magic of the age (5th to 6th cc. A. D.), appear in the names of Gabriel, the Cherubim and the Seraphim. I have mercilessly cut out many repetitions and incoherencies.

[1] Even the highest Angels derive all their glory from God; they have nothing of themselves.

[2] This is the invisible Virgin Silence of GG 4:1, the Deep of GG 12:1.

[3] God comes only to those wholly pure of heart, who keep also their bodies pure from fleshly lusts.

91. A Song of Praise to the Aeon[1]

1. Hail to thee, All-Cosmos of subtle Spirit! Hail to thee, O Spirit extending from heaven to earth, and amidst the Cosmic Sphere from the earth even to the end of the Abyss! Hail to thee, Spirit that enters into me, that clings to me or separates from me according to God's will in the goodness of His heart![2] Hail to thee, Beginning and End of Nature[3] none can move! Hail to thee, unwearying Liturgy of Nature's elements![4] Hail to thee, Brightness of the Sun-beam that shines to serve the world! Hail to thee, Disk of the night-shining Moon that shines unequally![5]

2. Hail all Spirits of the subtle Statues of the Gods![6] Hail, all of you whom holy

---

[1] This hymn is to the pantheistic God who, though involved in the whole universe, is yet pure Spirit, eternally free from involvement.

[2] The universal God is also in the spirit of His worshipper, revealed or hidden from time to time at His own good will.

[3] From Him all came, and all shall return to Him.

[4] The prayer-song of creation, the harmony of the spheres eternally glorifying their Creator.

[5] As perfect Light, this One God is symbolised by the light of the Sun and Moon, our two great Luminaries.

[6] It is He whom all images in temples of every Faith represent; behind the gross outer form of the idol is its living subtle body, invisible to ordinary men, but used by the God in His activity—as is known to many of the devotees.

brothers and holy sisters [1] hail in giving of their praise !

3. O mighty Spirit, mightiest circling and incomprehensible Form of the universe,[2] hail ! Celestial, subtle, inter-ethereal ; like water, earth, fire and air, like light and darkness,[3] shining as do the stars—Spirit moist, hot, cold—I praise thee, God of Gods, who ever restorest the universe and storest away the Deep [4] upon its throne of settling, which no eye can see; who fixes heaven and earth apart, and coverest the heaven with thy golden everlasting wings,[5] establishing the earth on thrones ! O thou who hangest up the Ether in the lofty Height, and scatterest the Air with thy self-moving blasts, who makest the Water eddy round in circling wheels; O thou who raisest up the fiery Whirlwind and makest thunder, lightning, rain and earthquakes;

---

[1] *i.e.*, the priests and priestesses of various Faiths. Perhaps an allusion to some monastic community like that of the Therapeuts in Egypt or the Essenes near the Dead Sea.

[2] *or*: universal Form. This whole universe, with all its revolving worlds and galaxies and star-systems, is His body.

[3] Really infinitely subtle, yet manifesting as the outer elements of Nature, in opposed pairs.

[4] The 'Deep' is here clearly the infinite vastness of outer Space.

[5] An allusion to the outspread wings of the Egyptian Solar Disk in flight.

GNOSTIC HYMNS AND PRAYERS   261

O God of Aeons, mighty art thou, Lord God,
O Master of the All!

This is a dignified hymn to the pantheistic Cosmic
God worshipped by Hermeticists as well as by most of
the Gnostics and the wiser-minded of the pagans of
the early centuries. In places its language is of great
beauty, and we may specially note the acceptance of
God's will equally in joy or sorrow (*cf.* GG 54 : 4), the
knowledge that it is the spirits behind divine statues,
and not the idols themselves, which are to be worshipped, and that the universe is the true form or image of
the One real God, manifesting in all its various and
even opposite forms.

It has been drawn from Mead's TGH 408-409
and was published by Wessely in Denkschr. d. K. K.
Akad. (1888), p. 72, ll. 1115 ff.

92. Wisdom's Wedding-Song

1. The Maiden [1] is a daughter of the Light
   in whom is set . . . the leaping radiance
   of the Kings; [2]

[1] Gk. *korē*; she is the *Korē Kosmou* of the Hermetists, the Wisdom Above, foreshadowed in the later Jewish Canon: "Wisdom has built herself a house and underpropped it with pillars seven. . . . Wisdom is on the lofty Heights; she stands in the Midst of the Paths, for she sits by the Gates of the Mighty and sings hymns at the entrances (of the Fullness)" (Prov. 9: 1 and 8: 2 LXX).

[2] Syr. *zywa d' mlka ayt lh*; Gk. *hēi enestēke kai egkeitai to apaugasma tōn basileōn to gauron* shows obvious accretion here. This 'radiance' is the *hvareno* of Zarathushtrian scripture, whereby the Royal blood might be distinguished; the Soul, Wisdom, is of the Royal Race Above. This alludes to the Light-Crown on the rescued Soul of GG 59; the King is, as Mead says, God, Ātman. "(Wisdom) is the breath of God's Power and a pure influence flowing from the glory of the Almighty, therefore can no defiled thing enter into

And delightful is the sight of her
> shining with luminous beauty,

Whose garments are like spring flowers,
> and from them a breath of fragrance is wafted [1]

While on (her) head the King is found
> feeding on His Nectar there turned to Him [2] (1-8).

2. Now Truth reposes on her head,[3]
> while with her feet she rays out joy;

Her mouth is gracefully open—
> thirty and two [4] are those who sing her praises.

[The Son's twelve Apostles are there,
> and the seventy-two are thundering therein.][5]

---

her. For she is the brightness of the everlasting Light, the unspotted mirror of God's Power, and the image of His goodness" (Wisd. 7: 25-26).

[1] The sweet odour of the Spirit, as in GG 22: 3.

[2] Grace is not efficient only to the soul to whom it is entrusted, but to all who seek God in touch with her.

[3] *i.e.*, prevails over her and always leads her.

[4] Mead suggests this refers to the 'teeth' which are the 'palisade' in App: I: 5: 4. This may be the 'Boundary' between the Real and the unreal. Mead suggests that the 'thirty-two' may be the 22 letters of the Hebrew alphabet, plus the ten Sephiroth, used in the Jewish Gnosis of the time.

[5] This rather weak couplet, which obviously replaces one with deep significance to the Gnostic, is found only in the catholicized Syriac version.

Her tongue is like a curtain of the door [1]
    which is shaken for those who enter; [2]
Her neck rises like a flight of stairs [3]
    which the First Creator has fashioned.
Now her two hands make signs.
    and suggest that the choir of the happy
        Aeons are preaching,
While her ten [4] fingers
    suggest [5] the gates of the City.[6] (9-22)
  3. Her bridechamber is brightly lit,
    breathing an odour of balsam and spice,[7]
And giving out sweet scent of myrrh and
        foliage,[8]

---

[1] *i.e.*, the Veil of the Treasure of Light in GG 51: 1.

[2] *viz.*, the inner shrine; that is, the priests in an exoteric sense; esoterically, approved candidates for the Gnosis.

[3] The head is 'Jerusalem Above', the Shrine on the top of the stairway which, Mead says, has six stages, the Monad being at their summit. It is the Ladder up to Heaven in GP 33.

[4] The perfect number, twice that of the Five Limbs of GG 93: 1, a hymn found in the same Acts of Thomas.

[5] The Aeons are paired off as male and female (GG 13 : 1 and note), arranged in opposing rows, self-sufficient and self-complementary, says Mead.

[6] This is the Shrine or Bridechamber of GG 19 : 2 and all contemporary Mystery Religions, the inheritance of the Light-Kingdom wherein the Soul is made one with its Spouse; it is approached down here through the Gate of Life (PS 52, 198).

[7] Gk. *hēs ho pastos phōteinos | apophoran apo balsamou arōmatos diapneōn*.

[8] It has been suggested this is the scented leaves of the *tulasi*, India's holy basil-plant.

while myrtle (branches) are spread within
And heaps of sweet-breathed flowers;
  the folding-doors are beautified with reeds
  (23-28).
4. Her bridesmen have closely surrounded her,
  whose number is seven,[1] whom she
  herself selected;
While her bridesmaids too are seven[2]
  who lead the Dance before her.[3]
But twelve[4] is the number of those who serve
  before her
  and under her have watch and gaze on
  the Bridegroom,
That at the sight of Him they may be filled
  with light,
  And for evermore they will be with Him
  for that eternal joy;
And they shall remain in that Wedding
  whereto the Nobles are gathered together,

---

[1] Mead compares with the seven Gods of the Mithraic Rite; seven is a lunar number, a quarter of the month of 28 days. It also refers to the attendant planetary lords who serve, no longer rule, the victorious Soul.

[2] Mead compares with the Seven Virgins of the Mithraic Rite.

[3] She too dances in rhythm with them; cf. GG 30 : 2.

[4] The twelve zodiacal signs, also subdued, adore the central Sun of Perfection, her Spouse.

And stay in the Feast
> whereof the Eternals are held worthy;[1]

And they shall be clad in Royal Robes of Light,[2]
> and in both joy and ecstasy[3] (29-44).

5. Then they shall glorify the universal Father
> whose superabundant[4] Light they have received,

For they have been filled with Light
> at the very sight of their Master,

Whose Nectar they have obtained
> which has no waste at all,[5]

And they have also drunk of the Wine
> that gives them no thirst and bodily desire.[6]

---

[1] Those who have transcended the temporal and put on immortality are alone worthy to share the Feast of the Heavenly Bridegroom.

[2] Gk. *kai amphiasontai stolas lampras*. This is, of course, the Robe of Light, so often met in this group of religions, even in GP 28.

[3] Gk. *kai en kharai kai agalliasei*.

[4] Gk. *gauron*, as in para 1; or: leaping.

[5] In Clem. Strom. 3 : 7 : 59, Valentinus tells us that in the body of Jesus there was no waste or decay, even of food, which is a *siddhi* among certain Hindu yogis. Decay occurs only among corruptible mortals, not in the Immortal.

[6] Three sacramental Foods are named: Light, Nectar (or Water, used by certain sects), and Wine; to this day Catholics mix Water with the Wine.

And so they glorified and hymned,
together with the Living Spirit,
The Father of the Truth
and the Mother of the Wisdom [1] (45-56).

Mead has shown that this Gnostic hymn, preserved in the Acts of Thomas as sung at a wedding-feast, is more original in the Greek than in the present version of the original Syriac—which has been more carefully doctored in the interests of orthodoxy to make it seem to refer to the Church, Spouse of Christ.

Actually, the Maiden is Wisdom (GG 14 ff, 50-69), the human Soul—not here in its fallen state but glorified, redeemed, espoused to her Saviour (GG 19 : 2). She shines with the Light of her Father, who is a crown upon her head (GG 59 : 1), pouring out His rays on all the worlds (GG 7 : 3), while her robes spread around them the fragrance of the Spirit (GG 22 : 3). She is all beauty as her dancing feet and the songs in her mouth spread joy around her, and within her is the Shrine of the Temple into which the chosen Priest may enter; her neck rises to the glory-crowned head as a ladder to the skies, and her gestures make one think that divine Powers are telling of Heaven's glories.

There is brilliance and every kind of fragrance in her bridal-chamber, the heart where she is made one with the King, and scented boughs and flowers are strewn upon the floor. She is surrounded by the conquered planetary lords and their consorts, who solemnly dance around her (GG 30 : 2), while the twelve eternal worlds, or zodiacal signs, carry out her will; they gaze on the Sun of Righteousness, her

---

[1] The catholicized Syriac version replaces this with an orthodox Trinitarian formula.

Spouse, irradiated by His Light, joyful in His perpetual presence among them, robed in the royal vestures of Light that only His chosen ones may wear. They praise Him for the endless glory He reveals and for His gifts of Light (the Gnosis), Wine (Truth or Life) and Nectar (Immortality); they worship also the Spirit of all Life, the God of Truth, and the Universal Mother of the Wisdom.

93. Invocations by St. Thomas

1. Come, thou holy Name of the Christ![1] Come, Power[2] of the Highest and the perfect Compassion! Come, O highest Gift![3] Come, O Mother compassionate! Come, province[4] of the Male! Come, Revealer of the hidden Mysteries![5] Come, O Mother of the Seven Houses, that there be rest for thee in the Eighth House! Come, O Messenger of the Five Limbs,[6] commune with these younger ones! Come, holy Spirit, and purify their reins

[1] Gk. adds here: "that is above all names"—almost certainly an accretion.

[2] Gk. adds "of grace".

[3] Gk. *kharisma*, a word used by St. Paul in 1 Cor. 12 : 4.

[4] Gk. *oikonomia*, i.e., almost the sphere of activity.

[5] Gk. *elthe hē ta mustēria apokaluptousa ta apokrupha*. Though it is generally Christ who initiates, this prayer preserves the more ancient tradition that it is the Mother who is true Initiatrix.

[6] Gk. adds their names, much the same as in Mani's books: *noos, ennoia, phronēsis, enthumēsis, logismos*—sometimes translated as Mind, Thought, Planning, Imagination and Will, though there are other perhaps better words in English.

and heart, and seal them also in the (holy) [1] Name (Acts Thom. 27)!

2. Come, O highest Gift! Come, perfect Compassion! Come, O province of the Male! Come, Skilled in the Mysteries of the Chosen One! [2] Come, Sharer in all the combats of the noble Champion! [3] Come, Stillness that reveals the feats of all the Greatness! [4] Come, Shower of the hidden things, Explainer of the ineffables! Holy Dove that bears twin Nestlings,[5] come, hidden Mother! Come, thou Manifest in her deeds and giving joy and rest to those at one with her! [6] Come, and commune with us in this Thanksgiving we make in thy Name, in this Love-Feast to which we have gathered at thy call [7] (Act Thom. 50)!

---

[1] This word is only in the Syriac; it is followed by an obvious interpellation naming the Three Persons of the Christian Holy Trinity—out of place here.

[2] Gk. *hē epistamenē ta mustēria tou epilektou.*

[3] The Mother-Spirit always assists the fighter for spirituality against the snares of Matter; *e.g.*, GPM 4-6.

[4] God's wonders can be known in the silence.

[5] As Virgin of the Light, her two daughters are "Shame of the Dry" and "Image of the Waters"; that is, she is the mother of the physical and the astral or emotional bodies.

[6] Gk. *parekhousa kharan kai anapausin tois sunēmmenois autēi.*

[7] In early days the Eucharist, received fasting, was closely associated with the Agapē, or Love-Feast, wherein the Christians met together as members of one family and rejoiced together; this is a mark of the early date of this passage.

It is most likely that in these two similar prayers we have fragments of an actual eucharistic invocation of blessing upon the sacramental species of some Gnostic 'sect'. It is striking that, as the Holy Spirit is mainly invoked, the feminine gender is used throughout—in early days even the orthodox Christians of the East looked on the Spirit as the maternal nourishing aspect of God. The prayers are full of significant Gnostic phrases, whereon volumes of commentary could be written; there is very little distinctively Christian in them. We have both Greek and Syriac versions, whereof the Greek, though in places a little expanded, seems nearer the original.

94. Prayers of St. John

1. Jesus, who hast woven the crown that is thine own garland,[1] who hast woven the crown of all the Saints and these various plants, having changed men into thy flower which never fades;[2] O thou who hast spoken in our hearts thy words, thou who alone carest for thy servants; O Physician of our bodies who freely healest them all;[3] thou who alone dost what is good for us, . . . Lover of every man

---

[1] The Crown of Light on the Saviour's head is made up of all the 'Sparks' whom he has saved; cf. GG 83:4. Copt: *pentafsōnt mpeklom pai ethm peksōnt pōk.*

[2] A beautiful conceit; redeemed men become a fadeless flower-garland on the breast of Jesus; a like idea for Mani's Church is found in GPM 45:5.

[3] Copt: *ō psaein mpensōma eftalco mmoou tērou nijinjē.* In all these allied religions Jesus is often called the Physician of Souls; here he heals our bodies without fee.

... who art in every place and art from everlasting, ... it is thou who shelterest every one who trusts in thee (Rep. John, 3-4).

2. We give glory to thee, the Way; we give thee glory, the Seed, the Word, the Salt, the true Gem, the holy Storehouse, the Plough, the Net, the Greatness that has been sent for us children of men. ... We give thee glory, O Truth, Rest, Splendour, Power, Commandment, Frankness, Freedom, our place of Refuge. For thou art the Lord, the Root of Immortality and the Fountain of incorruption and the Strength of the Aeons [1]—for thy name has been set on all these things, so that through these we too might call on thee [2] (Rep. John, 4).

3. Let not the good God grieve on your account, the kind, the compassionate,[3] the

[1] *Cf.* this list of Names with other similar lists of our Gospel, *e.g.*, GG 34 : 1. All have their own deep meaning in a Gnostic sense. A passionate prayer in the Gnostic Acts of Peter is worth quoting here: " I give thee thanks with the silence of a voice wherein the spirit in me loves Thee, speaks to Thee, sees Thee and prays to Thee. Thou art perceived of the spirit alone; Thou art to me father, Thou my mother, Thou my brother, Thou my friend, Thou my slave, Thou my steward: Thou art the All, and the All is in Thee; and Thou art—and there is nothing else that is save only Thee! (39) " A prayer worthy of Vaishnava devotees.

[2] We approach the Divine through His creatures, over which His Name has been uttered.

[3] Copt: *pnaēt ṅsanhtēf*; almost the same as the Qur'ānic " *arRaḥmānu arRaḥīmu* ".

spotless, the immaculate, the one and only, the changeless, the one without guile or anger, the Name that is over every thinkable name.[1] Let Him rejoice with you while you share happy citizenship with Him;[2] let Him rejoice with you while you live in peace and innocence; let Him be glad with you while you busy yourselves in reverence;[3] let Him be free of care while you live in celibacy; let Him be delighted at your brotherly sharing in good and (in) things offered (to Him); let Him revel that you love Him, let Him laugh that you are ready[4] (Rep. John, 3).

Though found also in Gk., and thence translated by M. R. James, pp. 108-109, I have preferred to use the Coptic version of this fragment of the old Acts of John, already so familiar to us from the fragments in GG 29-40; John uttered these beautiful prayers just before 'falling asleep'. The long list of names of the Lord in para 2 may be compared with those of the Cross in GG 34 : 1; on each of them a sermon might well be preached, and most of them relate to some parable of Jesus in a canonical Gospel. Such a list is found also in Gita 9 : 17-18.

[1] As having all names He is nameless; what name can be equal to His who is the All? Who can give Him a name save He Himself?

[2] Copt: *etetnpoliteue naf kalōs.*

[3] Copt: *etetnanastrephe hn oumntsemnos.*

[4] *i.e.*, for any sacrifice for Him, for anything He may choose to send.

95. Marcosian Prayers

1. I do not separate the spirit, the heart, and the merciful Power above the heavens;[1] may I enjoy Thy Name, Saviour of Truth!

2. Over all the Father's power I invoke what is called Light and Good Spirit and Life; for thou hast reigned in the body.[2]

3. In the Name of the unknown Father of the universe, in Truth,[3] Mother of all, in the one who came down into Jesus[4]—in union and redemption and sharing of the powers, . . . peace to all on whom this Name reposes (PG 7: 662-665)!

4. May the Grace beyond thought and speech (that was) before the universe fill thy inner man and increase in thee the Gnosis of itself, sowing in the good earth the grain of mustard-seed![5]

---

[1] Gk. *ou diairō to pneuma, tēn kardian kai tēn huperouranion dunamin tēn oiktērmona.* I cannot imagine any explanation of this sentence which would deny its advaitic content.

[2] *i.e.*, the Spirit of Goodness has controlled the body, so it can be safely adjured.

[3] Gk. *alētheia*, a feminine noun, perhaps the mother-aspect of Deity; some have suggested the name of Valentinus's Gospel refers to this great 'Aeon'.

[4] *i.e.*, the Holy Spirit which, according to the Gnosis, descended into Jesus at the Baptism. We have here the Gnostic Trinity.

[5] *i.e.*, Gnosis, which grows from a tiny source to a vast tree overshadowing the whole world of mind.

5. O Helper of God and of mystic Silence before the Aeon,[1] ... we take thee as Guide and Introducer [2] lifting up their forms which that greatly daring one imagined,[3] (and) through the Forefather's good emanated us the images (of Him?), ... do thou present to the Judge, as representing both (of us), the case of us both as being one.[4]

6. I will to impart my Grace to thee since the Father of the universe sees thy Angel throughout before His face.[5] Now the place of the Greatness is in us, we must be one.[6] Take first from me and through me the Grace; prepare thyself as a Bride awaiting her Spouse,[7]

---

[1] *i.e.*, that Silence in whose womb creation was planned by God as a Seed (*cf.* GG 12:2).

[2] Gk. *hodēgōi soi kai prosagōgei khrōmetha*.

[3] *i.e.*, who seeking the Infinite plunged out of the Fullness into the dark Chaos beyond; the 'Wisdom' of GG 13-14 ff.

[4] Identifying himself with his pupil, the Teacher asks Wisdom, who helped God produce the world, to speak for them both to the Judge of actions, that all sins be forgiven them.

[5] The pupil is one of the 'little ones' spoken of by Jesus in Mt. 18 : 10. As at baptism the Soul is reborn, so in the Initiation it is a little child. In his Gospel, Valentinus says: "In their turn came the little children to whom belongs the Gnosis of the Father; when they had been confirmed, they learned the aspects of the Father's face; they recognised (and) were recognised; they were glorified (and) they glorified " (CJ 19).

[6] As the same God lives in both Teacher and pupil, they must feel their own oneness in Him.

[7] Grace adorns the maid as a Bride to meet her Lord, as told in many religions; *e.g.*, GGS 47: 3.

so that thou mayest be what I (am) and I what thou (art).¹ Enthrone in thy Bride-chamber the Seed of the Light;² then receive from me the Spouse,³ and make room for Him and be given place in Him. See, the Grace has descended on thee, open thy mouth and prophesy⁴ (PG 7: 581-591c)!

7. I, a Son from a Father—Father pre-existing but Son in existence⁵—have come to see all things,⁶ (both) of others and my own—yet not altogether alien (to me)⁷ but of Aḥamōth who is (my) Consort⁸ and made these for herself. But I derive the Race from

---

¹ So that the pupil may become adult enough to be a Bride, as the Teacher already is, and so that the Teacher may in the pupil relive that sacred at-onement. Gk. *hina esēi ho egō kai egō ho su.* *Cf.* GG 84: 3.

² Enthrone the little 'mustard-seed' of God as King in your heart's shrine.

³ Christ comes to the pupil in the form of the Teacher—an idea familiar to Catholics as well as to Hindus.

⁴ *i.e.*, speak what He bids you speak, do always according to His will.

⁵ *i.e.*, the Manifest God, in whom we all are, derived from the Non-Being God of GG 20: 2 ff.

⁶ We have come to this world to learn what it has to teach; having learned, there is no further need of birth in physical bodies.

⁷ Even those most unlike the Soul, everything in the universe is actually related to us, because all are a part of Nature—as we too are—and so akin to us.

⁸ *lit.* female (Gk. *thēleia*); *cf.* Skt: *śakti*, in the sense of Consort with creative powers.

the Pre-existing,[1] and go again to my own whence I came.

8. I am a Vessel[2] far nobler than the Female (Power) which made you;[3] if your mother knows not her Root, I know myself and realise whence I am,[4] and I invoke the imperishable Wisdom that is in the Father and (is) Mother of your mother,[5] yet having neither mother nor male consort. A female born of a Female made you, (one) not even knowing her Mother and thinking herself to be alone.[6] But *I* invoke her Mother (PG 7: 665-668).

Irenaeus published these invocations and declarations in trying to refute the Marcosian 'heresy' derived from Valentinus; but the Marcosians themselves denied their authenticity. Yet there is nothing in them of which

---

[1] The Initiate declares her origin in the Non-Being God and her goal to return to Him.

[2] *i.e.*, I hold the Spirit (Gk. *skeuos*).

[3] I am far above mere Nature. "I created Man from unseen and seen Nature; his death and life are an image of both" (2 Eno. 30: 10).

[4] Nature does not know she is derived from the feminine aspect (*śakti*) of God, but the Initiate does know his source (*cf.* GG 84: 3).

[5] Wisdom is the Mother of Nature (Ahamoth), the distorted 'abortion' which came from her premature attempt at full Gnosis (GG 14 : 1). The Initiate is the Child of Wisdom herself.

[6] *i.e.*, Nature, child of Wisdom, and unaware of the very existence of Wisdom herself, still more unaware of God.

any follower of the Gnosis need be ashamed, and some contain great truths.

The first asserts that the individual is one with the universal Lord, while the third calls down all Divine blessings on devotees of the holy Name, of which Valentinus's "Gospel of Truth" has so much to say. The fourth prays that Grace may enter and grow mighty in the heart, while the fifth asks for the help of the unseen God in facing the judgment of the Soul—though I suspect some confusion in Irenaeus's text. The sixth exhorts to a oneness with God found through the Teacher (*Guru*), while the seventh proudly asserts that the Soul is from God and has come into the world only to learn of Matter, and the last repeats that the Soul is not of the world but from Above, and she knows her origin is divine.

96. From the Bruce Codex

1. Hear me while I praise Thee, Thou First Mystery who has shone out in His mystery [1] and caused IEOU [2] to establish the Aeons, and appointed Rulers and Ministers and Servants in the Aeons,[3] whose imperishable names are — and — . Save all my Limbs scattered abroad since the foundation of the world in the Rulers and Ministers and Servants

[1] God Manifest, appearing as the universe.

[2] The name is, as always, overlined in Coptic, showing it is an abbreviation. He is the Angel who organises the universe, the highest below God Himself. He is the 'God of Truth' who emanates all things (GIG); associated with the Three Voices A-O-U or A-O-E, he cries Ie Ie Ie! and shines forth as emanations.

[3] *i.e.*, in the eternal worlds. Copt: *henarkhōn mn-hendekanos mn-henlitourgos*; these are the rulers of signs and decanates and single degrees.

of the Aeons; gather them all in, and take them to the Light [1] (GIG 78-82).

2. I hymn Thyself, O God unattainable,[2] for it is Thou who hast shone forth in Thine own Self and evolved a Light-Image; Thou didst establish it around Thy very Self.[3] For what then is Thy will? To make all these things exist, O inaccessible God.[4] I hymn Thee, O God unattainable in other regions; to them Thou art an Inaccessible in these regions of these 'Great Words about each Mystery'.[5] Thy Greatness Thou hast placed in them, Thy will being also to let them approach Thee in them.[6] For what then is Thy will? To let all these things exist,[7] O God Unattainable (GIG 97).

---

[1] *Cf.* GG 84: 3, etc. God is asked to save from the Chaos of universe all the scattered individual Souls.

[2] Copt: *pnoute piatnratf*.

[3] The universe is itself God, in another 'form', reflecting the Divine Light.

[4] Copt: *pnoute piatnratf*, written with the usual hieroglyphic sign.

[5] This is the title of the book whence this prayer is taken; it describes the rites and magic words and numbers appropriate to each 'mystery' up to the Highest.

[6] "How could anything have endured if it had not been Thy will?" (Wisd. 11: 25). Through objects we come to their Source.

[7] God has set His glory in every creature, so that all may come to Him through the image of the Divine in themselves and in other creatures. This is God's great Plan, that through the darkness of Matter the One Light may be followed to its Source in Him.

3. Hear the prayer of the Man [1] in every place who prays with full [2] heart (GL 274)! For because of Thee we have put on this glory, and through Thee we have seen the Father of the universe AAAŌŌŌ,[3] and the Mother of all things who is hidden in every place,[4] who is the Thought of every Aeon, ... the Gnosis of every Invisible.[5] ... Because of Thine Image we have seen Thee [6] and have fled to Thee and received the fadeless Crown which through Thee has come to be known [7] (GL 242).

In the first para. Jesus prays to the manifest Father-God; in the original it is repeated for each of the Aeons, or eternal worlds, only the magical names, here represented by blanks, varying with each Aeon. He asks that His children, scattered through all the universe, may be once more gathered together into one

---

[1] To be taken as representing all mankind.

[2] *lit.* whole (Copt: *hēt tērf*).

[3] The Alpha and Omega, thrice manifested to represent its triple manifestation. " The universe has come out of Alpha, and shall return to the Omega when the fulfilling of all fulfilment takes place " (GIG 124).

[4] The universal Mother is the Divine Wisdom through whom God created all, and She is to be found in everything.

[5] While the outer self (*aeōn*) can think of Her, the unseen inner Self can know Her.

[6] God has been seen through His reflection in the universe as in a mirror.

[7] This is the Crown of Light, the garland of fair flowers spoken of by St. John in GG 94 : 1.

(GG 84 : 3, Jn 17 : 21, etc.) and glorified. The second para. likewise is a formula repeated 24 times in the original with slight variations; it forms part of the triumphant closing prayer of Jesus in the book so long wrongly styled after Schmidt "The Books of Iew". God has willed that a universe should manifest, so that through all creatures the Soul in each may draw near to Him.

The last para. is from the prayer of the creatures to God, thanking Him that through His manifestation they have seen Him, the Alpha and Omega, the Beginning and the End of all, the universal Source and Mind and Knowledge. It is through His beauty as seen in His Image, the world (GH 17 : 2), that they have received all their glory.

97. The Mother's Prayer for Her Children

1. Thou alone art the Infinite[1] and . . . the Unknowable . . . Deep,[2] and it is Thou whom everyone seeks but has not found Thee; for no one can come to know Thee against Thy will,[3] nor has anyone power to bless Thee save by Thy will alone. And it is only Thy will which has become place for Thee—for nothing

---

[1] Gk. *aperantos*, what cannot be transcended.

[2] *Cf.* GG 6 and 12 : 1; the word is often rendered 'Abyss'; there is little real difference between the various Gnostic "schools".

[3] Only by God's grace can we even wish to know Him; *cf.* Kathopaniṣad, 1 : 2 : 22: "Whom the Self chooses, by him is He attained."

(else) can be a place for Thee, as Thou art the place of all of them.[1]

2. I implore Thee to give order [2] to those of the world, and to give my children [3] commandment according to Thy pleasure; and do not grieve my children—for no one has ever grieved on Thy account,[4] nor has anyone known Thy counsel.[5] It is Thou of whom all stand in need,[6] within and without, for Thou alone art Unattainable, ... the Invisible and ... the Unsubstantial.[7] It is Thou alone who hast given qualities to every creature [8] and hast manifested them in Thyself. Thou

---

[1] Being infinite, God can be contained by nothing save Himself, His own will.

[2] Copt: *taxis*; the prayer is for peace and light to all beings.

[3] Copt: *tiwō*; lit. offspring. Nature does not give birth like a human mother; her children arise from within her as if spontaneously and parthenogenetically.

[4] It is never God who gives us pain; we suffer the results of our own folly and ignorance. The child touching fire is burned; God does not burn her.

[5] Nor has anyone understood why God lets us err and suffer; only God's direct control of all we do can save us from this.

[6] Copt: *ntok petousaat mmok tērou naphoun mn-napbol*. "That perfect Father who produced the All, in whom is the All, and whom the All needs" (CJ 18).

[7] Copt: *ouakhōrētos mauaak ... pahoratos ... panousios*. This last word is hard to render in English; *ousia* in Gk. means 'being, essence, substance' in a philosophical sense; we have here the negative form, prefixed by the Coptic definite article (p).

[8] The characteristics of each being come from God and are given by His will; so the acts resulting from those characteristics cannot be divorced from His will, even if they be what we call 'evil'.

art the Creator of those who have not yet manifested, for it is these whom Thou alone knowest—we know them not.[1] It is Thou alone who showest them to us, so that we may pray to Thee for them.[2] ...

3. It is Thou alone who hast brought Thyself to the measure of the hidden worlds until they have come to know Thee (and) that it is Thou who hast given them birth [3] in Thy incorporeal Body [4] and hast created them. For Thou hast produced Man in Thy self-grown Mind [5] and by Reflection and completed Thought. ...

---

[1] " Those who do not yet exist do not know Him who has produced them; I do not say, then, that those who do not yet exist are nothing, but they are in Him who desires that they should exist when He wishes it, like an event which is still to happen," says Valentinus (CJ 27-28), whose thought is very close to that of our author. We pre-exist in God's mind.

[2] God knows things before they come into being, and in due time brings them into being, so that we may ask Him for them—Copt: *jekaas eneaiti mmok etbēētou*. This does not mean to pray for their welfare, but that we may have them according to our need (*cf.* Mt. 6 : 11).

[3] God humbles Himself to the understanding of His yet unformed creatures, so that they may come to realize Him as their Source.

[4] *i.e.*, the universe, body of God, not made of flesh but of space and stars and creatures infinitely various; Copt: *hm peksōma nasōmatos*.

[5] God's Mind of itself arose in Him and was uncreated; Copt: *hm peknous nautophuēs*.

4. It is Thou who hast given Man all things, and he has put them on like clothes and has worn them like robes; he has wrapped himself with creation like a mantle.[1] This is the Man whom the universe prays to know,[2] (and) it is Thou alone who hast bidden the Man appear, so that through him Thou mayest be known;[3] for it is Thou who hast produced him, and Thou hast manifested (him) according to Thy will.

5. Thou art He to whom I pray, Father of all fatherhood, and God of every god, and Lord of every lord—this One whom I implore that He give order[4] to my forms and my offspring, to whom in Thy Name and in Thy Power I have given quiet.[5] O only Monarch and sole Changeless One,[6] grant me a power

---

[1] How beautifully does this describe man's control of that part of the universe in touch with him! Copt: *afcolf m̂psōnt n̂the ñourṣōn* "Now the most ancient Word of That-which-is is vestured with the universe as his robe" (Philo: de Prof. 20).

[2] *i.e.*, the Divine Man, Cosmic Perfection, God Manifest, the Christ.

[3] Through this Perfect Man God is revealed.

[4] Copt: *taxis*.

[5] Again we find calmness as the first requirement for the spiritual life, as in GG 81: 1. It is also the final goal—stillness.

[6] Copt: *patṣibe mauaaf*.

and I shall let my children come to know Thee, that Thou art their Saviour (GL 258-259).

This sublime prayer for the enlightening and enriching of all beings in God's universe comes very near the end of what is elsewhere known as the 'Untitled Apocalypse', for its real title has been lost with the first few pages. Its theology is surely unsurpassable by human language; God is shown as the unknown Beloved of all, in all, who showers His gifts on all, whose infinite Being can alone satisfy the longing heart of everyone, who has made all things that we may through them seek and approach Him by our very love for them—for He alone is the real Object of all our love.

He has humbled Himself to manifest in creatures, limited by their limitations, having been conceived only as thoughts in His creative Mind. He has lavished His richest gifts on Man, His child, and taught him to seek the Ideal in the Human God who came down for him into this lower world. To such a God of Love and Humility the Divine Mother prays for all her children, that they may be rightly governed, taught and led into all the Truth, once they have learned the secret of the quiet and silent Stillness.

CLOSING PRAYER

HEAR us, then, . . . O deathless Father, and God of the hidden things, and only Light and Life, . . . the Silence and Love and Fountain of the Universe! . . . Hear our prayer whereby we have prayed to the One hidden in every place; hear us, and send to us bodiless Spirits,[1] so that they may dwell with us and teach us what Thou hast promised us, and dwell in us and we shall be a body for them.[2] For this is Thy will to bring it to pass—so let it be![3] And govern our work and establish it according to Thy will and to the

---

[1] Copt: *henpneuma nasōmatos*. This clearly invokes guidance and help from the inner worlds where discarnate spirits dwell. I do not think attention has ever been paid to the extreme likelihood of the whole of the revelation of the Gnosis having come, like so much in our own days, from such psychic sources behind the veil of Matter.

[2] First the Spirits draw near to us, then as they come closer they can enter into us, so that we come to embody their wisdom, foresight and kindness.

[3] Copt: *je pekwōṣ pe pai etrefṣōpe, marefṣōpe.*

bidding of the hidden Aeons;[1] and govern ourselves, for we are Thine[2] (GL 262-263)!

We close this 'Gospel of the Gnostics', then, with a prayer to the omnipresent universal Lord of Light and Life and Stillness, that He may send to us spirits who may lead and teach us all the Gnosis, and enter into us that we may do their good will in the outer world. So shall God's will be done in us, and so shall our lives be rightly ruled by His wisdom and the leading of the eternal Powers behind His throne. This we claim from Him, because we belong to God, we are His children, in us He has chosen to manifest His boundless glory, and to Him is consecrated our all for evermore.

---

[1] *i.e.*, let all we do be guided and made successful by conformity with God's will and as the good Spirits of the inner planes inspire in us.

[2] Copt: *auō ngtoṣn hōōn, je anon pe nouk.*

APPENDICES

APPENDIX I

THE MYTH OF MAN IN THE MYSTERIES

PRESERVED in the heart of Hippolytus's interesting and valuable refutation of doctrines co-existing with early Christianity, we have a long and important text—most of which I reproduce here. Reitzenstein and Mead have shown that it is complex in origin; it seems certain that a Christian Gnostic (a Naassene) has in it commented on the commentary of a Jewish Gnostic (Simonian?) upon a pagan and pre-Christian Source. To a large extent I agree with Mead in the assignment of each sentence or phrase to these three origins, which are distinguished here as follows: The pagan Source is in Italics, the Jewish Commentary in Roman type, and the Christian additions, much of which I have omitted as irrelevant to ordinary students, in square brackets. The editorial comments of Hippolytus have been quietly omitted.

1. Introduction

These (Naassenes) . . . honour 'Man' and a 'Son of Man', . . . Male-female, who is called Adamas,

... and to him many different hymns are made, such as: "*From thee Father, and through thee Mother, the two deathless names, parents of Aeons, O Man, glory-conferring citizen of Heaven!*" ... [There are of him the intuitional, the psychic, and the earthy (types), ... but the knowledge of him is a source of being able to know God. ... Now all these, the intuitional, the psychic and earthy, have come out and descended at one time into one Man, Jesus, the one born of Mary; and they speak simultaneously, each ... from their own natures to their own (kind).]

2. The First of Men

1. *Now Earth, say the Greeks, first gave out a Man bearing a gift,*[1] *not wishing to become a mother of insensitive plants or irrational beasts (only), but of a gentle and God-loved creature. But it is hard to find out whether Alalkomēneus*[2] *rose as first of men for (the) Boeotians over Lake Kēphisis,*[3] *or whether Idaean*[4] *Kurētēs*[5] *were a divine race,*

---

[1] Emerging from Chaos, the Earth-Mother bore her son Uranus, who poured on her the fertilizing gift of rain, so that she spontaneously produced men.

[2] The first Man, who appeared near Lake Copais in Boeotia, near Athens, before the Moon was; he was Athene's tutor and advised Zeus against Hera, his wife.

[3] *or*: Lake Copais, into which flowed the River Kēphisos.

[4] *i.e.*, belonging to Mount Ida in Crete.

[5] Rhea's sons, who protected the infant Zeus from Kronos, and later vainly guarded Zagreus, who was lured away to death by the Titans; they were five in number, and were called the fingers of Rhea's right hand.

APPENDIX I

or the Phrygian [1] *Korubantes*,[2] *whom first the Sun saw springing up like trees; whether Arcadia*[3] *(saw) Pelasgos*[4] *before the Moon, or Eleusis*[5] *(had) Diaulon, dweller of Raria,*[6] *or Lēmnos*[7] *gave birth to Kabiros,*[8] *fair child of unspeakable orgies,*[9] *or Phellene the Phlegraean*[10] *Alkuoneus,*[11] *eldest of Giants.*

2. *Now the Libyans say (that) Iarbas,*[12] *first-born arising from arid plains, began with the sweet date of Zeus, but*

---

[1] In the west of Asia Minor, there was a very ancient orgiastic cult of the Divine Mother; here arose most of Greek music to the flute.

[2] Crested dancers born of Apollo, god of Music, and the Muse Thalia; at the winter solstice they danced to drum and cymbal, and they were priests of Rhea.

[3] The oldest and most backward province of Greece; the people were said to be Pelasgians; they worshipped Pan, long retained human sacrifice, and were hunters and herdsmen.

[4] The indigenous man of South Greece, who taught his descendants to make huts, sew skins and eat acorns; their sins led to Deucalion's flood.

[5] A small town west of Athens, very early famous for the Mysteries of Demeter and Persephone in the month Boedromion.

[6] On this plain Demeter taught Triptolemus the use of the plough and seed-corn.

[7] On this large Aegean island Hephaistos (Vulcan) had his worship among the volcanic caves.

[8] The Kabiri (great ones?) were perhaps of Phoenician origin and were worshipped in many places with orgiastic rites. H. P. B. speaks much of them.

[9] orgies: *i.e.*, inspirations, revelations.

[10] At Phlegra was the war between the gods and the giants.

[11] The Giant leader who twice raided the Sun's cattle and revived his strength every time Herakles threw him on the soil of his native Phlegra; at last on the advice of Athene Herakles dragged him into Boeotia, where he was easily slain.

[12] *or*: Garamas, son of Apollo and the daughter of Minos of Crete. He was born in Libya and was King of the Gaetulians, vainly suing for Dido's hand.

Egyptian Nile, to this day fertilising mud and breeding living things enfleshed by damp heat, gives out living bodies.[1] *But (the) Assyrians (say) fish-eating Oannnēs*[2] *appeared among them, while Chaldaeans (speak) of Adam.*[3] And him they allege to be the Man whom the Earth alone gave forth, and that he lay unbreathing, unmoving, motionless like a statue,[4] being an image of That Above, [the hymned Man Adamas].

3.[5] So in order that the Great Man from Above might be perfectly obeyed [from whom . . . every fatherhood is named on earth and has been formed in the heaven] a Soul was also given him, so that through the Soul the enslaved model of the great and most fair and perfect Man might suffer and be chastened. Now . . . Soul is very hard to find and difficult to understand, for it does not remain always of the same appearance or form, or of one mood, so that one could express it by symbol or grasp (it) by essence. Therefore (they doubt . . . whether) it is

---

[1] Gk. *ilun epilipainon mekhri sēmeron zōogonōn hugrāi sarkoumena thermotēti zōa sōmata anadidōsin*; perhaps from an Ode of Pindar.

[2] The fish-headed deity who came ashore near what is now Basra and founded the Mesopotamian culture; this may indicate that the earliest Sumerians came from beyond the Persian Gulf—could it have been from India?

[3] So the book of Genesis calls the first man; it has early Chaldean parallels. "They called him 'Adam' symbolically, through four elements out of the whole Sphere calling him according to the body", says the Apocalypse of Nicotheos, an early Jewish (?) Gnostic, referred to by GL.

[4] *i.e.*, God Manifest, being Man in the image of God.

[5] Mead ascribes most of this paragraph to the Source, which is itself a commentary on the Ode given in App. I: 8: 2.

sometimes from the Pre-existing, or from the Self-borne, or from the fluid Chaos . . .[1]

3. The Love of Adonis and Attis

1.[2] For of Soul every nature is enamoured, each differently, for Soul is the Cause of all things produced; whatever is nourished and grows needs Soul, for it is impossible to get any nourishment or growth unless Soul be present. For even the stones are ensouled, for they have the power to grow; and without nourishment there would never be growth, for things that grow increase by adding, and the adding is a nourishing of the nourished. . . . Therefore every nature . . . yearns after Soul.

2. *Now (the) Assyrians call such a one* [3] *Adōnis* [4] *or Endumiōn;* [5] *and when he is called Adōnis, Aphroditē* [6] *loves and*

---

[1] *i.e.*, Kronos, Zeus, or Rhea (Hyle, Spouse of Heaven); *cf.* GG 88: 1.

[2] Mead attributes this paragraph also to the Source.

[3] *i.e.*, so-called.

[4] A Sun-hero, whose name is the Heb. *Adonai*, lord. Born of a sword and a myrrh tree, he was brought up by Persephone, but Aphrodite claimed him, and he was given to each for 4 months in the year. When Aphrodite cheated, Ares, or Apollo, became a boar and gored him to death before her; from his blood sprang the crimson anemone; drops of myrrh-gum were tears shed for him in the spring festival on Lebanon; he was known as Tammuz to the Mesopotamians.

[5] The Moon granted him eternal youth when she fell in love with him in a cave. As King of Elis he celebrated the Olympic Games.

[6] The Greek goddess of love, who came from the sea-foam near Paphos in Cyprus; she was born of Zeus and Dione, and wed Hephaistos, but loved Ares; the Romans called her Venus.

desires the Soul of such a name. But when Persephonē,[1] and Korē, is in love with Adōnis, the said Soul separated from Aphroditē [meaning generation] [2] *is subject to death. Now if Selēnē*[3] *enters into desire for Endumiōn* [4] *and loves (mere) form (yet) the nature of the higher beings needs a Soul also. And if the Mother of the Gods* [5] *castrate Attis,* [6] *while she has him as sweetheart, the blessed nature of the supernal and everlasting ones above recalls to itself the Soul's male power.* . . . For Attis was castrated, that is, from the earthy parts of the down-tending creation, and departed upwards to the everlasting Being, [where there is neither female nor male but a new creation, a New Man, who is male-female.] . . . This is the unspeakable and mystical teaching.

---

[1] *lit.* ' bringer of destruction '; she was carried off by Hades to be his Queen in the underworld, but escaped from a cave in Eleusis, and because she had eaten seven pomegranate seeds below ground she had to return there every year for three winter months; she is also called Korē, the Virgin.

[2] M attributes these two words to the Source; I cannot agree.

[3] The Moon, who fell in love with the sleeping Endumion in a cave.

[4] The Moon granted him eternal youth when she fell in love with him in a cave. Asking of Elis he celebrated the Olympic Games.

[5] *i.e.*, Cybele, a Phrygian form of the Mediterranean Mother-goddess.

[6] A lovely Phrygian shepherd who, being unfaithful to Cybele, was made mad by her, deprived of his manliness, and changed into the fir-tree under which he bled to death. This was the origin of certain secret rites.

APPENDIX I

4. Osiris

1. *The Egyptians, of all men after the Phrygians most ancient,*[1] *and at the same time admittedly first to communicate to all the other men the rites*[2] *and sacrifices of all Gods, and in having proclaimed forms*[3] *and forces—have the Mysteries of Isis,*[4] *holy and venerable and not to be disclosed to the uninitiated;*[5] *and they say Osiris is Water,*[6] while the seven-robed Nature, surrounded and arrayed with seven ethereal vestures, . . . is *the ever-changing Genesis,* and is shown as a creation transformed by the Ineffable and Unportrayable and Incomprehensible and Formless One. And this is what is said in the Scripture: "Seven times shall the righteous fall and rise again",*[7] for these are the changes of the stars moved by the Mover of all.

---

[1] All Greeks admitted as beyond dispute the immense antiquity of Egyptian religion and ritual; but it is interesting to learn here that they considered Asia Minor yet older; we have not yet dug deep enough into the prehistoric levels on the Aegean coast to check on this belief. The Greek Hymn of Kumē, Isis speaking, says: "It is I who have revealed initiation to men; I have taught men to honour the statues of the Gods; I have founded the Gods' sanctuaries" (25-27).

[2] Gk. *orgia;* i.e., secret mysteries, often of human sacrifice.

[3] Gk. *ideas,* prototypes.

[4] Wife of Osiris, the mystical Mother of the Child Horus, the dawn-sun and the young initiate. Her cult spread widely in the early centuries, even as far as to Britain and Armenia.

[5] These words Mead ascribes to the Source; he may be right.

[6] For many explanations of Osiris see Plutarch's famous treatise, translated in Mead's TGH, vol. 1. In one aspect, he is the fertilising fluid.

[7] Quoting Prov. 24: 16 LXX; *cf.* Lk. 17: 4.

2. *The essence of the Seed, which is cause of all that come into being, is not of these, but begets and makes all things that are,* saying thus: " I become what I will, and am what I am."¹ That is why I say that the Mover is (Himself) unmoved, for what exists continues to make everything and becomes none of the things produced.² *This alone is Good,* [and about this is the saying proclaimed by the Saviour: " Why callest thou me good? One is good, my Father who is in the Heavens."]³ ... *and this is the great and secret thing of the universe, and an unknown mystery concealed and revealed among the Egyptians. For in a shrine Osiris is in front of Isis, and his hidden thing stands naked, ithyphallic and crowned with the fruits of all things produced.*⁴ *And he stands as first of idols in the holiest* [of holy] *shrines ... for the instruction of all,* [as it were a light (not) under the bushel but placed on the lampstand,⁵ a sermon preached on the housetops]⁶ *in all lanes and all streets and near the very houses, set forth as a kind of ' Boundary ' and ' Limit ' of the house; and this is said by all to be the Good,* [for they call it good-producing, not knowing what they say].

---

¹ This seems to be a quotation from some Gnostic Gospel, perhaps that of Eve or that of Philip. It is probably a pre-Christian gnomon originally, Hermetic (?).

² Mead ascribes this sentence also to the pagan Source.

³ The usual reading of early manuscripts of Lk. 18: 19.

⁴ Mead reads: " crowned with the fruits of generation ". Here Osiris has been identified with the prehistoric phallic deity of Egypt, Min.

⁵ Quotes Mt. 19: 17.

⁶ Quotes Mt. 5: 15 and 10: 27.

5. Hermes, Leader of Souls

1. *Now especially honouring the thumb*[1] (they say) *'Learned', for Hermes is a Logos who, being at the same time Interpreter and Maker of things that have been, are being, and will be brought into being, stands honoured* (among them), *represented by some such figure as a man's genital urged from things below to things above.*

2. *And he . . . is Soul-leader and Soul-Sender*[2] *and cause of Souls; nor does this escape the poets of the Gentiles, speaking thus:* "*Now Kullenian Hermes*[3] *called out souls of mindful men*"—not of Pēnelopē's[4] suitors,[5] O unhappy ones! but of the awakened and recollected ones —"*from so great honour and such great bliss (have I fallen here on earth to mix with mortals!*")[6] That is, they have been brought down here into the clayey plasm from the Blessed [or Primal] Man Above, [or Adamas] so

---

[1] Gk. *kullēnion*; in his frequent phallic form Hermes was called Kullenian, honoured on a pedestal at Kullene, says Pausanias.

[2] *lit.* evoker; he sends souls back to rebirth.

[3] The son of Zeus and Maia was born in a cave on Mt. Kullēnē in Arcadia; he was at first the phallus of an archaic fertility cult, and early associated with the fire-drill; to him were sacred the crane and the alphabet. He rescued Korē from Hades in his chariot, and so became conductor of the dead, leading them to the ferryman over the Styx. He wore a winged helmet and sandals, and carried in his hand a wand with intertwined serpents —the *kuṇḍalini* (?).

[4] Pēnelopē was the faithful wife of Odusseus, who promised to consider her many suitors in his absence once she had finished her weaving, which she undid every night.

[5] The Gk. *mnēsterōn* has both meanings: suitors, reminded.

[6] Quoting Empedocles 'On Purifications'; the line in brackets was probably omitted in error by Hippolytus himself.

that they might serve Ialdabaōth,[1] the Maker of this creation, a fiery god, fourth in number.[2]

3. "*Now he holds in hand a Wand, / beautiful, golden, and with it enchants the eyes of men / whom he will, and further awakens those who sleep./ This is the one who alone holds authority of life and death.*"[3] Of him it is written: "Thou shalt shepherd them with an iron rod",[4] but the poet, wishing to adorn the ill-contrived of the blessed nature of the Word, put for him the rod not (of) iron but of gold. "*And he enchants the eyes of the dead, and further awakens those who sleep*"—those who have been roused from sleep and have become mindful. [Of these the Saviour says: "Awake, O slumberer, and arise, and the Christ will enlighten thee!"[5] This is the Christ who in all that exists is 'Son of Man' portrayed from the unportrayable Word.][6]

4. This is the great and ineffable Mystery of the Eleusinians: "*O Wetter, beget!*",[7] and to him all things have been subjected;[8] and this is the saying: "Into all

---

[1] or: Esaldaios; i.e., El-Shaddai, the mighty God; cf. GG 52: 4, where this Ruler is made up of fire and darkness mingled.

[2] Mead points out that Ptah=Hephaistos, the fiery one, is the 'Fourth.' in chapter vi of TGH I.

[3] Quoting Odyssey 24: 2 ff.

[4] Quoting Ps. 2: 9 LXX.

[5] Quoting Eph. 5: 14, apparently a verse from an early Christian hymn.

[6] Mead renders this: "whom no expression can express".

[7] Gk. huĕ kuĕ, each word a dissyllable. We need not go into the literal meaning of this evocation; it is in effect a call for new life. Cf. Plutarch de Iside, 34.

[8] Mead refers this clause to the Philonic Jewish commentator.

APPENDIX I 297

the earth their voice has gone out "[1]—*as Hermes leads, waving the Wand, and the Souls twittering continually follow, just as the poet has shown by means of the figure, saying:* "But as when bats into an awesome cave's recess/ fly squeaking, when one falls/ of a cluster from the rock, they cling to one another"[2]—'rock' means 'of Adamas'. This is the Adamas, "the cornerstone become the head of a corner[3] ... which I insert as a diamond[4] in Zion's foundations"[5]—he speaks allegorically of the plasm[6] of the Man. Now the Adamas is entrapped within the ... teeth,[7] as Homer says, "a palisade[8] of teeth"—that is a wall and palisade wherein is the Inner Man, fallen therein from the Primal Man Above, Adamas, that "cut without hands",[9] dividing and bringing him down into the earthy clayey plasm of forgetfulness.[10] ... "*Twittering, the Souls, follow him, the Word; / as these were twittering together, then gracious Hermes went*

---

[1] Quoting Ps. 19: 4; *cf.* Rom. 10: 18.

[2] Quoting Odyssey 24: 5 ff.

[3] Quoting Ps. 118: 22.

[4] Gk. *adamanta*, the hardest of 'stones', a pun on the name of Adamas.

[5] Referring to Isa. 28: 16.

[6] Gk. *plasma*; model (?).

[7] Mead corrects as: "For the Adamas who is inserted is (the Inner Man, and the foundations of Zion are) the teeth." This may be right.

[8] Gk. *kharakōma*, a Gnostic term for the 'Boundary' of GG 14: 2 etc.

[9] Refers to Dan. 2: 15.

[10] These parentheses may well be from the Christian Gnostic.

to, that is, led, *them down dreary paths* [1]—that is, to the eternal places freed from all badness. For whence did they come? "*Now they passed over Ocean's streams and White Rock,*[2] / *by the Sun's gates and a land of dreams!* " [3] This is the Ocean, Genesis of Gods and genesis of men, ever whirled by ebb and flow, now up, then down.

5. Now when the Ocean flows down, it is the birth of men, and when (it flows) up to the Wall and Palisade and the White Rock, it is the birth of Gods. This is the writing: " I have said you are all gods and sons of the Highest [4]—if you hasten to flee from Egypt and cross over the Red Sea into the desert "—that is, from the intercourse below to the Jerusalem above which is the Mother of the Living.[5] " But if you turn back again to Egypt "—that is, to the intercourse below— " you shall die as men." For all the lower birth is mortal, but that which takes place above (is) deathless, [for it is born of water and spirit alone, spiritual not fleshly, while that below (is) fleshly.] . . . This is the spiritual birth,[6] this is the great Jordan which, flowing

[1] Quoting Odyssey 24: 9-10.

[2] *Cf.* Iliad 14: 201, 246; and Orphic Hymns 83: 2.

[3] *or*, Leucas, an island in the Ionian Sea; at its south end criminals were thrown over a high cliff at Apollo's annual festival; it was also a ' leap ' for unlucky lovers.

[4] Quoting Ps. 82: 6.

[5] *Cf.* Gal. 4: 27: " But Jerusalem Above is free, which is our Mother ", and Philo (de Som. 2: 39): " The Hebrews call the City of God Jerusalem, which means the ' Sight of Peace'; wherefore seek not the City of that which is in earthly regions, . . . but in the Soul that does not war, but offers to those of keen sight a life of contemplation and of peace."

[6] These words Mead ascribes to Hippolytus himself.

downwards and preventing the Israelites from going out of Egypt—meaning, from the intercourse below, for Egypt is the body—Joshua [1] drove back and made flow upwards.

6. The Threefold Source

1. *He who says all things are derived from One errs; he who says (they are) from Three is right and will give the (true) explanation of the universe.* For one is the blessed nature of the Blessed Man Above, [the Adamas]; and one the mortal (nature) below; and one the Kingless Race which is born from Above—where are Mariam the sought-for and Iothōr the great Sage, and Sepphōra the seeing,[2] and Moses whose generation was not in Egypt,[3] for " children were born to him in Midian ". *And neither did this escape the poets: " And all things were triply divided, and each (had) a share of honour."* [4] For the feats [5] must be declared, and be thus declared by all in every way, . . . for if the feats were not declared, the world could not hold together. These are the three

---

[1] *or*, Jesus. In Gk., of course, the same name. As Joshua led Israel into Canaan, so Jesus leads the Race Above into the true Holy Land, Jerusalem Above. As Joshua turned back the waters of Jordan to let them cross, so Jesus reverses the 'waters of generation' to produce gods, not men.

[2] Mead thinks this may come from a drama " The Leading-Forth " by some Hellenistic Jew, Ezechiel; all spellings are from the Septuagint.

[3] *i.e.*, his 'children' were not born of the flesh, Egypt, but of encratism, the desert, that is, spiritual children.

[4] Quoting Iliad 15: 189.

[5] *or*, greatnesses, often a technical Gnostic term.

tremendous words: KAULAKAU, SAULASAU, ZEĒ-SAR:[1] 'Kaulakau' of the Above, the Adamas; 'Saulasau' of the Below, mortal; 'Zeēsar' of the Jordan flowing upwards.

2.[2] *This is the great and ineffable Mystery of (the) Samothracians,* [which it is lawful only for us the perfected to know], for the Samothracians explicitly pass on that Adam(as) in the Mysteries which are solemnised among them, as Primal Man, *and in the Samothracian temple there stand two idols of naked men, having both the hands stretched up to heaven, and ithyphallic like that of the Hermes in Kullēnē.*[3] Now the aforesaid images are idols of the Primal Man [and of the newborn spiritual one, in all respects coessential with that Man]. . . .

3. *This is the male-female Man in all, whom the ignorant call three-bodied Gēruonēs,*[4] *as though from ' Gē-reonta', earth-flowing; but (the) Greeks generally (call him) ' Mēn's*[5] *celestial horn', because he has mixed and blended*[6] *all things with all.* [" For by him were all things made, and without him not even one came into being; and what

---

[1] *Cf.* Isa. 28: 13 (Heb.); " trial on trial, hope on hope, still little, still little—*i.e.,* the depth of trial, the height of hope, and as yet very little. *Cf.* PS 354. The name Zeēsar seems to appear in GG 88: 2.

[2] I have accepted Mead's rearrangement of these two paragraphs.

[3] Kullene was the highest mountain of Arcadia; the name is used as a pun between the phallic Hermes, born there, and the phallic symbol of the thumb.

[4] A three-headed, six-handed monster born in Spain, whose daughter married Hermes; Herakles robbed him of his red cattle and finally killed him.

[5] The Phrygian Moon-god.

[6] Gk. *kekerake*, a play on *keras*, horn.

came into being in him is Life ¹ " ; this is the ' Life '—the ineffable Race of the perfect men.] . . . This is the drinking-cup, " the goblet in which a King divines while drinking ",² and this was found hidden in the fair seeds of Benjamin.³ *And the Greeks also speak of it thus with frenzied tongue:* " Bring water, bring wine, O boy! / Intoxicate me and stupefy; / My cup says / from what land I must be born, / (speaking with silence unspeaking)." ⁴ This alone is enough for men to understand that the Cup of Anacreon,⁵ without speaking, utters an ineffable mystery; for Anacreon's Cup is speechless, yet Anacreon says it speaks to him with wordless sound " of what country he must be born ", [that is, spiritual not fleshly], if he would hear the mystery hidden in silence.

7. He of Many Names

1. *This one the Thracians ⁶ living around (Mount) Haemus ⁷ call* KORUBAS,⁸ *and the Phrygians equally with*

---

[1] Quoting Jn. 1: 3-4.

[2] Quoting Gen. 44: 5.

[3] lit. ' son of the Right ' (*ben-yamin*), and so here a type of the spiritual man born from Above; *cf.* GG 38: 2. The story of his sack is found in Genesis.

[4] Cruice adds this line, probably omitted in error by Hippolytus or his copyist.

[5] A famous lyrist of B.C. 550-465, who celebrated the praises of wine and love, like 'Omar Khayyam' and with perhaps a like hidden meaning.

[6] A cruel warlike people with savage blood-rites; from their midst Orpheus and Linus are said to have come.

[7] The Balkan range north of Thrace, now in Bulgaria.

[8] *Cf. koruphē*, head; a play is made on the word: *ho apo-koruphēs-bas*, the one coming down from the head. After Korubas the Corybantes were named.

Thracians, because from the head above and from the unportrayed [1] brain of *taking the beginning of the descent and coming through all the sources of the things below—how and in what way he comes down we do not understand.* This is the saying: "We have heard his voice, but his form we have not seen." [2] For when he is set apart and portrayed a Voice is heard, but the Form that came down from Above, from the unportrayed, no one knows what it is like; it is in the earthy plasm,[3] but no one recognises it.

2. This is the "God dwelling in the flood" according to the Psalter, and "crying (and) shouting from many waters." [4] 'Many waters' is the various genesis of the mortal men, from which he calls and shouts to the unportrayed Man, saying: "Save my aloneborn from lions!" [5] To this effect is a saying: "My child art thou, Israel, fear not! If thou pass through rivers they shall not drown thee, if thou pass through fire it shall not burn thee up!" [6] By 'rivers' he means the moist essence of birth, while 'fire' is the urge and desire for birth. "Thou art mine, fear not!" and again he says: "Even if a mother forget her children, not to pity them or give them suck, yet shall I forget

---

[1] Mead takes this word as 'expressive'.

[2] Perhaps from some Jewish apocryphon, now lost; *cf.* Jn. 5: 37 and GG 33 : 3.

[3] Gk. *plasma*; the word occurs in our 'protoplasm'.

[4] Quoting Ps. 28 : 10, 3.

[5] A conflation of Ps. 24 : 17 and 21 : 21, LXX.

[6] *Cf.* Isa. 41 : 8 and 43 : 1.

you?" Adamas says to his own men: "Nay, even if a woman forget these things, yet shall I not forget you! On my hands have I painted you."[1]

3. And about his Way Up, [that is, the rebirth that he may become spiritual not fleshly], the Scripture says: "Lift up (the) gates, O Rulers, and raise yourselves, eternal Doors, and the King of Glory shall come in!" This is a wonder of wonders, for "who is this King of Glory?"[2] A worm and no man, a scorn of man and contempt of people,[3] "he is the King of Glory, the one mighty in war!"[4] He says 'war'—that in a body, because the plasm has been made up of fighting elements, as it is written: "Remember the war waged in a body."[5] Jacob saw this Entry and this Gate when travelling into Mesopotamia—[6] ... now 'Mesopotamia' is the current of the great Ocean flowing from the midst of the Perfect Man—and he wondered at the heavenly Gate, saying: "How terrible this place! This is nothing but the House of God, and this the Gate of Heaven!"[7] [This is why Jesus says: "I am the true Gate"].[8] Now he who says these

[1] Isa. 49: 15-16, LXX.
[2] Ps. 24: 7, 9-10.
[3] Ps. 21: 6.
[4] Ps. 24: 10, 8.
[5] Job. 40: 27.
[6] The land 'between the rivers', *i.e.*, the spiritual going up, and the material coming down.
[7] Gen. 28: 7, 17.
[8] Probably from some apocryphal Gospel; *cf.* Jn. 10: 9.

things is the Perfect Man portrayed from the Unportrayable Above; [so the Perfect Man cannot be saved unless he is reborn by entering through this Gate.]

4. *This same one (the) Phrygians also call PAPA, because he ' calmed '* [1] *all things moved disorderly and inharmoniously before his own manifestation. For the name of PAPA is of all things simultaneously*—of the celestials, terrestrials and infernals—*saying " Calm, calm* [2] *the discord of the earth and make peace for those afar "*—that is, for the material and earthy—" *and peace for those at hand "*—that is, for the spiritual and intuitional* [3] Perfect Men. *And the Phrygians also call this same one CORPSE,* [4] *as it were in a sepulchre and tomb when buried in the body;* . . . [and again he says: " The dead shall leap out of the sepulchres ", that is, out of the earthy bodies, being reborn spiritual not fleshly. This is the Resurrection which takes place through the Gate of the Heavens; all those who do not enter through this remain dead] *and again the same Phrygians call this very one GOD-AFTER-TRANSFORMATION,* [5] [for he becomes a God when, having risen from the dead, he enters through such a Gate into Heaven. . . . These are by all called the ineffable mysteries [6] . . . of the

---

[1] Gk. *epausen.*

[2] Gk. *paue, paue.*

[3] Gk. *noerois.*

[4] Gk. *nekun.*

[5] Gk. *ek metabolēs theon.*

[6] Mead has: " These are the mysteries, ineffable (yet) spoken of by all ".

Spirit, which we alone know, . . . for it is very hard to accept and receive this great and ineffable Mystery; . . . none has become a hearer of these mysteries save only the perfect Gnostics. . . . This is the Fullness whereby all that exist, born from the Unborn, both came into being and were filled.]

5. *Now this same one is also called FRUITLESS*[1] *by the Phrygians*, [for he is unfruitful so long as he is fleshly and works the desire of the flesh, . . . for these ' fruits ' are only the rational,[2] the living, men who enter in through the Third Gate.] . . . If you eat dead things and make living ones, what will you make if you eat living things?[3] Now by 'living' **I** mean Words and Minds and Men—the 'pearls' of that Unportrayable thrown down into the plasm[4] below. [This is what he says: "Do not throw the holy thing to the dogs, nor the pearls to the swine";[5] now the work of swine and dogs is the woman's intercourse with man.]

6.[6] *And the Phrygians also call him VERY FRUITFUL*,[7] because "the children of the solitary are more

---

[1] Gk. *akarpos*.

[2] Gk. *logikoi*.

[3] Perhaps a quotation from the Phrygian Mysteries. Precede it with "At any rate they say" . . . (J). *Cf.* Lk. 23:31. It is obviously full of meaning.

[4] Gk. *Plasma*.

[5] Mead asks if this can be a play on *hue* (*hus*, pig) and *kue* (*kuŏn*, dog); *cf.* Mt. 7:6.

[6] I have accepted some rearrangement of paragraphs suggested by Mead.

[7] Gk. *polukarpos*.

than hers who has the husband ",[1] [that is, the things reborn deathless and ever-remaining are many, even though those born were few], . . . and Jeremiah also laments for the Jerusalem Below—[not the city in Phoenicia,[2] but the corruptible birth below], for Jeremiah also knew the Perfect Man [who is born again from water and spirit, not fleshly]; at any rate the same Jeremiah said: " He is a Man, and who shall know him? "[3] [Thus the knowledge of the Perfect Man is very deep and hard to grasp], for " source of Perfection (is) knowledge of Man, but knowledge of God (is) absolute Perfection ".[4]

7. *Now this same one the Phrygians call AIPOLOS,[5] not because he pastures she-goats and he-goats as the* **ignorant**[6] *name (him), but that he is Aipolos, that is, the ' ever-revolving ' and turning and carrying the whole world round by turning.* For ' polein ' is to turn and change affairs—whence all call the two centres of heaven ' poles '. Now the poet says: " Which unfailing old

---

[1] Isa. 54: 1. Philo says that the Soul which ceases to bring forth passions becomes mother of all virtues through God. Mead sees here a sign that the Jewish commentator may have been of Philo's school.

[2] Of course, an error, which no Jew could have made; the Naassene was unacquainted with the niceties of Palestinian geography.

[3] Jer. 17: 9.

[4] Mead thinks this is from some Gnostic mystical apocryphon; I agree.

[5] *lit.* goatherd. Here used in a different sense.

[6] Mead rightly suggests that ' psychics ' in the text must have replaced this word in the hands of the Naassene commentator.

man of the sea hither comes and goes?[1] / Egypt's undying Prōteus."[2] He is not 'bought and sold',[3] but as it were revolves and 'goes round himself'. Yet further the cities wherein we live are also called 'poleis', because we turn and circulate in them. So the Phrygians call AIPOLOS this one who always turns everything everywhere, and changes (them) into what is fitting.

8. *And further the Phrygians say the Father of the universe is an ALMOND* [4]—not a tree, but he is that pre-existing 'Almond' which, *having in itself the perfect Fruit as it were vibrating (?)* [5] *and stirring in the depth, rent its Womb* [6] *and produced its invisible* [and unnameable and ineffable] *Child* [of whom we speak]. For *amuxai* is as it were to break and cut open, just as in the case of inflamed and abscessed [7] bodies the surgeon lancing it says *amukhas*. Thus the Phrygians call him 'Almond' (*amygdalos*), from whom the Invisible proceeded and was produced, [through whom all came into being and without him nothing came to be].[8]

---

[1] Gk. *pōleitai*.

[2] Odyssey 4: 384. Egypt is here, Mead says, the Nile, the 'Great Green' of outer Space. Prōteus was the oft-changing servant of Poseidōn, Atlantean god of the sea.

[3] Gk. *piprasketai*, often a synonym of *pōleitai*.

[4] Gk. *amugdalon*.

[5] Reading for *oion idiāi sphuzonta—hoionei diaphuzonta*.

[6] or: bosom. Gk. *diēmuxe tous kolpous autou*. The word derives from *amuxai*, here by a play associated with *amugdalon*.

[7] *lit.* containing some boil.

[8] Jn. 1: 3, reading, as usual in early copies, *ouden* for *oude hen*.

Now the Phrygians say what has come into being from him is a PIPER,[1] *because what came to be is a harmonious breathing,* [*and the Spirit is there where both the Father is named and the Son born from this Father.*]

9. *Now the Phrygians also call him REAPED GREEN CORN-EAR*,[2] *and after the Phrygians the Athenians*,[3] *initiating* (*in the*) *Eleusinian Rites, also show the neophytes there a reaped ear of corn as the great* [*and wonderful and most perfect*] *supreme Mystery in silence. Now this ear is* among Athenians *also the* [*perfect great*] *Light from the Unportrayable—as is the Hierophant himself, not emasculated like Attis, but made a eunuch by hemlock . . . by night in Eleusis under a great fire*[4] *when, enacting the great and ineffable Mysteries, he cries and shouts, saying:* " *Queen Brimo*[5] *has borne a holy Son, Brimos!* "[6]—*that is, a Mighty one a Mighty. Now* ' *Queen* ' *is the* [*spiritual*

---

[1] Gk. *suriktēs*, player on the seven-reeded Pan-pipes called the Syrinx.

[2] Gk. *khloeron stakhun tetherismenon*. The Bull of Mithra often has a tail ending in a wheat-ear, or else the like flow from its heart; it represents the sperm of man, fruitful of new life.

[3] From an early date Athens more or less controlled the Rites at Eleusis.

[4] Mead has: " to the accompaniment of much fire ", *i.e.*, when it blazes forth. All lights in the ' Telēstērion ' were put out, then the door was opened and in a blaze of light the mystical drama began.

[5] *lit.* raging. Mystagogues entered dressed as shepherds, shouting as they showed a winnowing-fan holding the holy Child, said to have been the fruit of rubbing the phallic object on a woman's top boot. At the New Year Demeter, the Earth-Mother, was called Brimo.

[6] Also known as Iacchus son of Iasius and Demeter; the hymn was sung to him on the sixth day of the New Year Rites during the ' entry ' called ' *eleusis* '.

heavenly] Birth Above, and 'mighty' is he thus born. For the Mystery is termed ADVENT (*eleusis*) and ROYAL (*anaktoreion*) [1]—'Advent' because we [the spiritual] have come [2] from Above, pouring down from the Adamas, and 'Royal' (from) *anagesthai*, (to lead back, that is from) 'returning up'. This is what those say who are initiated in the Mysteries of the Eleusinians.

10. *Now it is a law that those initiated in the Lesser be further initiated in the Greater, for* "*greater destinies win greater lots*".[3] *Now the Lesser Mysteries are those of Persephone Below—about which mysteries and the way leading there* [being wide and spacious] *and leading* (*the perishing*) *to Persephone, a poet also says:* "*Beneath her, moreover, there is a rugged path,*[4] */ deep-cut* (*and*) *miry, but best as guide / to greatly honoured Aphrodite's charming grove.*"[5] *These are the Lesser Mysteries* [those of the fleshly birth], *having been initiated into which Lesser ones men ought to pause and* (*then*) *be initiated into the Greater* [the heavenly] *ones.* "*For those who share portions*[6] *receive greater destinies*". For this is the Gate of Heaven and this the House of God, where the Good God dwells alone, into

---

[1] Gk. *anaktoreion*, said to be derived from *ana-ktorein*, to return upwards.

[2] Gk. *ēlthomen*, derived from the root *eluth—*.

[3] Heracleitus has: "For greater deaths win greater lots."

[4] Mead reads: "Beneath this there is another path death-cold."

[5] This quotation may be from either Parmenides or Pamphus of Athens.

[6] Mead has "deaths"—which were shown portrayed in the Greater Mysteries.

which no one unpurified shall enter, [neither psychic nor fleshly], but it is kept for (the) spiritual alone, and having come to be there (they) must throw away the garments, and all become Bridegrooms emasculate [1] through the Virginal Spirit. Now this is the 'Pregnant [2] Virgin', conceiving and bearing a Son [not psychic, not bodily, but a blessed Aeon of Aeons].

8. Is One Soul

1. This is the many-named, myriad-eyed Incomprehensible, whom every nature desires in various ways. This is the Speech of God [which is an utterance of " an Announcement of the Great Power "],[3] wherefore it will be sealed and hidden and concealed, stored up in the Dwelling where the Root of the Universe is founded, . . . an indivisible Point out of which gradually the tiniest thing begins to expand, which, being nothing and composed of a nothing—being an indivisible Point —will become by its own thought some inconceivable Vastness. [This is the Kingdom of the Heavens, the seed of the mustard,[4] the indivisible Point existing in the body, which no one knows save the spiritual alone.]

[1] Gk. *apērsenōmenous*. I see no reason to follow Mead in changing this into *apandroumenous*, becoming true men. The present word gives correct Gnostic sense; *cf.* GG 84: 2. The whole text reads: *kai pantas genesthai numphious apērsenōmenous dia tou parthenikou pneumatos*.

[2] lit. the having in belly—*hē en gastri ekhousa*.

[3] The title of Simon the Gnostic's great Book, which may indeed be actually a Simonian commentary on a pre-Christian apocalypse.

[4] *Cf.* Mt. 13 : 31.

APPENDIX I

This is the saying: "There are no words or language whereof their voices are not heard."[1] . . .

2. So then, when the crowd assembles in the theatres, and someone clad in exotic dress comes on the stage carrying and playing a lute,[2] he speaks thus, chanting the Great Mysteries (though) not knowing what he says:

> "*Whether Race of Kronos,[3] or blessed one of Zeus or Great Rhea,[4] Hail Attis, Rhea's mournful strain![5] Assyrians call thee thrice-longed for Adōnis, and all Egypt calls thee Osiris; the Greeks, Mēn's heavenly horn (and) wisdom; Samothracians, venerable Adama; Haemonians Korubas; while the Phrygians sometimes Papa, and then Corpse, or God,[6] or the Fruitless, Ever-turning, or Reaped Green Ear of Corn, or the one whom Many-fruited Almond brought forth—Man, or Piper!*"

This is (the) many-formed Attis, and when they sing to him they speak thus:

---

[1] Ps. 18: 3.

[2] The lute or kithara was triangular and had seven strings.

[3] Mead reads: "Whether blest Child of Kronos, or of Zeus, or of Great Rhea." Kronos, the youngest of the Titans, was son of Sky (Ouranos) and Earth (Ge), and husband of Rhea. He deposed his own father and was in turn deposed by his son Zeus, whom he vainly tried to devour.

[4] Daughter of Sky and Earth, identified with Cybele, Mother of the Gods, in Asia Minor, who emasculated Attis.

[5] Gk. *akousma*. The probationers of Pythagoras were called the *akousmatikoi*, hearers. The Song begins when Rhea changes from chaos to cosmos.

[6] Mead suggests: "or alive", from Gk. *theein*, to run.

"*I shall hymn Attis with boomings of Rhea's bells, not to the tune of the pipes of Idaean Kurētēs, but I shall blend (it) with music of Phoebus' lyres—Evoi Evan! Like Pan,[1] like Bacchus,[2] as a Shepherd of shining Stars!*"

APPENDIX IIa

THE PRODIGAL SON

There was a man who had two sons, and the younger of them [3] said to his father, " Father, give me the share of the property that comes to me." [4] So he divided his wealth between them. Not many days later, the younger son sold off everything and went abroad to a distant land,[5] where he squandered his means in loose living and excess.[6] After he had spent everything, a terrible famine set in throughout that land, and he began to be in want; so he went and hired himself to one of the citizens of that country,[7] who sent him to

---

[1] Arcadian god of flocks and shepherds, usually a son of Hermes, who invented the shepherd's flute or syrinx, and wandered here and there, hunting or dancing with the nymphs.

[2] Another name for Dionysos, god of wine; son of Zeus and Semélē, he was brought up by nymphs, later placed among the stars as the Hyades; wandering over the known world, he established the cult of the vine.

[3] The elder son is the 'Viceroy' of GG 72 : 2; he stays at home.

[4] *i.e.*, the rich bundle of precious things given the Prince in GG 70 : 1.

[5] *i.e.*, Egypt, the physical body.

[6] *i.e.*, the food given him in Egypt, whereon he became 'drunk'.

[7] The service of the king of that country, GG 72 : 2.

his fields to feed swine.[1] Then he longed to make a good meal of the pods the swine were eating, but none gave him anything.[2]

But when he came to his senses,[3] he said: "How many of my father's hired men[4] have more than enough to eat, while I am here perishing of hunger! I will be up and away to my father, and I will say to him: 'Father, I have sinned against heaven and against you; I do not deserve any more to be called your son; only treat me like one of your hired men.'"[5]

So he got up and went to his father. But when he was still a good way off,[6] his father saw him and pitied him, and ran and threw his arms round his neck and kissed him.[7] The son said: "Father, I have sinned against heaven and against you; no longer do I deserve to be called a son of yours." But the father said to his servants: "Quick, bring the best robe[8] and put it on him; fetch a ring for his finger and sandals for his feet. And bring the fat calf and kill it,

---

[1] *i.e.*, to indulge in the pleasures and lusts of the flesh; *cf.* App. I: 7 : 5.

[2] These pleasures can do nothing to satisfy his need, which is spiritual.

[3] *i.e.*, was roused from the drunken sleep, as in GG 73 : 1.

[4] Those who are inseparably dependent on God in heaven, and could not exist apart from Him.

[5] So the Prince kissed the Letter in humble acknowledgment; GG 73 : 1.

[6] *i.e.*, at the 'Boundary' of the East (GG 74).

[7] "He rejoiced in me and welcomed me" (GG 77).

[8] *i.e.*, the Robe of Light, shot with countless colours; GG 75 : 2.

let us eat and enjoy ourselves;[1] for my son here was dead and has come to life again;[2] he was lost and is found again." So they began to make merry. . . . (Lk. 15::11-24).

APPENDIX IIb

THE STORY OF CYRIACUS[3]

1. By the same Gate of the Lord the righteous enter in.[4] Because I prayed to my God, my Mother made for me a Robe and adorned it with pearls.[5] . . . And at the signal of the Spirit's Letter[6] I was sent into the Dark City, where there is no light, nor sun, nor moon, nor stars.

2. Now when I came into the City, whose name was Marsh-Sea,[7] I found ass-centaurs and horse-centaurs,

---

[1] The wedding feast of the returning Soul; cf. GG 92 : 4.

[2] The true resurrection from the dead for all Gnostics.

[3] Derived from the 5th century Syriac Acts of Cyriacus and Julitta—text printed by Reitzenstein in his 'das iranische Erlösungsmysterium', pp. 77-79—this quaint fragmentary story still bears traces of the old Gnostic quest of the Pearl narrated in our GG 70-77.

[4] Cf. App. I: 7: 3.

[5] Here we have the begemmed Robe of Light given the seeker.

[6] It is at God's will the Soul enters the darkness; cf. GG 54 : 2. This 'Dark City' corresponds to 'Egypt', the body.

[7] Perhaps this name, Gk. Limnothalassa, suggests the marshes of northern Egypt, where, round Alexandria, in early days the Gnosis throve. Horus was born in these marshes, the mystical son of Light.

and wise serpents, and a horde of demons;[1] and they tried to destroy me, but the Letter chased them away from before me.[2] And then I came into Babylon,[3] ... to the river called Sandy, which men can only cross on the Sabbath day, for it is decreed also for it to keep (each) one of the Sabbaths.[4] Now in the river there was the overflow from the Deep, and all was sand, nor could anyone see the waters of the river.

3. Then I crossed the river and came to the City, ... and there I found (ass-centaurs and) horse-centaurs, and serpents, and the Reptile-King of the Earth, whose tail lies in his mouth and a path of destruction runs before him. His teeth are as sharp swords, his ribs of brass, and his spine of iron; his talons are an eagle's, his couch like sharp points, and his food papyrus and cattle-fodder. Out of his nostrils comes a breath as of smoke, and whenever his mouth opens it takes in for seven days the River Jordan, nor does it flow out of his mouth.[5] This is the Dragon which by passions led astray the Angels from the heights; this is the

---

[1] These correspond to the 'men of Egypt' with their 'filthy ways'.

[2] The Letter of God protects the Soul from his worldly foes.

[3] Here too, as in GG 71 : 1, Bābel plays a part; centre of the world's commerce at one time, it naturally came to stand for worldliness.

[4] Only through obedience to God's Law can the 'river' be crossed.

[5] This terrible description of the 'Dragon' may be compared with that by Mani in GPM.

Dragon which misled and threw out of Paradise the first Adam, ... which opened the storm of the torments which pervert the truth and the souls of men.[1]

4. Seeing me, this one sought the right to drink me up, but my Letter muzzled his mouth; ... it burned up that great Dragon, and chased from before me all the power of the Evil One, and gathered all the surviving power out of Israel,[2] and made them dwell in that City,[3] so that they might shine with one accord.

5. Now this (is) the sign in the City: the threshold (is) of iron and the gate of iron, whose top (is) three hundred cubits (high) according to the cubit of giants. And in the last days, so it was said, the iron threshold will be worn away under the trampling of the footsteps of the men who pass over it, until nothing is left of the iron in that place where it is crossed.[4]

6. And when I came into the City of the Kingdom, I fulfilled my vow.[5]

---

[1] The text has many other less relevant deeds of the Demon King. It may be noted that this late text refers to the old legend of the Fallen Angels or the 'Watchers' of GY.

[2] *i.e.,* gathered the limbs which were scattered abroad; *cf.* GG 84: 3.

[3] This City is the Heavenly City, the Jerusalem Above, to which the returning exiles are gathered in.

[4] A way of expressing the vast number of its citizens.

[5] Probably, since we are not told what the vow was, it was to challenge the evil beings in the Dark City and return victorious to his Home.

APPENDIX III

FROM THE CHALDEAN ORACLES[1]

1. The Universal Source

1. All things have the One Fire for their Father,[2] . . . for Mind is not without the Intelligible, nor does the Intelligible subsist apart from Mind. . . . He is the all-embracing Monad who begets the Two; . . . from both of these flows the body of the Three, first yet not first; for it is not by this that intelligible things are measured (1: 42, 29, 42-43).

2. God is wholly good, . . . He who governs all things with the Mind of the Eternal, . . . vehicled in rare Drawers-of-straight-lines,[3] flashing inflexibly in furrows of inflexible Fire. . . . For nothing that is imperfect spins from the Paternal Source; . . . the Father does not sow fear, but pours forth persuasion (1: 30, 52, 64, 30).

3. Conceiving with His will in all its prime, the Father's Mind emanated Ideas that can take all forms upon themselves, and taking flight, they sprang forth

---

[1] These Syrian Oracles, of unknown but great age, survive only in quotations by Proclus, Damascius, and other late pagan writers, and give us a good idea of the pre-Christian Gnosis. The text was published, so far as it has hitherto been recovered, by Scott in his 'Hermetica', and by this I have checked on Mead's excellent translation which I have mainly followed here. Reference is to the page number of his two little volumes on The Chaldean Oracles.

[2] The author insists on a single Source of the all.

[3] *i.e.*, geometricians.

from One Source. For from the Father was both Will and End; these were differentiated by Knowing Fire (and) allotted into different knowing modes. For the King laid out an intellectual unchanging Plan for the many-formed world. Kept to the tracing of this Plan that no word can express, the World gladdened with the Ideas that take all shapes grew manifest with Form.[1] There is but One Source of these Ideas, from which others evolve in differentiation that no one can approach—bursting forth round the bodies of the world —which circle around its awe-inspiring Deeps like swarms of bees flashing incuriously around and about them, some hither and some thither—the Knowing Thoughts from the Paternal Source which fully cull the flower of Fire at height of sleepless Time. (But) it was the Father's first self-perfect Source which welled forth these original Ideas (1: 66-67).

2. The Universe Evolves

1. The cosmos-transcending Paternal Deep [2] ... is all things, but intelligibly, ... what cannot be cut up,[3] the holder together of all sources, ... Source of sources, Womb that holds all things together. ... She is the Energizer and Forth-giver of life-bringing Fire, ...

[1] Creation, as in the Hebrew books, was by an act of Divine Will, but continued through an evolutionary process.

[2] The reader will note the parallels with 'The Gnosis of the Light'.

[3] *i.e.*, the indivisible atom; Copt. *patpōs*, ultimately, the individual.

possessed of mighty Power, . . . and flows fresh and fresh into the wombs of things (1 : 55-58).

2. Thence leaps forth the genesis of Matter manifoldly worked in varied colours; thence the down-streaming Fire-flash dims its flower of Fire as it leaps into the wombs of worlds. For thence all things begin to shoot down their admirable rays, . . . for from Him leap forth both inexorable Thunderings and the Fire-flash-receiving Bosoms of the all-fiery radiance of Father-begotten Hekatē, and that by which the flower of Fire and mighty Breath is girt beyond the fiery poles (1: 61-62). The Whirls created by the Father's Thought are themselves intelligent,[1] being moved by wills ineffable to understand, . . . for all Cosmos has inflexible intelligent sustainers. . . . But to the Knowing Fire-whirls of the Knowing Fire all things yield, subject to the Father's will which makes them obey (2 : 15-16, 19).

3. The Father's Mind uttered that all should be divided into three; His Will nodded assent,[2] and at once all things were so divided. . . . You must know (that) after the Father's thinkings **Nature**, the Soul, dwells, making all things live by heat. . . . For He does not lock His transcendent Fire, the Primal Fire, His Power, into Matter by means of works, but by energy of Mind.[3] For it is Mind of Mind who is the Architect

---

[1] The words *noētos*, *noeros*, and other cognate expressions abound here.

[2] This reminds us of the Kosmopoiia published in 'Abraxas'.

[3] *i.e.*, by thought, and not by action, He creates.

of this fiery world;[1] . . . it is a Copy of Mind, but what is brought forth has something of Body (in it also). . . . The Father caused to swell forth seven firmaments of worlds, . . . (and) the centres of the material world are fixed in the aether above it (1: 51, 48, 38, 85, 75-76).

3. The Light-Spark Appears

1. These things the Father thought, and made mortal to be ensouled; . . . the Father of men and gods placed Mind in Soul and Soul in inert Body, . . . a portion of the Divine Fire. . . . For Soul, being shining Fire by reason of the Father's power, both keeps immune from death, while Body is of Life and has the fullnesses of many wombs (2: 30-32).

2. The Father's Mind has sown Symbols in the Souls; . . . He gave to some to receive the Token of the Light, to others even while asleep He gave the power of bearing fruit from His own might. . . . For the Mind of the Father has sown Symbols through the world—(the Mind) that understands intelligibles and thinks out ineffable beauties (2: 43, 76, 43). For the Aloneborn, the Father's Mind,[2] perceiving His works, sowed Love's bond into all that overmasters all with His Fire; so that all might continue loving on for endless time, and that these weavings of the Father's

---

[1] *i.e.*, the real Demiurge is the Mind which fancies all things and so brings them into being—wherewith the Vedanta would agree.

[2] As among the Gnostics, the Mind of God is styled the Aloneborn (*monogenēs*).

Knowing Light might never fail. It is with His Love, also, the elements of Cosmos keep on running.[1]. . . With the bond of admirable Love, who first leaped forth clothed round with Fire,[2] his consort bound to him, that he might mix the original Mixing-bowls by pouring in the flower of his own Fire (1: 69-70).

3. Having mingled the spark of Soul with two in unanimity—with Mind and Divine Breath—He added to them as a third pure Love, the august Master binding all. . . . In every Cosmos there shines a Triad, whereof a Monad is (the) Source; . . . all things are served in the gulfs of the Triad. . . . From this Triad the Father mixed every spirit, . . . arming both Mind and Soul with triple might.[3] . . . (Then) the Father withdrew Himself, yet shut not up His own peculiar Fire within His Knowing Power, . . . for Power is with Him, but Mind from Him, . . . calm . . . Silence, Nurturer of the Soul (1: 71, 53-54, 33, 35).

4. The Soul Travels Home

1. The Soul of man, with nothing in it subject to death,[4] should press God closely to itself; but (now) it is all drunk, for it glories in the Harmony under

---

[1] "It's love that makes the world go round", in the words of an old song!

[2] Love, as for Valentinus, was the cause of creation (GG 12: 2).

[3] This is the origin of the phrase 'three-powered' in GG 50, etc.

[4] *i.e.*, turning from all things mortal.

whose sway the mortal frame exists [1] (1: 31, 2: 36). Seek out the channel of the Soul-Stream—whence and from what order it is that the Soul (fell) into slavery to Body, (and) to what state thou shalt rise again, atoning work with holy word.[2] . . . (Those who do this) flee the reckless fated wing of Fate and stay themselves in God, drawing to themselves the Fires in all their prime as they descend out of the Father, from whom as they descend the Soul culls the flower of empyrean Fruit which nourishes the Soul (2: 44, 59).

2. But verge not downwards! Beneath thee lies a precipice sheer from the earth, which draws one down a Stair of seven steps, below which is the throne of dire Necessity! . . . See that thou verge not down into the world of the Dark Rays, under which is ever spread the formless Abyss where is no light to see, wrapped in defiling black gloom which rejoices in shadows, void of all understanding,[3] precipitous and sinuous, for ever winding round its own blind depth, eternally wedded with an invisible body inert (and) lifeless (2: 88, 86-87).

3. Do not invoke the self-revealed image of Nature, . . . (for) her name is identical with Fate; . . . do not increase thy fate (2: 40-41). Do not soil the spirit, nor turn the plane into the solid (1: 84); the mortal once endowed with Mind must put bridle on his Soul,

---

[1] The usual idea of Gnostics and Hermetists, etc. Its attachment to the lower world subjects it to the fate ruling that world, and so to rebirths.

[2] *i.e.*, the Gnosis, through at-onement, simplicity.

[3] The Chaos of dark emptiness, in the story of Pistis Sophia.

that it may not plunge into the ill-starred earth,[1] but win to freedom. . . . Dowsed in the earth's frenzies and the needs of Nature, . . . thou shouldst not look on them before the body is perfected; they ever fascinate men's souls and draw them from the Mysteries. . . . If thou extend fiery Mind to flowing work of piety, thou shalt preserve thy body also (2: 51, 66, 58).

4. Let the immortal depths of thy Soul be opened, and open all thy eyes at once to the Above, . . . for if the mortal draw near to the Fire he shall have Light from God. . . . Thou shouldst speed to the Light and to the Father's Rays, whence has been sent to thee a Soul richly arrayed with Mind. . . . But when thou beholdest the most holy Fire flashing formless with dancing radiance through the depths of all the worlds, then listen to the voice of the Fire.[2] . . . Believe thyself to be out of body, and (so) thou art; . . . for Divine things are not accessible to mortals who fix their minds on body; it is they who strip themselves naked[3] who speed aloft to the Height (2: 50, 54, 52, 72, 93, 53).

5. Yes, there is the End-of-Understanding which thou must understand with flower of Mind. For shouldst thou turn thy Mind inwards upon It and understand It as understanding something, thou shalt not understand It (at all).[4] For there is a power of

---

[1] In recurring rebirths.

[2] The Divine Wisdom appeared to the neophyte as radiant Fire.

[3] *i.e.*, abandon all worldly things, as in GG 84: 2-3.

[4] Truth, or Reality, is not something apart from the self to be *understood*; it is itself the Self.

the (Mind's) prime which shines out in all directions, flashing with intellectual rays. Yet indeed thou shouldst not (strive) with vehemence (to) understand that End-of-Understanding, nor even with the spreading flame of wide-extending mind that measures all things—save (only) that End-of-Understanding. Indeed, there is no need of strain in understanding This,[1] but thou shouldst see thy Soul in purity, turned from everything else so as to make thy Mind empty, attentive to that End in order to learn that End-of-Understanding, for It subsists beyond the Mind (1: 23-24). Keep silence, thou who art admitted to the sacred rites [2] (2: 64).

6. The Soul-lord, he who sets his feet on the ethereal realms, is the Perfectioner;[3] . . . alive in power he runs, an Angel (2: 23, 78), a Name of august majesty and with sleepless whirling, leaping into the worlds by reason of the Father's swift Announcement[4] (2: 24). For he alone, culling to the full the flower of Mind out of the Father's might, has the power to understand the Father's Mind, and to bestow that Mind both on sources and on all principles—both power to understand and ever to abide upon His tireless pivot. . . .

---

[1] Krishnamurti says "Let go!" Effort awakens egoism and hides the Real.

[2] That which is to be understood is God, the One Intelligible; He cannot be found save calmly and effortlessly by the perfected Mind, which is beyond this lower mind that studies and learns all other things. Leaving them, the Soul finds God silently and in perfect peace. But this cannot be spoken of to others who have not experienced it. How can they understand through *words*?

[3] Gk. *teletarchēs*, one who can make others perfect in his turn.

[4] At God's word only he may henceforth enter into birth.

Armed at all points, clad in the bloom of Sounding Light, arming both Mind and Soul with three-barbed power (1: 59, 54), he must set in his heart the Triad's every Symbol and not move scatteredly along the empyrean ways but collectedly,[1] ... urging himself to the Centre of Sounding Light [2] (2: 45-46, 48).

---

[1] *Cf.* the gathering in of the Soul's power in GG 84: 3.
[2] Where, at the Heart of things, the senses merge into one, and all is still for evermore, in the Silence that is God.

INDEX

ABSOLUTION, forgiveness: 2, 45, 54-55, 57, 78, 81
Adam: 24
Adamas: 48, 62-63, 66-68
Aeons: 3-4, 7-8, 10-15, 17, 45, 48-49, 51, 55-57, 60, 62-68, 80, 85, 88-92, 94-96, CP
Ahamōth: 16-19, 95
Aloneborn: 9, 11-15, 17, 90
Angels: 3, 15, 17, 19-20, 48, 83, 85, 90, 95
Arrogant: 50, 52-64, 66

BĀBEL: 71, 73-74
Baptism: 57, 85
Barbēlō: 45
Body: 5, 11, 17-19, 45, 78-79, 81-83, 86-87, 90, 94-95, 97, CP
Boundary: 7, 14, 16, 46, 74, 81
Bride, spouse: 19, 92, 95

CHAOS: 52-55, 57-65, 57-69, 84, 88
Cherubim: 90
Child: 21, 41, 46
Christ: 15-17, 19, 26, (34), 39-40
Church: 12-13, 15, 18
Creation: 5, 11, 23, 26-27, 87, 97
Cross: 7-8, 14, 16, 33-35, 39-40, (86)
Crown: 7, 9-11, 59, 63, 86, 94, 96
Crucify: 1, 33, 45
Cup: 5, 79

DANCE: 30-31, 33, 36, 92
Darkness: 5, 9, 16, 29, 33, 52-55, 58, 60, 63-64, 67, 69, 78, 80, 91
Deep: 6, 11-12, 14, 39, 91, 97
Destiny: 46, 48, 78-79
Dodecad: 30
Door: 11, 30, 34, 92

EGYPT: 70-73
End of the world: 2, 19, 43, 48
Ennead: 7, 11, 39

Elijah: 45
Elisabeth: 45

FAITH: 11, 34, 39, 80
Fire: 5, 14, 26, 52, 78, 90-91
Firmament: 23-24, 47-48
First Mystery: 41, 45-46, 49, 51-52, 54-56, 58, 60, 78, 82, (85)
Fountain: 5-7, 39, 94, CP
Fullness: P, 2, 7-8, 11-16, 18-19, 39, 42

GABRIEL: 45, 60, 63, 96
Gate: 41, 66, 69, 72, 76-78, 82, 92
Gather: 10, 35, 39, 84, 86, 93, 96
Gnosis: 16-17, 19, 25, 27, (33), 39-40, 55, 86, 88, 95-96, (97);
    What is Gnosis? P, 2, 11, 26, 80
Gospel: 26-27
Grace: 9, 12, 27, 29-30, 34, 40, 57, 80, 95

HEAVEN and Earth: 1, 5, 18, (42), 43, 90-91
Hebdomad: 18, 24-27
Hope: 11, 39, 80
House: 9, 30, 70, 73, 75, 93
Hymn: 15, 29, 43, 47, 50-51, 54-55, 57, 59, 64-66, 69, 92, 96
Hyrcania: 75

IALDABAŌTH: 52
Iaō: 45
Iaō Zeēsor: 8
Ieou: 55, 96
Ignorance: 3, 14, 16, 18-19, 23-26, 48, 55, (69), 95
Image: 8, 11, 17, 75, 95-96
Indian: 70
Individual: 7-8, 11
Ineffable, mystery of : 2, 7-8, 11-12, 26, 44, 46, 85-86
Inheritance: 55, (70), 78-79, 85
Inmost: 10, 43
Intelligent: 2, 7, 19, 56, 82
Invisible God: 2, 8, 13, 17, 97
Israel: 86

JAZZAK: 70
Jerusalem: 33
Jesus: P, 15, 27, 29, 34, 41-44, 49, 94-95
Jews: 29
John: 33, 45

LAST Mystery: 41, 45
Life: P, 2, 9, 11-13, 15-16, 18, 34, 39-40, 83, 86, 95, CP

INDEX 329

LIGHT: 5, 9, 11, 16-17, 21, 26-27, 29, 33-34, 41-42, 44, 47-48, 50-60, 62-68, 73-74, 78-81, 83, 85-86, 88-89, 91-92, 95-96, CP; children of: 2, 83; excess of: 9, 11, 42, 44, 47-48, 63, 92; faith of: 83; kingdom of: 2, (38), 46, (70, 72, 77), 78, 81-83, 85; land of: 69; mysteries of: 2, 79, 81-83, 85; Maiden of: 45, 79; Treasure of: 2, 41, 45-46 49-50, 52, 55, 66, 81, 83
Light-Aeon: P, 10, 12, 52, 82
Light-Stream: 60, 63, 85
Lion-faced Power: 52, 54-57, 61, 63
Love: 10-12, 14, 39-40, 57, 70, 74, 76, 80, 83, 87, 94, CP

MAISHAN: 71, 74
Male-female: 4, 12, (84)
Man: 1-3, 5, 7-8, 12-13, 15, 18, 20-21, 28, 31, 36, 38-40, 83-85, 94-97
Mary: 27, 45
Matter: 5, 10-11, 17, 19-20, 45, 4?, (50), 52, 54-55, 59, 63, 80-81, 83
Michael: 60, 63
Midst: 1, 4-5, 18-19, 45-46, 79, 85-86
Mind: 1-5, 7, 9, 12-15, 30, 34, 88-89, 97
Mirror: 30, 75
Monad: 3, 8-11, 39
Moses: 21, 24
Mother: 8, 10, 12, 17-19, 39, 45, 72-73, 80, 83, 92-93, 95-96
Mount of Olives: 33, 42

NAME: 7-8, (20), 22, 26, 40, 46-47, 50, 57, 64, 72-73, 83, 89-90, 93-95, 97
Non-Being God: 20-24, 26

OGDOAD 12, 18, 23-26, 30

PAIR, Twin: 14-15, 41, 46, 50, 52-53
Parthia: 72
Peace: 10-11, 72, 76, 80, 94-95
Prayer: 7, 9, 96-97, CP
Psychic: 17-19, 28

QĀSHĀN: 70

RACE (of Mind): P, 2, 35, 71, 95
Realities: 7, 11
Receiver: 45, 57, 79
Refine: 22, 24, 50, 59, 82
Renunciation: 1, 81-83
Repentance: 40, 53-57, 60, 78
Rest, Repose: 15, 19, 31, 34, 39, 79, 86, 93-94
Resurrection: 11, 34, 39, (41)
Robe (Light): 5, 11, 45-47, 50, (70, 72, 75, 84), 92, (97)

Ruler(s): 1, 18, 23-26, 41, 45, 47-51, 55, 65-68, 78-79, 83-84, 96
Root: 5, 13, 34, 40, 94-95
SABAOTH the Good, Great: 45; Little: 79
Salome: 84
Sarbug: 71, 73-74
Saviour (s): P, 9, 15, 17, 19, 41-43, 45-46, 54-55, (58),64, (78), 86, 95, 97
Seed: 18-23, 28, 34, 63, 79, 94-95
Seraphim: 90
Sētheus: 11, 80
Serpent: 5, 29, 70-71, 73
Silence: 4, 6-8, 11-13, 24, 31, 39-40, 43, 95, CP
Similes: abortion 27, arrow: 61; artisan 21, blind men 78, child 21, camphor 26, city 8-9, dead men 48, eagle 73, egg 21, field 8, fig-tree 3, fish 25, fountain 5, fragrance 5, 22, king 9, serpent 5, ship 8, shrine 5, spider 21, spring flowers 92, star 5, 8, sunbeam 5, sword 57, wing 22, womb 5
Snake: 61, 63
Sonship: 11, 22-24, 26-28
Sons of God: 24, 26-27
Source: 3, 5, 12
Spark: 5, 10-11, 39
Spirit: 5, 26-27, 34, 39, 77, 82, 89-93, 95, CP; the holy: 15-16, 22, 24, 26-27, 29, 32

THIRTEENTH Aeon: 45, 50, 52, 55, 57, 61, 63, 65-66, 69
Thought: 3-6, 12, 22, 95-97
Three-Powered: 10-11, 46, 50, 52
Time: 7, 12, 54, 58, 60, 66-68, 78, 85
Tōbe: 42
Triple: 5, 22, 85
Truth: P, 8, 10-12, 15, 34, 44, 48, 53, 80, 86, 92, 94-95

UNIVERSE: 2, 5-7, 9, 11, 24, 26, 28, 41, 45-47, 80, 82, 91, 95-97, CP

VEIL: 11, 17, 41, 41, 48, 50, 52, (92)
Virgin: 5, 10, 90, (92)
Voice, Sound: 6, 21, 33-35, 39, (41, 46), 73-74, (76), 77, 84

WATER: 5, 45, 79, 91
Willed: 13-14
Wisdom: 3, 7, 11, 13-14, 16, 18-19, 34, 50-57, 59-63, 65-69, 79, 92, 95
Womb: 5, 12, 45, 89
Word: P, 1, 3, 5, 7, 9, 12-13, 15, (22), 29, 31-32, 34, 36, 39-40, 86, 94, 96

In the above skeleton Index to this Gospel references are given to the Section of the Text; P stands for the Prologue, and CP for the Closing Prayer.

ALSO AVAILABLE FROM THE BOOK TREE

PISTIS SOPHIA: A Gnostic Gospel, translated by G.R.S. Mead. The Gnostics were part of early Christianity and were composed of a number of mystical sects. This was one of their gospels. Virtually all Gnostic teachers were persecuted and their documents destroyed because the Church needed a uniform set of beliefs to operate under. Only now have we begun to better understand these early Christian mystics. This work remains an important milestone in Gnostic research, on par with Nag Hammadi, and should be part of any serious study. It tells the story of how we, as spiritual beings, have fallen into the world of physical creation. The soul is asleep here, bogged down in physical surroundings, unaware of our true nature. The purpose of Pistis Sophia is to awaken us, and to aid in the process of spiritual freedom. **400 pages • hardcover $55.00 • softcover $27.95**

THE BOOK OF JUBILEES, Translated by R. H. Charles. This rare and important holy book sheds new light on Judaism and early Christianity. It was written sometime between 250 BC and AD 100 by one or more Hellenistic Jews, and reflects a form of Jewish mystical thought at around the time of Christ. It retells much of the Old Testament story, but includes additional material not mentioned in the Bible. It also relies heavily on *The Book of Enoch*, which was, like this book, translated from the Ethiopic text. It covers Adam and Eve, the Fall of Man, Cain and Abel, the fall of the angels and their punishment, the deluge foretold, the ark and the flood, the tower of Babel and confusion of tongues, evil spirits, corruption of the human race, God's covenant, the Messianic Kingdom, Jacob's visions, prophetic dreams, and Moses, among other interesting topics. **224 pages • paper $18.95**

THE LOST BOOKS OF THE BIBLE OR THE APOCRYPHAL NEW TESTAMENT, assembled by William Hone. Translated by William Wake and Jeremiah Jones. First published in 1820 under the title The Apocryphal New Testament. These documents were written soon after the death of Christ, during the early days of Christianity. Yet when the Bible was compiled near the end of the fourth century, these texts were not included and were suppressed by the church. **295 pages • 6 x 9 • paper • $24.95**

THE BOOK OF ADAM AND EVE or The Conflict of Adam and Eve with Satan, Translated by Rev. S.C. Malan. This book reveals the life and times of Adam and Eve after they were expelled from the Garden of Eden, up to the time when Cain killed his brother Abel. It covers where they went, where they lived, and their various troubles and temptations, including those coming from Satan. This is an interesting book because it provides one with more information to work with beyond the standard Biblical account. The work includes a number of helpful notes by the translator, issued for clarification, and they appear consistently throughout the text. **256 pages • 6 x 9 • paper • $21.95**

To order call 1.800.700.TREE 24 hrs. OR visit www.thebooktree.com

www.ingramcontent.com/pod-product-compliance
Lightning Source LLC
Chambersburg PA
CBHW032014230426
43671CB00005B/84